THOSE
Rockefeller
BROTHERS

THOSE
Rockefeller
BROTHERS

AN INFORMAL BIOGRAPHY OF
FIVE EXTRAORDINARY YOUNG MEN

by

JOE ALEX MORRIS

HARPER & BROTHERS PUBLISHERS
NEW YORK

Library of Congress catalog card number: 52-11692

Foreword

EVERY MORNING AND EVERY AFTERNOON THE MAIN HALLS and underground streets of Rockefeller Center are turned into a stream of chattering, hurrying New Yorkers. It is their habit to go to work and to go home with a certain degree of fuss. The stenographers and clerks, the shopkeepers, waitresses, salesmen and executives scurry out of elevators, clatter along the marble corridors and swish through the revolving doors, a little like children—who, each morning are not quite tardy and, each afternoon, are not quite sure there will be enough time for play before dinner.

Sometimes a neat, not-very-tall man walks erectly and with steady step in the middle of all this bustle. He usually wears a dark Homburg set precisely on his graying head. If he nods pleasantly to the respectful doorman and, perhaps, lifts his hat sedately as he passes the young lady at the information desk you can be pretty sure that he is John Davison Rockefeller, Jr. His sons own the place.

There is not, however, any very good way to pick out Mr. Rockefeller's five sons as they come and go to their offices in the crowded Center. They dress and act and look very much like all the other executives from all the other offices. No tourist wandering amid the architectural wonders of the Center will ever spot one of them among the passers-by. Very few office workers will recognize them in the elevator.

The fact that the Rockefeller brothers—whose grandfather was the world's first billionaire industrialist—have been able to grow up and pursue their independent careers without being marked men in a crowd, without looking either up or down to their contemporaries is considerably more of an achievement than it may appear at first glance. A famous name has more often than not proved a major hazard for young men who felt they were compelled to live up to something, or to live down something, or who decided just to coast through life as happily as possible.

None of these things happened to the Rockefeller brothers in any marked degree. They have had their problems but they also have had, thanks to their parents, a carefully planned opportunity to acquire balance. As a result, they learned to take life in a pretty regular, normal stride. This became of particular interest and importance when they reached manhood in the decade of the great depression, and had an opportunity to demonstrate what conscientious men might do with accumulated wealth in a world already wracked by tremendous economic convulsions.

That, in a broad way, is what this book is concerned with: how they grew and what they have done—although it is better to say what they want to do because, at this mid-century mark, they are still young men who can be credited only with an impressive beginning. My own interest in the Rockefellers' story began in the summer of 1949 when I did an article for the *Saturday Evening Post* about Rockefeller Center. At that time I was struck by the fact that people who worked with the brothers were highly enthusiastic about them, yet the public generally knew very little about their careers except for Nelson's wartime operations as Co-ordinator of the Office of Inter-American affairs and as an Assistant Secretary of State.

Thinking it over, I discovered that I could not remember

even the names of the five brothers who represented the third generation of what had been the world's richest family, and was still one of its most famous. The reason for this was plain once I had checked the records. Almost nothing—again excepting Nelson's wartime career—had been published about them. John Davison, 3rd, was born in 1906, yet it was almost literally true that neither he nor his brothers were mentioned in the country's newspapers in the next decade and a half. And after that there were only the most formal and insignificant items, concerning such things as graduation from college or a ticket for illegal parking, until 1938 when an article was published concerning their childhood and college careers.

As a result of this, I thought it would be interesting to examine the careers of five still young men who were the grandsons of a man whose income amounted to thirty million dollars a year. My feeling was that times had changed considerably during the period in which they had grown up. Income taxes had been introduced; so had inheritance taxes. Labor unions had developed and expanded enormously to demand a share of industrial income. Under the New Deal, as one self-made Republican political figure remarked to me about that time, it had become impossible for an honest man to make a million dollars. In such an era of economic upheaval, what were the Rockefellers doing with their accumulated wealth; how did such a great personal fortune as theirs fit into the modern industrial pattern? The editors of the *Saturday Evening Post* were interested in the idea and I opened negotiations in the fall of 1949 to get the co-operation of the Rockefellers.

The first thing I discovered was that, on such a proposition, you couldn't get the consent or the co-operation of only one or two of the brothers. Either they all agreed or none agreed. Nothing much happened for a couple of months but at least the proposal was under consideration. Then came word that the time didn't seem exactly right. Wait a while. I waited. In fact, I waited about a year and was just ready to start a four months' tour in the Rocky Mountain area when I received word that they had agreed to co-operate and would be available for interviews the following week. I postponed my Western trip and spent a week talking to all five brothers and filling several notebooks. Once they had agreed to the interviews, no one could have been more pleasant or co-operative. At the end of the week I explained to them with some embarrassment that I had other commitments requiring me to be away for a while but that I would see them later. Actually, about another year passed before I got back to the Rockefellers and I was sure that the whole arrangement was badly fouled up.

But when I walked into Rockefeller Center again they all acted as if I had just been away for the week end. We took up about where we had left off some twelve months earlier—I could still read my notes and their memories seemed to be excellent—and nobody hinted that I had caused any inconvenience by wandering away in the middle of the job. The articles finally appeared some twenty-seven months after I had first taken up the work.

The articles, and this book, for that matter, were basically a reportorial job from my viewpoint, but here I think I might interject a few ideas of my own that were acquired along the way. The Rockefeller brothers, it seemed to me, are fundamentally "good" men. That is a dangerous word to use and, of course, it is inaccurate, particularly when used collectively, but it kept recurring whenever I tried to describe them or rather to express my own feeling about them and their activities. I suppose that what I meant was that they devote a great deal of their time, efforts and money to an intelligent attempt to make the world a better place in which to live.

That does not have anything to do with whether they are

good businessmen or whether they indulge in sharp practices at times or whether they occasionally take undue advantage of the great weight that their position and wealth can exert in business and financial circles. Nor does it, perhaps, seem very much to ask of five men who have never had to worry about making a living. But, on the other hand, it is more than you'll get in the normal run of millionaires, and the important thing is that the Rockefellers work at their good intentions.

"It is easy," a distinguished friend of the family said shortly after World War II, "to say that the Rockefeller boys have had a downhill drag in life and to discount what they have done. But I look at it another way. It would have been so very easy for one or all of them to have made a botch of things. If they had handled themselves and their affairs in an unhappy manner the result could have been a very serious blow to our complex, competitive economy in these dangerous times of world struggle. Because of their name they would have become Exhibit A for the propaganda of the enemies of our way of life, not just in this country but all over the world."

This is an interesting idea and doubtless true, but it seems to me that it misses the point. Anybody can spend a lifetime sitting on his own hands and be reasonably sure of keeping out of trouble. The Rockefellers, however, have been punching away at the job of "doing something" ever since they were old enough to double up their hands into fists. And perhaps the best commentary on how they fared can be found in two newspaper clippings.

The first one, dated in the year before World War I, concerns a low point in the Rockefeller family's relations with the working people of America. It is an account of the Ludlow massacre that occurred during a strike at Rockefeller-controlled mines in Colorado, a brutal story that seemed likely to make the

Rockefeller name a permanent epithet of hatred in the ranks of labor.

The second clipping was dated not long after World War II. It concerned a meeting in New York City to honor citizens who had contributed to the progress of community affairs, and the chief speaker was the New York state president of the C.I.O. The Rockefeller brothers, he declared in the course of his address, were perfect examples of what a rich man's sons should be. "All of the labor leaders present," the account added, "stood up and applauded."

J. A. M.

Guilford, Connecticut
October 2, 1952

THOSE
Rockefeller
BROTHERS

⌘ I ⌘

ONE HOT SUMMER DAY IN THE MIDDLE 1930'S TWO TEXAS oil field workers climbed out of a big hole they had been digging and sat down with their dinner pails in the shade of a truck. One was youthful, broad-shouldered, six feet three inches tall and weighed more than two hundred pounds. The other was small, wiry and in his fifties.

"Rocky," said the little man, after both had cleaned up the last crumbs of their thirty-five cent luncheons, "how much money have your folks got?"

Winthrop Rockefeller rubbed a big hand thoughtfully over his sweaty chin.

"Well," he finally replied, "I can't answer that for a good reason. I've always had a roof over my head. I've always had food and clothes and, so far as I know, the family isn't running out of cash. So I just never asked that question myself and I don't know the answer."

Winthrop's reply, more honest than evasive, was typical of the third generation of Rockefellers to share custody of a family fortune that boosted John Davison Rockefeller, Sr., a self-made billionaire, to fame as one of the world's richest men back at the beginning of the twentieth century. It was a reply that might have been made by any one of the five sons of John D. Rockefeller, Jr., who by the 1930's were busy starting careers at the point where most Americans would feel that they had reached the finish line—the point where they were assured of great wealth, prestige and security.

The Rockefeller heirs were relieved by the accident of birth of the necessity of accumulating personal goods but none of them was willing or able to let it go at that. As much as and possibly more than any other American family they labored at the difficult problem of finding a formula by which they might make their own contribution to our complex modern society on a scale as impressive as their grandfather's business triumphs or their father's philanthropic achievements.

"Even if we wanted to, we couldn't do what grandfather did," one of the brothers remarked at a time when they were all more or less well launched on careers. "And the big philanthropic enterprises that father developed began in an era that was pretty well ended by the time we were grown up.

"Anyway, we never wanted to walk with little steps in the big footprints of those two generations. I believe that all of us have felt since we were in college that there was something we could do to help meet the challenge of our own time. One way or another, all of us have worked at that idea. We expect to keep on working at it."

When you take a second look at it, this turns out to be a stilted kind of statement, a little modest, a little strained and even a little pompous. It is not so much an offhand conversational remark as it is a well-prepared and long-considered prospectus or plan of operations. It contains an appreciation of the past and a goodly measure of ambition about the future. It is confident in a quiet way, not about anything specific but about the desire of the brothers collectively to make the best use of their wealth and their position—and to let others judge what results, if any, are achieved.

It is also typical to a greater or lesser extent of all the Rockefeller brothers. They have thought about and talked about such things for so long that not only do their ideas fit into a general pattern but they are likely to use about the same words to express their broad, philosophical attitudes. And this is especially true in regard to their desire to make constructive use of their money, and of the position their money has given them.

To suggest that the brothers have solved the problems of fitting accumulated wealth efficiently and beneficially into today's complex economic structure would be sheer flattery. They have, despite excellent coaching, rung up at least the normal number of errors in the box score. They have occasionally thrown the ball to the wrong base and they have sometimes struck out, swinging. They have never quit trying, however, and even the casual observer can see a pattern emerging from their sometimes fumbling, sometimes idealistic but always grimly determined efforts. Just what the pattern will finally show remains to be seen. "The world," John D., 3rd., remarked in 1950, "is in a state of rapid transition and I think that at present we as a family are in a transitional stage, too, trying to bring into firm focus our future work. I'm not sure yet just what it will add up to in the end."

This was not more than a mild understatement. The Rockefellers are accustomed to long-range planning and to broad perspectives. Big and solid structures are not thrown up overnight, and it is only occasionally that a touch of the spectacular creeps into their operations. But even in 1950 it had been demonstrated that their ideas were not by any stretch of the imagination—as not a few critics had suggested—merely a web of impractical theories woven by five wealthy young men. On the contrary, their efforts, at best, were already channeled along lines that might mean a step forward in the long struggle of nations to find a way to live peacefully together. And later events showed that the Rockefellers will rate at least an "A" for effort in their studied and open-minded attempt to make a contribution to the solution of the major problems of their era.

The five brothers are a tightly knit family group, almost a team, in many things that they do, but any attempt to explain their attitude in a collective sense immediately runs into serious difficulties. It evokes an impression of labored earnestness and do-goodism filtered through a screen of able but conservative public relations advisers. It suggests a kind of puritanical ab-negation of the traditional rights of princely scions either to squander or multiply a fortune; a kind of overeagerness to conform and an over-all submergence of individuality. Nothing could be further from the truth. It is true that for good reasons of family and fortune the five brothers present a common front in many affairs; that they are well and carefully advised. But, in fact, they are so unalike that it is doubtful anyone would pick them out as brothers in a crowd and the main things they have in common are boundless energy and the family name.

John Davison, 3rd, born March 21, 1906, is six feet two inches tall, a slender almost ascetic man who gives the impression of shyness and who was once acutely embarrassed in his college days because a campus restaurant refused to cash his check on the grounds that the name he signed was a boyish gag.

Nelson Aldrich, born July 8, 1908, at Bar Harbor, Maine, is shorter, husky and aggressive and once, as a child, shattered the nerves of his nurse by calmly climbing down into a manhole in a New York street because he "wanted to know what was down there."

Laurance Spelman, born May 26, 1910, is intense and de-termined; dark-haired, firm-jawed and the holder of the fam-ily seat on the New York Stock Exchange. From the business viewpoint, he is perhaps the most vigorous and ambitious of the grandsons of the business-wise founder of the family fortune.

Winthrop, born May 1, 1912, is the largest of the five, a handsome and gregarious young giant who once teamed with Actress Mary Martin to win a dance contest, occasionally has been seen in cafe society circles and, until 1951, was the only Rockefeller on an oil-company payroll since his grandfather retired.

David, born June 12, 1915, is a robust, precise and scholarly man who won entomological fame by gathering one of the finest insect collections in the world, who once was in politics under the New Dealish wing of New York Mayor Fiorello La Guardia and who eventually went to work "down at the bank" where he became Vice-President in the foreign department of the Chase National. Later he switched to the commercial banking department and, in September of 1952, became a senior vice-president.

Any story of the evolution of the brothers' ideas and plans must find its beginning in their childhood and the background of the Rockefeller family but, as far as they are concerned, it is a background that goes back only to their grandfather. There is in existence a Rockefeller Family Association, comprised of descendants of Johann Peter Rockefeller, a German who settled in New Jersey about 1720 and eventually acquired very large land holdings. Although he never took an active interest, John D. Rockefeller, Jr., became a member of the association. The brothers are not members. Various volunteer experts have attempted from time to time to trace the forebears of John D., Sr., in Europe and have come up with such possible ancestors as the Marquis de Roquefeuil and George, Duke of Clarence, who was a brother of Edward IV of England.

The Rockefeller family has greeted these efforts with a polite expression of thanks and a stifled yawn. They are not much interested in ancient family trees and were amused on one occasion when a crusty Philadelphia socialite referred to Nelson as "that New York boy who married into the Clark family." For them, the family history begins with the rise of John D.,

Sr., to domination of the oil industry at the end of the nine-teenth century, and the establishment of the family's fortune—sometimes estimated over the years to have totaled two billion dollars—on the foundation of the Standard Oil Company. The wealth of John D., Sr., was such that it fascinated amateur statisticians of the day and in 1906 one of them calculated for the newspapers that if it were left to accumulate at the then current rate for approximately thirty years it would amount to ninety million million dollars. That is no misprint, the figure being $90,000,000,000,000.

When the elder Rockefeller surprisingly retired while still in his fifties, he put into the hands of John D., Jr., not only the business but the philanthropic work which he had started and which his son later developed and expanded. This work is represented by such famous enterprises as the Rockefeller Foundation, the Rockefeller Institute for Medical Research, the General Education Board and many other contributions to science, culture and learning. In all, the family's philanthropies to date amount to about $800,000,000.

Thus the third generation of Rockefellers found, as boys, that the cycle was being completed, with their grandfather famous as a money-maker and their father famous as a money-giver. Their father had, moreover, promoted an entirely new concept of philanthropy designed to secure the widest benefits for humanity generally. In such circumstances, it would have been easy for the sons of John D., Jr., to reach the conclusion that there was nothing left for them to do except expend their great energies in enjoyment of life.

It would not only have been an easy course to take; it would have been more or less in the pattern of the generation that was growing up after the First World War in the reckless, careless and somewhat befuddled jazz age. The sons of a great many wealthy men were growing up that way.

"Anybody with your money and five sons," an acquaintance remarked one day to John D., Jr., "has a right to expect at least four black sheep in the family."

Almost anybody would have agreed that the remark was reasonable. But it was a prediction that didn't come true in the case of the Rockefeller brothers for a number of reasons, the most important being their mother, their father and their grandfather.

❈ II ❈

IT WAS INEVITABLE THAT THE FIVE ROCKEFELLER BROTHERS should be set somewhat apart in the public mind from the time they were babies. The mere fact that they were grandsons of John D., Sr., was enough at that time to give them an unusual status in the mind of the people, not just in the United States but throughout a great part of the world. The mere accumulation of money on a fabulous scale, to say nothing of the power it entailed in a period of lusty American economic growth, had long since become firmly associated with the word Rockefeller in even the meanest household. Characters bearing distorted versions of the name—Mr. Rockybags or Mr. Richfeller—were immediately recognizable to any reader.

Furthermore, John D., Jr., was an only son and the public attention on the name remained centered on a single personality in the second generation instead of being divided among several individuals as it might have been if there had been other sons. The boys' parents were always strongly aware of this situation and devoted themselves to avoiding the unhappy effect it might easily have on the lives of their children. Mr. Rockefeller was a quiet, perhaps overly modest young man, inclined to be extremely cautious in his personal relationships, acutely conscious of his responsibilities and prone to deprecate his own charm and abilities. He had managed to keep himself fairly well out of the limelight and go calmly about the business of raising a family during the long period when his father—first

8

as a financial giant and then as a frail but pleasant old man whose face stared out of the rotogravure sections of the Sunday newspapers with great regularity—was so strongly in the public eye. He was determined that his sons, too, should have a chance to develop their own personalities beyond the range of the spotlight of newspaper publicity.

The Rockefeller money and influence made this possible but only because of skillful parental guidance. The five sons were born in the decade before the First World War—their sister Abby was the oldest child—and attended school in New York, traveled all over the United States and sometimes to Europe and attended well-known eastern colleges with so little publicity that not even the average newspaperman in New York City could have said offhand how many children there were in the family. No journalistic sob sisters wrote about the Rockefeller children. Their pictures were not available for publication and not even their names were published except on rare occasions, as when Nelson shot himself with an air rifle in 1922.

The purpose of this policy was not so much to make the world unaware of the children as it was to enable them to grow up—so far as it was possible—without feeling any undue pressures because their family was one of the richest if not the richest in the world. It was not possible, of course, to relieve all such pressures, especially as the boys grew older and began to acquire a better understanding of the world around them. But by that time their personalities had been formed and their family training was well established, and they were accustomed to keeping their balance in the world in which they would live.

An interesting example of how this worked out for the boys can be found in their relations with their grandfather.

The elder Rockefeller was a more important influence on his grandsons than might be generally expected in view of the fact that he was in his sixties and pretty well retired from business affairs—he withdrew gradually over a period of years —when John D., 3rd, was a mere baby. This vast gulf of years that separated the boys from their grandfather, however, seemed to have helped rather than hindered the development of their affectionate and respectful feelings toward him. Various other things that are a part of the nation's business history helped, too.

Mr. Rockefeller, Sr., was to his grandsons a man of many facets, some of which they learned about at first hand, some of which they heard and read about as they grew up and some of which may always be dimly obscure to them. There was first the self-made business giant, careful, shrewd, penny-watching and yet able to envision the future of the scattered, cut-throat oil industry and to manipulate the forces that would build his billion-dollar empire. Then there was the piratical monopolist of the popular imagination of half a century ago, the man whose very name became a synonym for great wealth no matter where it was uttered in the civilized world; the primary target of labor agitators and political cartoonists—and just ordinary politicians, for that matter—who might look around for a symbol of the evils of monopoly.

There was the almost fanatical religious atmosphere associated with the Rockefeller name, a faith that was zealously nourished by the distaff side of the family. Both the mother and wife of John D., Sr., were devoted to the Church and its works with a puritanical fervor and with a strict regard for religious precepts that regulated their family's daily activities. Card-playing, dancing and similar relaxations were not for the Rocke-fellers, and on many occasions the wife and mother of John D., Sr., were members of the little bands of women temperance workers who marched into the saloons, knelt down on the sawdust-sprinkled floors and prayed for deliverance of the nation from the evil of legalized liquor. This was strong stuff, even in the days of militant women of the white ribbon league, of Carry Nation and her hatchet. The ladies of the Rockefeller family served God fearlessly and faithfully, and their influence was to be felt down through the years in a manner that profoundly affected the lives of the five brothers.

Still another side of their grandfather's character was that of the philanthropist, the prince of industry who had amassed great wealth and then set out to give away hundreds of millions of dollars in a systematic, scientific manner designed to bring the greatest benefit to the largest number. This was quite a different man from the monopolist pictured by the muckraking cartoonists, and so many varied sides to grandfather's character might have been highly confusing to the third generation except for the fact that their first and most vivid impression of him was something entirely unrelated to any of these things. They thought he was a consummate wit.

From their earliest memories, from the days when they donned Eton collars and striped trousers to go to his home for dinner, he was a relaxed, perceptive, pleasant old man who had been mellowed for the public by the press agentry of Ivy Lee. The bitter newspaper and political attacks, the labor strife, the Congressional investigations were something that the young brothers would read about as history, just as they would read about his business achievements and his philanthropies. They could later balance the good against the bad; they could approve or they could regret. But they could never be detached or objective because the thing they all remembered most clearly was this shrunken, smiling old man with the wrinkled, parchment skin and the thin threads of silver hair, this old man with a pocketful of bright new dimes and an ability to tell a funny story better than anybody they ever knew.

The young brothers unhesitatingly agreed among themselves that their grandfather was a better humorist than Will Rogers, then at the top of his career, and today they are inclined to smile happily—all of them—and agree that their youthful judgment was sound. Even when they heard him tell the same story over and over through the years he always made it seem different and they still thought he was good.

Any historian pursuing this comparison of the elder Rockefeller with Will Rogers will conclude that it was not flattering to the Oklahoma monologist but he will see what the boys were driving at. They remember family dinners, perhaps with a few guests present, when their grandfather stood up at the end of the table, a spotlessly white napkin clasped lightly in his fingers, and began telling about some character that he might or might not pretend to know. Such examples of the Rockefeller humor as are available suggest that he liked best to tell a long, dead-pan story of how this character had fallen into tragic circumstances. Or had gotten drunk and was dumped by his friends into the watering trough on the town square. He would raise the napkin or draw out a handkerchief to wipe imaginary tears from his eyes and appear so moved that his listeners— particularly any guests unfamiliar with his ways—would be on the verge of tears themselves. But his grandsons, holding their breath and sitting on the edges of their chairs, knew what was coming and were ready to burst into gales of laughter when he ended up with some sudden twist that made it all a huge joke. To them it was always a masterly performance.

And, when they were older, they liked the way Mr. Rockefeller, Sr., sometimes took the wind out of the sails of a rival storyteller. On one occasion he sat, dead-pan, through a long-winded joke told by an acquaintance and then, when the teller paused for laughter, the old man cupped his hand to his ear and said: "Would you mind repeating that? I didn't quite get it."

There was, of course, a great deal more to their relationship than a sense of humor. They enjoyed visits to his home in Lakewood, N. J., or at Ormond, Florida, where they sometimes played with him around his little golf course. John, 3rd, who was not too strong as a child, spent most of one winter in Florida and the other boys made shorter visits there. Their grandfather was never in a hurry, he seldom talked about himself or the past, he listened gravely to their troubles, encouraged them to talk about their own ideas and doled out undisturbing bits of philosophy and bright new dimes almost every day. Sometimes he even declared a dividend and gave one of them a dollar. And, at other times as they grew older, he occasionally cooled off their youthful business enthusiasms by remarking that their ideas were "all very interesting but what do the figures show? It's the figures that count."

On one occasion when two of the boys had been on a vacation trip in Central America while still in college they returned with an idea that they knew how to make money by business ventures in several undeveloped areas. Their grandfather listened to their story in considerable detail but he made no pretense of humoring their boyish ideas of business and, when they had finished, demolished the whole scheme with a few pointed questions about problems that had never entered their minds. He didn't, however, make a habit of moralizing to them on business affairs and he didn't often interest himself directly in their training. In the end, they felt that he was an old and companionable man sitting back and watching the world go by, almost completely detached, unwilling to hurry about anything, eating slowly, walking slowly and waiting patiently.

"I'm like your bike when you're coasting downhill," he once told Laurance. "I can coast just so far and nothing much can be done about it."

It was, of course, on their father—whom they always addressed as Pa—that the real responsibility of training the five boys fell. Whereas their grandfather could relax, joke with them and give them the feeling of a vacation when they visited him, their father had to make them into responsible men and he never forgot that he and they had a number of difficulties to overcome as well as a number of advantages to enjoy. It is easy to be humorous or scornful about the "poor little rich boy" and what a hard time he has getting along with all that money. He is, in most cases, going to get along very well— probably much better than he would without all that money.

But with Mr. Rockefeller it wasn't a matter of just getting along well and it wasn't a matter of just being rich. They weren't just rich. Considering the conditions that existed when the boys were born, it would have taken a fertile imagination indeed to see how all five of them and all of their children could, merely by spending, make much of a dent in the family fortune in the course of a couple of generations.

The real question in their father's mind was whether they would grow up to be useful and respected citizens with an understanding of the obligations and responsibilities which he felt went with the money the family had accumulated. And when he looked around the New York scene it wasn't difficult to find examples of how wealth sometimes interfered with that understanding; to see the disadvantages of undue publicity and, especially, to see what could happen to his sons if they had nothing to offer the community except the fact that their name happened to be Rockefeller. Above all, perhaps, he wanted them to realize that they had to contribute something other than inherited money in order to get something back from life.

An interesting indication of the painstaking seriousness with which he approached family affairs is given in Mary Ellen Chase's description of his courtship of Abby Aldrich. "John was a deliberate as well as a reticent young man," she points out. "He describes himself as even 'a bit cold-blooded' about this major decision of choosing a partner for life, since he had been constantly pursued by the nightmare of making a fatally wrong choice and discovering it too late. His future entailed duties and obligations of which he was well aware; and his choice of a wife consequently meant to him searchings not only of heart but of head as well." In later years, he also searched his head as well as his heart in dealing with his children.

Mr. Rockefeller, Jr.—his associates referred to him that way even after his father's death because he retained the "junior" as part of his signature out of respect for his father—brought to his sons a measure of the religious training he had known all his life. Each morning at a quarter of eight the family began the day with prayer and Mr. Rockefeller read a passage from the Bible before breakfast—a custom, incidentally, that is still maintained in Nelson's household.

Breakfast, in fact, was the brothers' main boyhood contact with their father except for Sundays when he regularly devoted several hours a day to them. On Sundays he often took them on long walks near the family home at Tarrytown, some thirty miles from New York, or, in the summers, at Seal Harbor, in Maine. Mr. Rockefeller had an extensive knowledge of wild life and he knew intimately the trees and wild flowers and he often delivered little lectures to his sons on these subjects. Just how much these lectures were appreciated—Laurance's adult interest in the New York Zoological Society is about the only hint—remains open to question, but Mr. Rockefeller didn't depend entirely on nature to make the walks attractive. He always carried in his pocket pieces of chocolate or maple sugar and there was a stop somewhere along the way for a treat.

Mr. Rockefeller taught his sons to swim and to ice skate, and from their boyhood he schooled them in an orderly and sensible attitude toward the handling of money. All these things, as

John Cushman Fistere pointed out in one of the rare articles about the Rockefeller brothers that appeared in the *Saturday Evening Post* about the time they were out of college, were very much in line with the training that Mr. Rockefeller had received from his own father. The elder Rockefeller, with a straw hat perched on his head, had taught his son to swim and had given him lessons in skating in the back yard of their New York City home. Very good lessons they were, too, because even after his own sons were grown Mr. Rockefeller, Jr., was easily the best ice skater in the family and a superior horseback rider and driver.

The boys' father had been brought up with the feeling, which his mother emphasized, that the family's money belonged to God and that he was to be merely a steward. He impressed something of the same idea on his sons and he followed his own father's system of requiring them to keep detailed accounts of their allowances and what they spent, starting in their childhood when they might get only a quarter a week. Each week he examined their account books and he might fine or reward them to the extent of a nickel or so depending upon the accuracy of their records. He also insisted that it was a good idea for them to give a modest sum regularly to charities. This custom of keeping books continued through their college days when their allowances had advanced to perhaps $1,800 a year and they were buying their own clothes and managing their own recreational affairs. As in ice skating, they learned the intended lesson but not as well as had their father in his youth. Occasionally, after the boys were at college, there came an appeal for a little extra money, which sometimes was granted and sometimes wasn't. John was usually the best at keeping his accounts and Winthrop suspects that he was usually the most often broke.

"Looking back," David said long after his graduation, "I'm

sure father was wise about the amount of money we had. I never felt I had plenty. But it never really occurred to me that I could get more."

Mr. Rockefeller himself wasn't always so sure of his own wisdom, or perhaps it would be fairer to say that he was never overconfident. When, in the 1930's, it was remarked that the boys were measuring up to all that could be asked of them, he agreed but added that "not a day passes but Mrs. Rockefeller and I pray that they will continue to measure up." And later he remarked in a speech at Princeton University that "even in this machine age there are certain things so important that they demand personal attention. The business of being a father is surely one." In the business of being a father, Mr. Rockefeller was not one to encourage rowdy or roughhouse play even in the family's most relaxed moments but he spared no efforts to establish a relationship of respect and affection with his sons.

The third and, in many ways, the most vital influence on the boys however was their mother, the former Abby Greene Aldrich, daughter of U. S. Senator Nelson W. Aldrich of Rhode Island, one of the powerful Republican leaders of his day in Congress. Of the many thoughtful things Mr. Rockefeller did in his efforts to assure his sons of a balanced, normal life, there is considerable reason to believe that the most important step was taken when, still a senior at Brown University, he fell in love with Abby Aldrich. Mr. Rockefeller even as a young man had little taste for social affairs and when he did attend such functions was retiring almost to the point of shyness, but his wife was at home in almost any company whether it included Left Bank artists, social leaders or politicians. Where the Rockefeller family was strait-laced and socially very conservative, she was accustomed to the more liberal attitudes of Washington society.

This turned out to be a happy combination for the five Rockefeller boys. There was a considerable difference in the attitudes and ideas of their parents but at the same time it was an unusually happy and congenial family atmosphere in which the children grew up, with the diversified attitudes of their father and mother so skillfully blended that each supplemented and reinforced the other in the task of rearing the children to live balanced and busy lives.

The boys and their older sister, Abby, relaxed every afternoon at teatime with their mother, who taught them simple card games such as Flinch and Numerica, read to them or discussed whatever they were most interested in at the moment. These were warm, gay and cheerful hours in which they combined fun with learning and in which their father sometimes, but not often, joined for a short while before dinner. Mrs. Rockefeller, an enthusiastic and able patroness of the arts, encouraged the boys' interest in painting and music without uncovering any remarkable talents. Mr. Rockefeller had learned to play the violin as a boy but none of the children showed a particular interest in music. Nelson plugged away at learning to play the cello— he was the kind of boy who liked to take a big grip on anything he did—but gave it up in disgust when the strings on his instrument snapped just as he was about to make his first public appearance in a church performance. It also was typical that, having learned about painting, Nelson made a stab at applying his youthful knowledge in a practical way. For some years he painted his own Christmas cards but without producing anything that has stood the test of time.

Mrs. Rockefeller's letters to her children, many of which have been collected in the story of her life by Mary Ellen Chase, give a good indication of the great amount of time she spent—in addition to running four houses and supervising the activities of a large staff and attending to her social duties—in widening the interest of the boys in people and ideas. "My enthusiasm for all sorts of people," she wrote once, "is likely to carry me away." "I am glad that you like The Wind in the Willows. Of course, I knew you would. What are you going to read next?" "I hope that you will find time to finish Vanity Fair, for it will well repay you." "I hope you will memorize lots of good poetry because, as you grow older, you will find that it will give you great pleasure." "I bought you a little magnifying glass yesterday, and I am sending it to you. You can look at flowers and bugs and all sorts of things through it." David eventually became an expert collector of beetles. "There are so many jays here in Florida that the air is filled with cries of thief, thief, thief. They are beautiful birds to look at, but their table manners are very bad." "Don't forget to keep your accounts. Papa will want to examine them." "I'm terribly sorry over the death of your mother rabbit. Do you suppose she could have died from eating your shoe-strings?"

For as long as she lived, this correspondence with her children continued whenever they were separated, and she repeatedly emphasized their responsibility to take an interest in schoolmates who were lonesome or failed to make friends easily. She also reminded them on many occasions to be polite to older persons with whom they came into contact either on social occasions or in school affairs. "Old people like to be made a part of things," she wrote. "Don't forget to go out of your way to make them feel wanted and at home." And she never let them forget that their father was the real center of the family. "Your father is so modest, so unassuming, and often so doubtful of his own ability that I wonder if you always realize what a tower of strength he is to me and to us all." "Your father is so wonderfully thoughtful himself and so considerate of all the people with whom he comes in contact that I am sure he must occasionally find the rest of us somewhat difficult. Perhaps there is a little bit too much Aldrich in us and not enough Rockefeller!"

Mr. Rockefeller would never have admitted that he sometimes found them somewhat "difficult," but he was always pleasantly uncertain about what his wife might do or say next. She had a great many interests and a habit of doing things in her own way and none of the men around the house ever felt that there was even "a little bit too much Aldrich" in the Rockefeller family.

✳ III ✳

A NUMBER OF AMUSING STORIES SURROUND THE BOYHOOD
of the Rockefeller brothers, most of them untrue. As
with most legends, however, there was usually a slight basis
for the stories and they were illustrative of the boys' upbringing.

Of these supposedly real-life incidents, the best known concerns a meeting with several young friends during a vacation
at Seal Harbor in Maine. The boys spent a great deal of time
in the water and their father had bought them a small sailboat
with which they were delighted. One of their friends, however,
was not much impressed, and pointed out that there were far
more handsome and expensive models available.

"Why," he demanded, "doesn't your father buy you one of
those big new boats?"

The Rockefeller boys looked at him scornfully. "Who," one
of them asked, "do you think we are—the Vanderbilts?"

There was something so basically correct about this story
that it has clung to the boys for years, although none of them
can actually remember ever having had such a conversation, and
they have come to regard the story as both a little embarrassing
and more than a little tiresome. An element of truth, however,
lies behind the yarn. When the Rockefellers' first son, John,
was around kindergarten age he frequently went to play in
Central Park and sometimes sailed a toy boat on Conservatory
Lake.

At that time the lake was a favorite spot for children of rich families living near the park but very few children from poor or even middle-class families showed up there. One reason for this was that employees in the office of the Commissioner of Parks usually co-operated in discouraging the common folk from using the lake by telling those who inquired that a permit was necessary to sail boats there. This was perfectly true but the attendant usually forgot to tell the inquirer—unless he obviously was a person of wealth—that a permit could be secured without charge merely by asking for it.

As a result of this practice, most of the children who played there had expensive toys and four or five of them had toy sailboats that cost as much as fifty or a hundred dollars. The Park Department caretaker stored the boats in between visits, the Police Department always had at least two officers on duty during the busy hours to see that the children were not molested and most of the young visitors were accompanied by husky chauffeurs.

A young man who was then office boy for the Park Commission recalled long afterward that everybody called the Rockefeller heir Johnny and that he was usually easy to identify because his boat couldn't have cost more than five dollars. Johnny often played by himself but seemed to enjoy talking to adults around the park, particularly the police and park officials. One of them first reported that when he asked Johnny why he didn't have a bigger and fancier boat, he received the classic reply concerning the Vanderbilts. At the time, John was so young that the remark was probably put in his mouth by some older person and it is doubtful that it meant anything to him other than a way to get adults to laugh. Park attendants often sent visitors to question him about his boat and John always made the same reply, taking a normal childish delight in the horseplay.

John, when he was older, attended Browning School in New York, where his father had been a student, and later went to Loomis School at Windsor, Connecticut, but by the time the other boys were old enough for school their mother had become interested in some new educational ideas sponsored by Professor John Dewey. The progressive and coeducational Lincoln School was just being started in connection with Columbia University and was a kind of experimental laboratory for some of Dewey's methods. One thing about the school that interested the Rockefellers was that, by benefit of scholarships, every stratum of society and every race, color and creed were represented in the student body at Lincoln. The child of a Harlem day laborer had the same status on entering Lincoln as the child of a Park Avenue banker.

When Nelson was ready for school he entered Lincoln and the Rockefellers were so pleased with his experience there that the younger boys also attended the school when they reached the proper age. They made the daily trip of several miles by all modes of transportation. Sometimes they walked or roller-skated part of the way from their home on Fifty-fourth Street and rode the rest of the way in the family limousine, which had followed them along the street and was ready to pick them up whenever they became tired or the hour grew late. When they were older they took a bus part of the time or, depending on the family residence at the time, drove down from Tarrytown in a beaten-up old Ford. They liked the school, expanded in its highly competitive atmosphere and later, like most of their fellow students, felt fairly well prepared for almost anything except spelling and perhaps arithmetic.

Their after-school play, as children, was usually supervised by a student from the Union Theological Seminary who took them to Central Park for a romp on pleasant days and got them safely home again or turned them over to the family chauffeur.

In the winters, they lived in the nine-story family mansion at ten West Fifty-fourth Street, in what was then a dignified residential section of New York City. The big house, which has since been torn down to make way for the Museum of Modern Art, had an infirmary, a gymnasium, a playground and squash court on the roof, and large living quarters for the staff in addition to the family suites, workrooms, drawing room, library and music room. Mrs. Rockefeller was not one to be awed by the task of running a large establishment and once remarked that she didn't mind a little clean dust occasionally. She had the boys pick out the draperies and wall paper for their own rooms and, as they grew older, take charge of their own parties. She ran her household staff pleasantly and efficiently and at times kept four different houses open and running, without ever seeming to be heavily burdened by such duties.

There was necessarily a great deal of entertaining in the Rockefeller household as the boys grew up, despite the fact that their father took little pleasure in social functions that included other than members of the family and a few intimate friends. Even the most formal occasions, however, were comparatively unostentatious and touched the lives of the younger Rockefellers only indirectly or on some memorable night as when the King of the Belgians was a guest on Fifty-fourth Street. Even the debut of Abby was a modest affair when compared to the coming-out parties that were customary in New York society in those days. Abby's party was at the Fifty-fourth Street mansion. A few days before the occasion Mr. Rockefeller met a distinguished friend who asked him to attend a dinner at which a group of civic leaders planned to discuss some worthy cause. The dinner was the same night as Abby's debut and Mr. Rockefeller shook his head.

"I'm sorry," he said, "but I can't come because we're having company at home that night."

The Rockefeller children usually spent summer vacations at Seal Harbor, where they lived in the water and in the woods most of the time, but perhaps their happiest days were week ends and summers at Pocantico Hills, near Tarrytown, some thirty miles up the Hudson River from New York. Here their father owned some 3,000 acres high over the river, here he and his bride had planted sapling spruce and hemlock trees across a great hill sloping down from the big house, here he had built driving and riding trails and, later, a $500,000 playhouse with bowling alleys, tennis court, swimming pool and squash court. Pocantico Hills was home to the Rockefeller boys from their earliest memory of picnics in the woods and it remained home to them after they were grown. Four of them eventually established their own homes on or close to the estate and the fourth generation of Rockefeller children played under the tall trees which their grandparents planted half a century earlier.

The boys learned to appreciate good food as they grew up but there was nothing fancy or exotic about the meals served them at home, and they ate what was placed before them at the table. They also learned, with their mother's encouragement, to cook. Both Nelson and Winthrop developed considerable pride in their culinary skill and after they were grown they still liked to take a turn over a hot stove occasionally. During one summer vacation, Nelson and Laurance joined up as members of the famous Grenfell expedition on an arctic trip. They were members of the crew with routine duties, but when the regular cook became ill on the trip they were shifted to the galley and told to prepare the meals. As cook, Nelson was reported to have performed so successfully that the crew insisted he stay on the job for the rest of the trip even after the cook had recovered. This report has been received with some skepticism by those who have sampled Nelson's cooking in later years, although the skeptics usually have to admit that they, of course, never tasted the wares of the expedition's regular cook.

Throughout the period of their elementary schooling the brothers had been encouraged to keep themselves busy, especially in a way that would be useful or would bring them some satisfaction other than the pleasure of the moment. They raised rabbits, and Nelson and Laurance formed a partnership that made money by selling them to a laboratory. They ran errands, hoed the garden at so much an hour, cleaned shoes at a fixed price and killed flies at ten cents a hundred to earn pocket money, of which they never felt they had quite enough. They learned to ride, swim and sail a boat and won permission to drive an automobile a little later than the time they considered themselves qualified. (Nelson, Winthrop and David all managed to get tickets for speeding in the next few years.) They quarreled with each other, they experienced jealousies and disappointments, they resorted to boyish fights and generally enjoyed every minute of it. It was all in the pattern of the lives led by their young friends, ranging from the chauffeur's children, who fared very well, to the children of socialite families, most of whom fared a trifle better in worldly goods than the Rockefeller boys. They were not often denied reasonable requests for things that they wanted but at the same time it was almost a rule that they were never given the biggest, the best or the most elaborate of anything.

Their father and mother stuck closely to the job of rearing their children and were seldom separated from them for more than a few days at a time. Mr. Rockefeller wanted the boys to know their own country and occasionally he would take some of them or the whole family would go on a trip to the West or to some other area that he felt would be both entertaining and educational. And later they made a similar trip to Europe.

On such journeys, even when some of the boys were very

young, they all had responsibilities commensurate with their ages and experience. One of them was assigned to take charge of the railroad tickets, which he purchased and cared for throughout the trip. Another handled the job of reserving hotel rooms and of paying the bill when they departed. A third took over transportation of the party's baggage, and so on. Each was paid according to his job.

These trips were planned to avoid any mention of the Rockefellers in the local newspapers of towns where they stopped, but it didn't always work out that way. Sometimes word would leak out that they were arriving and the reporters and photographers would swarm around. On such occasions, Mr. Rockefeller was in the habit of explaining frankly to the reporters that he felt his sons would have enough trouble growing up like other boys of their generation and that he didn't want to have their problems intensified by photographs and articles in the newspapers while they were young. He would tell the newspapermen that he would "appreciate any help you can give me" and then he would offer to answer questions himself if the reporters had any they wanted to ask. An interview with Mr. Rockefeller was a rare event in the newspaper world and reporters were always happy to turn their attention away from the boys in exchange for almost anything their father was willing to say about national or international affairs. It wasn't, as a rule, very much.

How much the young Rockefellers appreciated, at the time, the efforts of their father to keep them from public attention may be open to doubt, but it is certain that in later years they all approved and applied many of the same rules to the rearing of their own children. Not only have the brothers avoided publicity in regard to their children but they have rather determinedly encouraged a strong spirit of self-reliance. As a result, there have been occasions when young sprouts of the fourth generation have come home from school or from play with a few bruises of battle on their faces as a result of old-fashioned fist fights.

In the same spirit, Nelson's son, Rodman, did a spell of farm work in Venezuela during one school vacation when he was about seventeen years old. On his return to New York his father took him from the airport to a plush Rockefeller Center restaurant for luncheon and ordered steaks. "Gosh!" exclaimed the young scion of the Rockefellers when the meal was served. "Steak! I haven't had anything but beans for weeks."

Allowing for a slight exaggeration, young Rodman was reflecting an attitude that has been prevalent in both the third and fourth generations of the family; a kind of aggressive determination to show that they can "take it" as well as anybody else. The Rockefellers always have their guard up against anyone who suggests that their name and wealth give them some special privilege. Laurance stood in a long line at City Hall to pay two dollars for his wedding license. Nelson ate in a cafeteria to save money at college. Winthrop lived the life of a common laborer when he worked in the Texas oil fields. They were determined to "belong" to whatever group they were associated with and one of the brothers still recalls with acute disgust the school instructor who, apparently trying to be both amusing and flattering, singled him out of a group visiting a factory and introduced him as Mr. Richfellow. Such incidents were not rare and even today one of the brothers' children occasionally brings up the problem of what to do when a classmate greets him on the school bus by shouting: "Hello, Mr. Moneybags Rockefeller. How many yachts do you have?"

"Just say, 'Good morning, Mr. Vanderbilt,'" the boy's mother told him. "'We have only sixteen yachts now but we're getting some more soon.' Then everybody will think it's a joke and pay no attention."

The idea of fitting into a congenial crowd probably influenced the older boys when they had to decide which college to attend. None of them chose Brown University, which their father had attended. John and Laurance went to Princeton, Nelson to Dartmouth and Winthrop to Yale. David, who had already shown signs of being the family scholar, went to Harvard and, later, to the London School of Economics and the University of Chicago. The boys had made extended trips away from home during their high-school days but college was perhaps the first real test of how well they could operate on their own. Their father offered each boy $2,500 if he wouldn't smoke until after his twenty-first birthday, but only David and Nelson—neither of whom became smokers later—earned the prize. John smoked a pipe at college but the family abhorrence of liquor was so strongly impressed on him that he didn't even drink from the customary loving cup during ceremonies of his club—although his father had agreed with him that such a formality could hardly be criticized if he felt he would be embarrassed by refraining.

None of the brothers was particularly interested in or expert at athletic competition. John played tennis and golf; Nelson made the soccer team at Dartmouth; Laurance played good but not brilliant competitive tennis. Their scholastic performance, too, was about average except for Winthrop who never finished his work at Yale. He remarked later, in trying to evaluate his college career, that he never quite knew what his trouble was except that he "just wasn't interested and wasn't getting enough out of it" to enable him to do the required work.

Nelson's roommate was an unusually able scholar as well as a close friend, John French, Jr. French easily made Phi Beta Kappa in his junior year while Nelson was plugging along making average grades and engaging in a number of campus activities and trying—vainly—to get elected class president.

The best he could do was vice-president. Nelson thrived on competition, however, and when French received his Phi Beta Kappa key it was a challenge that couldn't be ignored. He suddenly became a bookworm and, by sheer hard work, made the honorary society in his senior year. He was one of five seniors permitted because of their high standing to choose their own courses that year without reference to college requirements.

"When John French heard I had made Phi Beta Kappa," Nelson said later, "he took off his key and announced that he would never wear it again because if they would give it to a plugger like me it couldn't mean anything to a real scholar." This explanation was rather typical of Nelson's reactions to his own accomplishments. It was also, according to French, completely untrue.

John and Laurance came in for some gentle ribbing in college when they were chosen by their respective classes as the ones "most likely to succeed." David got his Ph.D. at Chicago and caused some lifted eyebrows by writing a highly technical thesis analyzing the causes of economic waste and stating that "the existence of monopoly offers prima facie evidence of a social evil." The idea that this might represent an attack on the methods by which his grandfather founded the Standard Oil Company was of no concern to David, who not only approves of the way John D., Sr., brought order and efficiency into a chaotic industry but thinks it was a fine thing that the government forced the breakup of the monopoly into a number of separate companies. "Some units," he pointed out later, "are now bigger and better than grandfather could ever have imagined even the whole company would be."

Although the brothers enjoyed most phases of their college careers, they also were becoming accustomed to the idea that they were going to assume responsibilities of considerable importance within the next few years. This was nothing to cause them any collective dismay. On the contrary, most of them were eager to get at the job and felt with typical college enthusiasm that the world should begin to show at least some slight improvement once they had a chance to start doing things. But they had been reminded a great many times that the family merely exercised a stewardship over the Rockefeller money and that they were under a stern obligation to conduct that stewardship in a manner that would serve the common good. It was an idea they never dreamed of questioning, any more than they would have thought of trying to shirk their responsibilities.

"I suppose," one of them said later, "that when we were in college all of us felt that responsibility was the only thing we had more of than our classmates."

This may well have been true, but it didn't deter them from taking on added responsibilities as soon as they got out of college. Except for Winthrop, all of the brothers married within a comparatively short time after graduation.

John's wife is the former Blanchette Ferry Hooker, whom he had known for some years prior to their marriage in 1932. They have three daughters and one son. They built a home near the Pocantico Hills estate and, in New York, occupy a duplex apartment on the East Side. In 1950 they built an ultramodern guest house near fashionable Beekman Place, with a nine-foot-high brick wall along the front topped by three ten-foot-high glass panels.

Nelson married Mary Todhunter Clark, daughter of a wealthy and socially prominent Philadelphia family and a vacation neighbor of the Rockefellers in Maine the week after his graduation from Dartmouth in 1930. They have three sons and two daughters. In New York, they occupy a triplex penthouse over Fifth Avenue, keep it well filled with primitive art and the works of modern painters, and occasionally fret about how they can arrange things in order to achieve a spare bedroom. This was a problem that proved difficult to solve and for a long time overnight guests had to get along as best they could in a study that could be transformed into an emergency bedroom.

Laurance married Mary French, whose family were close friends of the Rockefellers, in 1934. They have three daughters and one son.

Winthrop was thirty-five when he married glamorous Mrs. Barbara (Bobo) Sears. They have one son and, since late in 1949, have been separated.

David, who married Margaret McGrath the same year he completed his work at Chicago University, has two sons and four daughters.

There was practically a decade—in years—separating the eldest and the youngest of the Rockefeller boys, which is a considerable span when you're just out of college. Furthermore, David had spent a few extra years at graduate studies and it was 1940 when he left Chicago University, whereas John had graduated from Princeton in 1929. There was not, however, much of a difference in their attitudes or their way of thinking, or at least not as much as might have been expected, because they had long been in the habit of talking things over at family conferences whenever the opportunity arose.

In these talks, the brothers were constantly reviewing what they wanted to do, what they were expected to do and how they were going to go about doing it. None of them approached the choosing of a career lightly or without weighing the pros and cons. Circumstances differed with each, but on the orderly balance sheet of their collective assets and liabilities there were certain things that could be taken for granted.

None of them, for instance, was looking for a sinecure. They were not only trained to work and willing to work but there was about them a kind of tense, determined eagerness to achieve; an eagerness that might easily become pomposity save for a realistic sense of humor and an ingrained abhorrence of sham or pretense.

They were ambitious and individualistic enough for quarrels and jealousies and were inclined, for the most part, toward competition rather than reliance on one another. Yet they had a strong bond of family unity that overshadowed everything else in a pinch and they were emphatically aware of the necessity for and the advantages of sticking together wherever the broad interests of the family were involved. They had, among themselves, a variety of talents and a considerable amount of money.

Their attitude toward money was important, and a little involved. By training and example, they were far from "soft" about financial affairs. On the contrary, they were keenly interested in making money and, on various occasions, they have made full use of all the legitimate financial and business advantages—and they are, of course, considerable—the Rockefellers possess to do so. This attitude was illustrated when one of the boys, while still in college, distressed his mother by remarking that he was deliberately training himself to be cold and calculating in order to prevent his personal feelings from influencing his judgment in financial affairs.

Yet this interest in money-making was largely a matter of proving their ability. The third generation of Rockefellers knew that the mere possession or accumulation of money was not their problem, nor was it likely to be. Money itself was of secondary value in their scheme of things; money represented merely a tool with which they could work and the important thing was how they used the tool and what they built with it.

This attitude was frequently illustrated—and still is—not only in large affairs but in small things. When their sister Abby was married, for example, young Laurance's wedding gift was a box of stationery which he paid for out of his allowance. When John, years later, was looking around for a suitable Christmas gift for a distinguished educator, he picked out a fishing knife that cost less than five dollars. When one of the brothers wanted to help a woman employee who was worried about a thousand-dollar hospital bill he sent her a check not for the entire sum, which would have made little difference to him, but for half of it, explaining that he hoped she would not be embarrassed by his desire to help out since he knew that in different circumstances she would help him.

"The Rockefellers almost never give presents of much value," a business associate remarked after knowing them for a number of years. "But they understand the value of thoughtfulness. One of them may send my wife flowers on special occasions. Or if I'm on a business trip I'm always sure to get a telegram or a letter wishing me luck or thanking me for something I've done. Any one of them will go to a lot of trouble to show his interest in little ways—so that you usually feel that they mean it."

This de-emphasis of the importance of money in achieving either friendship or success as they want it is inherent in the brothers' thinking. But in quite another way they are also conscious of a different, but no less important, monetary factor in the broad field of business and finance. With the third generation, the family's accumulated wealth is being dissipated on a great descending curve by taxes, philanthropies and division among the heirs who, by 1952, included six children and twenty-two grandchildren.

This is not, of course, to suggest that Winthrop was wrong when he told a Texas oil-field companion that he failed to see any signs that the family was running out of cash. John D., Jr., retaining control of the great bulk of the fortune, was still at the middle of this century hundreds of times a millionaire—perhaps four to six hundred times. Or perhaps considerably more, because fluctuations in the value of securities held by the Rockefellers make a vast difference from year to year and even from month to month in the total of their over-all wealth.

Money has come to the boys directly and, indirectly, through trust funds set up for them and their children and their grandchildren. They have the use of income from these trusts during their lifetimes after which the income will go to their children. That, however, will mark the end of the present arrangement and the fifth generation will necessarily bring some kind of a turning point in the handling of the estate. Under New York law, the trust funds cannot be longer maintained in their present status and the Rockefeller wealth must be split up among the grandchildren of the five brothers and their sister, Mrs. Irving Pardee.

Owing to circumstances such as these it was probably difficult for the Rockefeller boys themselves to estimate with accuracy either their personal wealth or the extent of the family fortune when they were ready to start their careers. They knew that they would soon share with their father ownership of the $125,000,000 Rockefeller Center real estate project and would, later, become sole owners. And they knew that the bulk of their own and the family's investments were not in such enterprises at all but in other concerns, principally oil companies and the Chase National Bank.

All of this added up to a great deal of money but the sons were, nevertheless, in a far different position from their father, who was the only son of John D., Sr., in a day when inherited wealth could be passed more freely from one generation to another. "We just don't," Laurance remarked on one occasion in a comment that was strictly relative, "have money the way people used to have it."

Thus, when the young Rockefellers were starting their careers, they totaled up their assets and came to the conclusion that

their really important possessions were the Rockefeller tradition, their business connections, their time and talents and their
money—in about that order.

"What we really have," one of them pointed out later in an
effort to clarify their attitude, "is our name. That is our big
asset. It opens doors and, as our money is dispersed, it is of far
greater value than anything else as long as it remains a good
name. Seeing that it does must be our first consideration. There
is an old saying: 'Shirt sleeves to shirt sleeves in three generations.' Well, we have to avoid a third-generation anticlimax.
We have to put our time and our money to work building something new."

The most important elements of the Rockefeller brothers'
philosophy were packed into that paragraph and, without dis-
paraging the importance of money, it put that word more or
less in its proper place in their affairs. This was clear to a certain degree in their minds as they came of age and began taking
over various obligations that were essential to the continuity
of family affairs. But they began, too, the search for something
else; something that would lead them out from the shadow of
the family name and let them stand on their own feet. It wasn't
going to be an easy search but none of them objected to that.
If it had been easy, the Rockefeller boys wouldn't have been
interested in pursuing it.

✳ IV ✳

WHEN JOHN DAVISON ROCKEFELLER, JR., WENT TO WORK in his father's private office just before the turn of the century he learned his way around by doing all kinds of odd jobs, including filling the ink wells. Such menial tasks were more or less expected of a young man who was trying to get a start in business in an era of top hats, frock coats and dignified financial giants. Great things were happening in the United States, great cities were springing up in the West, great new industrial horizons were opening and William McKinley was in the White House. There was plenty of opportunity—something Mr. Rockefeller didn't have to worry about—for any young man in the country, but in Wall Street it was still deemed the better part of wisdom to start at the bottom and work up.

Some drastic changes had come about more than three decades later when Mr. Rockefeller's five sons were emerging from college and starting their careers. The vast personal empires of the nineteenth century were being transformed by introduction of the managerial system and by the pressure of government regulation. The day of the Wall Street barons who pushed the railroads and factories westward beyond the horizon was coming to an end. Even the aura of great personal dignity and discretion so long associated with financial leadership seemed to be overshadowed by the bustling, hustling showmanship that had come to the front in the Roaring Twenties. But most of all, the land was racked by an incredibly devastating

economic depression that had sent all sorts of unknown pro-
fessors and economists scurrying to Washington to set up something called the New Deal.

The influence of the times was not lost on the young Rockefellers, none of whom filled inkwells. Furthermore, there were
five of them and sometimes it may have seemed to their father
that they quintupled the effect of change that had occurred
since he was graduated from Brown University in 1897. But,
if so, he was not one to object. Nor was he one—any more
than his own father had been—to interfere or impose advice or
try to hold a tight rein on his sons after they had set out on
their own.

Mr. Rockefeller had always had an appreciation of traditional
things and, in the old days, his horse-drawn carriage had been
one of the last to give way to the influx of automobiles in Wall
Street. He liked horses and he preferred a calmly progressive
way of life to a hectic one. But he could understand and approve the fact that Laurance chose to race down the Hudson
River to his office in a chattering speedboat. He could appreciate
the reasons behind Winthrop's decision to gain experience by
shoveling dirt as a common laborer in the oil fields instead of
immediately parking himself behind a desk. He could understand David's extended pursuit of higher education at the
London School of Economics.

But when he was approached with the idea—in which Nelson
concurred—that the time had come for him to abandon his
lifelong advocacy of prohibition, Mr. Rockefeller felt that things
were being carried a bit too far. This proposal, however, and the
way it worked out illustrate a couple of interesting things about
the family relationship. One is that they like to argue things
out among themselves, especially the brothers, and to get the
benefit of each other's viewpoint, not infrequently changing
their minds as a result. Another is that these arguments, which

are sometimes hot ones, are kept very much inside the family and thus—as is not uncommonly the fate of those who keep their own affairs to themselves—give rise on occasion to cockeyed stories of how this or that came about.

One of these cockeyed stories concerned Nelson, his father and the Volstead Act. As reported on various occasions, the story was that Nelson became firmly convinced that the experiment in prohibition in the United States was a failure and that it was resulting in many evils, mainly gangsterism. He felt that it would be an important contribution to the campaign for repeal of the Volstead Act if his father would make a public announcement that he was in favor of repeal and he supposedly discussed the question with Mr. Rockefeller without success. The discussion, however, continued at the dinner table and Mr. Rockefeller remarked that he believed the evils of prohibition had been greatly exaggerated.

This was a challenge to Nelson and he invited his father to go for a short walk through mid-Manhattan after dinner. They walked only two or three blocks but in that time Nelson pointed out a score of speak-easies running full blast and ignored by the police.

"And, pa," he was supposed to have added as a clincher, "every one of the speak-easies you've just seen is on your property!"

Circumstances were such that this story might well have been true because there were considerably more than a score of illegal saloons and a sprinkling of other questionable establishments on the land that had been recently acquired for construction of Rockefeller Center. The neighborhood of old tenements and brownstone fronts was such that any visitor giving it a careful inspection might have changed his mind about prohibition. But the truth is that Mr. Rockefeller could never have made such a difficult and important decision in such a manner, nor would Nelson have had the temerity to suggest it to him in such an offhand way.

Liquor had never been and still is not served in the elder Rockefeller's household. His support of the Volstead Act had been based on deep religious and moral conviction, backed up by a long family tradition. "Neither my father nor his father ever tasted a drop of intoxicating liquor, nor have I," he said later. "My mother and her mother were among the dauntless women of their day who, hating the horrors of drunkenness, were often found with bands of women of like mind, praying on their knees in the saloons in their ardent desire to save men from the evils that so commonly sprang from these sources of iniquity."

This background made it extremely difficult for Mr. Rockefeller to approach the idea of changing his mind and joining the repeal movement. He didn't want to believe that prohibition had failed and it was with great reluctance that he found himself in partial agreement—but still unconvinced—with those who believed it had. The climax came one spring night in 1932 when he had dinner with a group of men, including some who were old friends and respected advisers, and his two eldest sons, John and Nelson. At such a meeting the boys were little more than spectators. John was twenty-six and Nelson twenty-four, while the other dinner guests were men of stature in New York affairs. One of them was Thomas M. Debevoise, their father's oldest and closest associate, a soft-spoken man but one whom the brothers treated with the utmost respect. Other guests included Harry Emerson Fosdick and Raymond B. Fosdick and George W. Wickersham, then head of a commission that was investigating prohibition problems.

It was a long and by no means a happy session. Mr. Rockefeller was seeking advice and he got a great deal of it in unvarnished terms, particularly in regard to the blossoming of gangsterism in connection with bootlegging, the breakdown of law enforcement and the manner in which speak-easies flourished on his own property in mid-Manhattan. It was perhaps the most difficult decision of his life, but not long afterward Mr. Rockefeller issued a statement in favor of repeal and was generally credited with influencing public opinion considerably toward that end.

This idea of talking things out before important decisions became almost routine with the Rockefeller brothers, who slowly developed an attitude of give and take, of subtly combined independence and interdependence and of willingness to profit by one another's experience. It is a system that requires a balance not always easy to maintain. Sometimes one or more of the brothers goes along with great reluctance. Sometimes one of them insists that he is being "bullied" into agreement. But in affairs that involve family interests they usually end up with a reasonably united attitude, conscious of the importance of each sharing in the job of carrying on the continuity of many affairs that began with their father or grandfather. This awareness of a common interest, however, tends to make each of them more intensely determined to strike out on his own as well.

Only John, the eldest of the lot, went into his father's office to take up as a full-time job the philanthropic work to which Mr. Rockefeller has devoted so much of his own lifetime. "I suppose it worked out that way because I got out of college first," he said on one occasion. "Father had the whole job when he was young because he was an only son. There were five of us and as the other boys came along they helped pick up the ball, so that each of us has had opportunity for other things. But I was always the one most concerned with philanthropies."

The Rockefeller philanthropies are on a world-wide basis and

John began his education in international problems while still a student at Princeton, but only after covering a number of other fields before and after he entered college. At Loomis School in Connecticut he was a thin and gawky boy, quiet but friendly and willing to pull his own weight. He was secretary and vice-president of the French Club and a member of the student council but his biggest extracurricular job was as business manager of the student publication, which in prep-school fashion was called the *Loomiscellany*. He liked the job and when he went to Princeton in 1925 he went to work selling advertising for the *Princetonian*. This got him a job on the business board of the college daily, but that was about the end of his publishing career.

John was too reticent and perhaps too unsure of himself to get very deeply into the swirl of campus life in the Princeton of the 1920's, when the rosy fog of F. Scott Fitzgerald and the "jazz age" still hung heavily over the college. He was also too pious, if that word is accepted in the sense of meaning reverent and religious. He spent a good deal of time in Y.M.C.A. work in Princeton and served as that organization's undergraduate vice-president. He taught English to immigrants in the community and in the summers he worked as a counselor in a summer camp for tenement boys in New Jersey. He made a bid to become manager of the fotball team without success, but was elected to Cap and Gown, one of the more exclusive social clubs at Princeton.

At this point, John's plans for the future were not particularly definite except that, more than his brothers, he is a conformist and more or less accepted the idea that he would follow in his father's footsteps. He was majoring in economics and, in addition to all his other activities, he managed to get in a couple of visits to Europe while he was still in college. One of these journeys was a bicycle trip with Nelson through France, where they spent most of the time wandering about historical spots on their own but occasionally made contact with the world of châteaux and town houses by presenting letters of introduction with which their parents had equipped them.

Later John spent one summer in Geneva as an assistant in the information section of the League of Nations, which was a kind of turning point for him. Despite his family's position, his own shyness had previously limited his view of world affairs and made him feel that the activities of famous personages, the events that made the newspaper headlines were beyond his experience. But at Geneva he had a job that required him to rub elbows with men who were making history and he found that they were occasionally quite willing to rub elbows with the eldest of the third generation of Rockefellers. Aristide Briand, the shaggy, eloquent French Foreign Minister who was regarded as the ablest diplomat of his day, chatted with him through a haze of cigarette smoke, squinted his eyes at John's thin face and told him he looked like Charles A. Lindbergh. "Maybe," he added, "*all* young Americans look like Lindbergh to me."

Prime Minister Mackenzie King of Canada stopped by the building where John worked one morning to say hello. John and another young man in the information section shared an office on the fourth floor and they were sitting with their feet on their desks when a boy from the lobby toiled up the four flights and presented the Prime Minister's card. By that time, John had expanded sufficiently in the diplomatic atmosphere of Geneva to wave grandly to the boy and quip: "Okay, send the Prime Minister up." But, while it was a good gag, it wasn't in the Rockefeller manner and John quickly got his feet off the desk and himself down to the lobby to see Mackenzie King.

"At Geneva, I began to get a glimpse of the world and its problems," John remarked later. "I got an idea of how great the problems were and how much effort was required to do anything about them."

The next year, when he had been graduated from Princeton, he was one of four young men selected to be junior secretaries at the 1929 conference sponsored by the Institute of Pacific Relations at Kyoto, Japan. On this occasion he was taken under the wing of James F. MacDonald, who was later United States minister to Israel and the two made a trip around the world, stopping off at Kyoto for the conference. In all, they visited a dozen countries, took the trans-Siberian railroad across Russian territory and came home by way of the Pacific. For John, it was a period of serious study as well as an exciting experience and he came back to New York a little appalled by the incredible handicaps which many parts of the world would have to overcome in order to catch up with the twentieth century.

"That trip showed me the world," he said long afterward. "I felt I had learned the real meaning of the word 'international.' I knew then that only by visiting a country could you understand its problems. It is like the difference between seeing an accident and reading about it in the newspaper. If our country is going to meet its obligations of world leadership our people will have to get abroad and see the world."

This journey and subsequent visits to the Far East and Africa, as well as to other underdeveloped or laggard economic areas, did a great deal to influence his later thinking in regard to the Rockefeller philanthropic enterprises. When he returned from Kyoto to New York in December of 1929, he immediately went into his father's office and in the next three years he became a trustee of the China Medical Board, the Rockefeller Foundation, the General Education Board, the Rockefeller Institute for Medical Research, the Spelman Fund, Industrial Relations Counselors, Inc., and Colonial Williamsburg. All of these represented enterprises, mainly philanthropic, which his grandfather and father had originated or strongly supported, and which made up the backbone of the family's continuing plan for using the Rockefeller money—or at least a considerable share of it— to promote the common good.

While these enterprises were ably managed, they were dealing with constantly changing conditions, and representing the Rockefeller interest in them—and in others as the years moved along—was a man-sized job for John from the beginning. As an example, the China Medical Board, in which he was especially interested, had been created in 1914 as an operating division of The Rockefeller Foundation, and was responsible for the erection and development of the Peiping Union Medical College. Regarded as an unusually fine center of medical training, the college was instrumental in bringing modern medical techniques to China and in creating throughout the Far East a greater respect for scientific methods. John took an active interest in development of the college until 1941, when it was closed by the Japanese during their war in China. In 1947, after thirty-two years' connection with the Foundation, the China Medical Board received a final grant of $10,000,000 and became an independent organization. At that time, John resigned from the Board which, in all, had received almost $45,000,000 of Rockefeller money.

"The genius of the Rockefeller family," a close associate once remarked, "is an ability to do many things without throwing their weight around." This definition probably can be applied more accurately to the family as a whole than to the brothers as individuals, but it is particularly true in John's case.

"I didn't give my sons fixed sums of money at any period," his father once told an interviewer. "As each grew older I increased the amounts. When they went to college, John was the only one to whom I felt I could give more money than I thought he might need. The others I held in a little."

John turned out to be the most reticent, the most cautious and the most careful of the five, and yet he soon had a reputation as being the easiest to work with. Unlike some of his more extrovert brothers who occasionally like to bang a fist on a desk, John approaches a problem with quiet, painstaking thoroughness. When he became a member in 1932 of the committee on juvenile delinquency of the Bureau for Men and Boys, he felt that he couldn't take anybody's word for conditions existing in the state's penal institutions. Instead, he went himself on long, exhausting visits to the worst as well as the best of such institutions and he felt that he knew what he was talking about when the committee published "Youth in the Toils," a report that called for far-reaching changes in the methods that had long been employed in handling youthful lawbreakers and which, he felt, in many cases merely made such youths confirmed lawbreakers. The American Law Institute used the report to work out a model program and John later took an active part in the campaign to introduce this improved legislation into the criminal justice system.

The inclination to take plenty of time and to study all of the facts is so pronounced in John's approach to his work that it sometimes puts his associates into a dither. Once when an important question had to be decided with as little delay as possible an expert on the problem involved gave him a full report and asked for an opinion as quickly as he could give it. Several days passed with no word from John. The matter was becoming urgent when John finally called on the telephone and the expert rushed to answer with a sigh of relief. Their conversation, however, was hardly decisive.

"I've been thinking about our problem," John said.

"Good. We are anxious to get it settled now."

"Well, how about playing a round of golf this afternoon?"

"Why—uh—a round of golf? Sure."

They played a round of golf and John shot a deliberate, unhurried ninety-two while his companion played nervously and erratically, waiting vainly for some word about their mutual problem but hesitating to bring it up himself. "It wasn't until we reached the eighteenth hole that he finally raised the question I had been worrying about," the man said later. "He said he had reached a decision about what he felt was the best course and he outlined it to me concisely. I was so relieved that I knocked my putt into a sand trap and conceded the hole."

This attitude of cautious deliberation is balanced by John's extreme thoughtfulness in his relations with others, by a very natural friendliness and a slow-burning enthusiasm that rises to the top when his interest is aroused. "You do the best job," he once observed, "on those things from which you get the most satisfaction." He lives with as little fuss as he can manage. Often (as did his grandfather) he has a snack of crackers and milk at his desk in mid-morning and (unlike his father) he serves liquor when entertaining, but he so seldom takes a drink himself that it is usually a surprise to his friends when he decides to join them. This usually happens only when he is tired as, perhaps, after a large party at which he has been host. On one such occasion in his New York home he finally settled down late in the evening, when most of the guests had gone, with several close friends who were having a last drink. "It's been quite a day," he remarked, "and I guess I'll have a drink." He sank back in his chair and poured himself a small glass of sherry.

In some ways, John's career stands out rather sharply from the activities of his brothers and, in many ways, the fact that he is the eldest son may have made his role most difficult. Being concerned primarily with philanthropic work, he operates in a field where it is customary to measure success in broad

terms of the progress of civilization rather than in financial
or business results or specific personal achievement. He has,
however, developed a practical and clear-cut philosophy of
giving which, in large part, guides all of the brothers.

A couple of years after he left college, he became a member
of the Spelman Fund, which was maintained to handle his
father's philanthropical contributions for a period of about
eight years, but in 1940 he and his brothers set up the Rockefeller Brothers Fund, of which John became president, to meet
what he called their "citizenship responsibilities." These responsibilities include assistance to such organizations as community funds and various religious charities. In addition,
however, there is an entirely different phase of giving that
John refers to as "venture philanthropy." This is a concept
that more or less parallels the various business projects into
which the Rockefellers have put their venture or risk capital
and, in later years, they were to make a significant effort to
show how venture capital and venture philanthropy could be
used effectively together in the rehabilitation of the world's
underdeveloped areas.

In the meantime, John had collected in the years between
1932 and the beginning of World War II an unusually large
number of jobs and scattered duties that suggested in vivid
fashion the demands made on the time of all the Rockefellers.
A mere glance at a list of the boards and committees, the
clubs and the associations to which he belonged—and he gave
time and effort to virtually all of those to which he belonged
—revealed an impressive record of activities.* Only by reject-

* All of the Rockefellers belong to a large number of boards and committees,
some of which are permanent and some of which are for shorter periods. What
this means in time out of each day or each week is difficult for the average
citizen to grasp, but to the Rockefellers it means long working hours and many
lost evenings. Just for example, following is a list of boards and committees
on which John D., 3rd, held membership—or acted as chairman—over a
period of about eighteen years: American Red Cross, American International

ing countless requests to associate himself with various public and charitable endeavors and by rigorously confining himself to those in which he was specially interested or with which the family had some past connection, could the number be kept under thirty. And though his duties in some cases were nominal there were other instances in which many hours of hard work were demanded.

This work was increased with the beginning of the Second World War. John was a member of the National Child Refugee Committee and of the special gifts committee of the United Service Organization and, in 1940, became a director of the Allied Relief Fund which was later taken over by the British War Relief Society, of which he was a director. In the next year, he also became a director of United China Relief and, eventually, was awarded China's Order of the Auspicious Star by the Chinese Nationalist government. In 1942, he took on the job of assistant to Norman Davis, chairman of the American Red Cross, and helped develop that organization for full participation in the war effort. Later that same year he joined the Navy and fought out the rest of the war in Washington.

Association for Economic and Social Development, Allied Relief Fund, Inc., American Museum of Natural History, American Youth Hostels, British War Relief Society, Bureau for Men and Boys, China Medical Board, Citizens Committee for Reorganization of the Executive Branch of the Government, Colonial Williamsburg, Community Service Society, General Education Board, Greater New York Fund, Industrial Relations Counselors, Inc., International House, National Committee on Maternal Health, Princeton University, Riverside Church, Rockefeller Brothers, Inc., Rockefeller Brothers Fund, Inc., Rockefeller Center, Inc., Rockefeller Foundation, Rockefeller Institute for Medical Research, Spelman Fund, Tarrytown Hospital, Union Church of Pocantico Hills, United China Relief, Williamsburg Restoration, Inc. Also he was a member of the Academy of Political Science of New York City, the Historical Society of the Tarrytowns, the Metropolitan Museum of Art, the National Child Refugee Committee, the New York State Committee on the Youth Correction Authority Plan, the New York Zoological Society, the Westchester County Conservation Association, and the New York State Chamber of Commerce. Not to mention the Century Club, the University Club, the Sleepy Hollow Country Club and the River Club. To get a rough idea of the total number of such organizations to which all of the brothers belong, multiply the above list by five.

He spent a year in the Bureau of Personnel, was shifted to Naval Military Government and in that job was working with the Combined Civil Affairs Committee and the State-War-Navy Co-ordinating Committee until his discharge in 1945 as a lieutenant commander. For a while after his discharge he continued his work as a special assistant to Under-Secretary of the Navy Artemus Gates, but he was glad to get back to New York at the first opportunity. "In the Navy," he remarked later, "I was strictly on the hard-working level, not the policy level."

The war period, however, was an interruption in his career and it gave him an opportunity to take a look at what he had done in a decade and to think and plan about what lay ahead. "Only after the war period," he once said, "did I realize that I had to limit my area of operations and focus on a few fields in order to get a maximum effect. It seemed to me that we—the third generation—were in quite a different position than father and grandfather. They could give large sums of money for work which others carried on. Today the character of philanthropic operations has changed because you have, generally, more givers but they give less. Giving, of course, is essential but it seemed to me that in our approach the most important thing was our personal effort. And I wanted to focus my effort where it would do the most good."

When he got back to his New York office John was a tall, thin man of forty years, with a slow, pleasant smile, thinning brown hair and eyes that reminded you of his grandfather. The war had changed him little perhaps, but it had put the beginning of his career behind him and made him eager to get back to his chosen work. By the time he had settled down at his desk, his brothers, too, were back from the war.

STUDENTS IN THE PSYCHOLOGICAL FIELD ARE SOMETIMES prone to assay the philanthropical and civic activities of the Rockefellers on the basis of an assumption that they are motivated by a sense of guilt growing out of the ruthlessly acquisitive business methods that were practiced in the era of John D. Rockefeller, Sr. Such probings into the subconscious, however, strike incredibly sterile ground when they get to the second son of the clan. Nelson Aldrich Rockefeller is an irrepressible optimist, a believer in man's ability to do the improbable and a more or less cosmic catalyst in the affairs of his busy, wealthy and beneficent family. He is the most assertive, the most unrepressed, the most impatient of the five brothers and perhaps the most likely to fly off on a tangent, but he is also a kind of unstoppable organizer of their efforts to do things—and do them in an impressive way.

He is so free of inhibitions that one writer who studied him carefully during World War II suggested that his temperament was much like that of President Roosevelt, completely free of inner tensions. And Mr. Roosevelt himself once seemed to recognize some temperamental kinship when he tossed off a good-humored quip that if he could keep Nelson under his wing for a year or two he'd "make a man of him."

"Nelson," a business associate summarized, "has a politician's flair for personal touches like chucking a baby under the chin but at work he doesn't worry much about the little things, the details. He likes big, broad ideas and large-scale action. And when he makes a mistake, which isn't often and is usually due to the fact that he's in a hurry, the mistake is likely to be a whopper, too."

This tendency to be global, or at least hemispheric, in his ideas and actions sometimes scared hell out of Nelson's associates when he was in his thirties and operating under what was probably a maximum head of steam. Once or twice when he was Co-ordinator of the Office of Inter-American Affairs during World War II he decided he'd heard enough arguments over what ought to be done on some particular problem and, banging his fist on the desk, said: "We're going to do this!" His close friends would then go sleepless for a month or so while they did it, but they eventually discovered that Nelson's analysis of the problem pointed in the right direction more often than not. Nelson himself slept soundly every night.

"It wasn't so much the fear of making a big blunder, as it was that no job ever seemed too big or too impossible for Nelson to tackle," one of his associates said later. "There was one time when we were breaking our necks to ship food to Latin America but the German U-boats were knocking off ships in the South Atlantic faster than we could get them loaded. Well, somebody came up with the idea that we might avoid the U-boats if we could make better use of shipping facilities on the South American rivers and, in some way, that might be done if a canal were dug to link the Amazon and Orinoco rivers. I never was very clear on the idea but Nelson didn't stop to talk about it; he just had a survey made and the survey showed that it was engineeringly possible to do it. The trouble was that it would have been something like digging half a dozen Panama canals. Anybody but Nelson would have shrugged it off right then, but he was ready to move Pike's Peak with a hand trowel if necessary to solve the U-boat problem and God knows what would have happened if the Navy hadn't suddenly begun knocking off Nazi submarines at a highly satisfactory rate."

Nelson is instinctively an organizer, sometimes a relentless and overwhelming organizer whether he is running Rockefeller Center, of which he was president until 1951, or organizing the National Conference of Christians and Jews Brotherhood Week, of which he was chairman, or operating in the Department of State, where he was an Assistant Secretary, or merely buzzing around one of his own cocktail parties seeing that everybody has a drink and that nobody is having a dull time. "Well, let's get organized," is a familiar phrase to his friends, family and associates, and one that he is just as apt to apply to plans for going to lunch as to a $3,000,000 project for development of farming and livestock production in Venezuela. Even his children, if they happen to have a dull or disappointing afternoon, are likely to explain: "It wasn't much fun. Nobody ever got organized."

Nelson likes crowds and action and punchy phrases such as "carrying the ball" and he often becomes so intent upon getting things done that there is little time for relaxation in his long and busy day. If he takes time out for a half-hour under a sunlamp he keeps right on reading or writing while he gathers in the violet rays. If he wants to write a book he sets aside exactly a month in which to complete this chore and break into the literary world—a project which, it turned out, he couldn't complete in a month and therefore abandoned. If he goes to a cocktail party he is likely to spend an hour talking business with an acquaintance in a corner and ten minutes being so darned charming to everybody present that his hostess is almost sure to forgive all. Even the guests at his home are usually persons whose views he wants on some particular subject and he seldom wastes time or resorts to subtlety in getting the conversation around to what interests him. He usually gets the information he wants from his guests, too, although an exception may have occurred when he was host to Russia's Andrei Gromyko, a man notoriously miserly with inside information.

Fortunately, Nelson is interested in almost everything and believes that everybody else should be, too. He was once amazed when a friend remarked during an argument that he had never actually read Karl Marx. Next morning, Nelson appeared at his friend's office with a copy of *Das Kapital* and said: "Here. You ought to know about this." Such acts have long since ceased to surprise his friends, who are in the habit of saying: "Oh, sure. That's typical Nelson." Old-timers connected with Rockefeller activities now have a wide collection of items that can be filed under the heading of Typical Nelsoniana.

There is about him a positiveness that sticks out in large and small affairs, and makes for good anecdotes. Once in Haiti, he ignored the stern warnings of doctors in charge of a native clinic and shook hands with dozens of patients suffering from virulent skin diseases, including yaws, saying that he understood there was little danger involved. As it turned out, he was right. "Sure. That's typical Nelson."

On another occasion, he got on a crowded elevator at Rockefeller Center and, careful not to push his fellow passengers around, stood with his toes just inside the groove for the sliding door. The operator politely suggested that he edge back to avoid having his nose knocked off by the sliding door.

"I know exactly where to stand," Nelson replied with the authority of the man who built the place. "Go ahead."

The operator still hesitated but Nelson motioned him to close the door and it slid swiftly down the groove within half an inch of the Rockefeller nose. He didn't move a muscle.

When he was making a trip through a rural area in South America with a group of high government officials their automobile was delayed by a traffic jam at a small bridge. The officials, embarrassed by the delay and inconvenience caused their distinguished guest, fumed and apologized profusely. They were a little startled when, after a few minutes, Nelson excused himself and walked up the dusty road to the bridge where he discovered that the delay was caused by a large truck, whose driver was fearful of a narrow bridge beyond a sharp turn. Nelson talked it over with the driver and then climbed up into the cab of the truck. He drove it across the bridge with a confidence that was, perhaps, justified by the fact that although the bridge creaked and swayed it didn't really break down. When the government automobile reached the bridge the officials found their guest directing traffic with the gusto of a New York cop at the corner of Fifth Avenue and Forty-second Street on the day before Christmas.

Nelson has countless acquaintances and a few close friends but even with those he knows best he can seldom relax. One associate who traveled often with him over a period of years noted only one occasion on which he suggested getting out of the stream of things in order to catch a little rest. That was when a group had made an inspection trip by airplane and, starting back to New York, Nelson said: "Let's miss the plane the others are on and go back alone. I'd rather not talk to anyone." They took a different plane from the West Coast and had to make a stop in a small Western city. Nelson wandered aimlessly but restlessly around the airport waiting room and finally spied a soft drink vending machine. He pushed in a nickel and pulled the lever but nothing happened. He was joggling the lever vigorously when the lunch counter waitress took a long look at his rumpled clothes, his tousled hair and boyish face and said: "Give it up, son. You got to have a *dime* to buy anything around here."

A couple of years after the war Nelson decided he needed

a few days' rest and invited several friends to go up the coast of Maine on his newly acquired yacht. A leisurely week-end cruise on a millionaire's boat seemed a wonderful luxury to at least one of those invited and he accepted with enthusiasm. It turned out differently. The yacht was an unconverted English channel patrol boat with some of the equipment missing, a defective lighting system and one man for a crew. She wasn't ready for a trip but Nelson couldn't wait. Everybody rolled up his sleeves and worked until dark getting the lights on and the boat under way.

There were a lot of odd jobs to do around the craft and the guests kept busy. The wheel was so stiff that it was hard labor to hold the course and everybody took short turns trying to do it. Nelson finally announced he would prepare dinner and disappeared in the galley. A few minutes later there was a mad commotion as the stove burst into flames and had to be doused with a fire extinguisher. Dinner, late at night, consisted of black bean soup—Nelson's favorite dish—and not much else. They were, however, afloat and that had been the host's objective.

This avoidance of ostentation is a Rockefeller trait but it is a very natural one with Nelson, who enjoys an almost complete absence of vanity. A well-equipped and well-run Hollywood type yacht wouldn't interest him for a minute; it would be too easy to order it built and have somebody else hire the crew. To enjoy anything, he has to have a hand in creating or planning it, and he has seldom displayed timidity in taking charge when the opportunity arose. In high school he once greeted a new teacher with an invitation to call on him if there was anything she didn't understand because "you're new here and I've been around for quite a while."

Nelson was popular in school, loved arguments—which teachers at Lincoln encouraged—and sometimes invited his whole class to picnics at Pocantico Hills. He decided to go to Dartmouth because he felt that a small college would be more democratic and interesting than one of the big three. He taught a Sunday School class for small girls while in college, did a lot of skiing, became an enthusiastic amateur photographer, played campus politics and served as editor of the Dartmouth pictorial magazine. He wore an old sweat shirt and corduroy pants a great deal of the time at college and rode a bicycle, although a good many other students had automobiles. He used so much of his $1,500 a year allowance to pursue his hobbies that he was usually broke and sometimes resorted to eating in the kitchen of his college club to save a few dollars a week. The thing he liked least about Dartmouth in the beginning was the fraternity system, which he bitterly attacked in an article in the campus newspaper, but eventually be became a member of Psi Upsilon. In his senior year he wrote his thesis on the subject of his own grandfather, refuting attacks by muckrakers of the day who had portrayed Mr. Rockefeller, Sr., as a ruthless economic pirate.

Nelson is not much inclined to looking backward, but he regards his grandfather's career "as a challenge rather than a stifling blanket" and he likes to feel that the third generation of Rockefellers also have a good measure of the political ability of their maternal grandfather, Senator Aldrich, for whom he was named. Upon his graduation, he was in a hurry to start meeting the challenge but he was also in love. A week after leaving Darmouth he was married in Philadelphia to Mary Clark and one of their wedding gifts—from the Rockefellers —was a year-long honeymoon trip around the world.

Whereas Nelson's journeys abroad in his college days had been made with the idea of roughing it, the young couple now traveled in style, called on high officials and distinguished persons, boned up on each country by studying its history seriously before they arrived and generally got a maximum educational value from their journeying. Geoffrey T. Hellman, writing in *The New Yorker*, later gave an interesting account of the Rockefeller's visit to India, for instance.

"At New Delhi," Hellman wrote, "they called on the Viceroy of India, Lord Irwin, now Lord Halifax. Rockefeller also had a letter to Gandhi and was rather put out, upon arriving in New Delhi, to find that the Mahatma was in jail and not receiving. The Rockefellers went to Bombay and later returned to New Delhi to call on Gandhi, who was by then out of jail and available in a restricted way, for social life. 'The first day we went to his house it was his day of silence,' says Rockefeller. 'He was spinning. You could damn well tell it was his day of silence because he didn't say a word. He wrote me a note saying, "Come back tomorrow. I'll talk to you." We got there at five in the morning, and then piled in his car and went to the Fort in the old part of the city. We'd been hunting with the vice-regal hounds the week before and it was quite a contrast. He told us his whole background, his relations with the British. It gave me the Indian point of view. I have a great interest in the other person's point of view. He showed no interest in me whatever.' "

When Nelson and his bride returned to New York in 1931 he began his business career by digging into the mysteries of the Chase National Bank every morning and acting as director in charge of real estate and renting for the new Rockefeller Center enterprise every afternoon. His uncle, Winthrop Aldrich, was president of the Chase National, but so far as the record shows Nelson left no indelible imprint on the nation's banking system. He quickly demonstrated, however, that he knew how to sell, and knew how to make use of his connections.

With two other young men—Webster Todd and Fenton Turck—he got together a small enterprise to act as a brokerage firm, with an office in the Standard Oil Building on lower Broadway. Just what this firm, known as Turck & Company, did was never quite clear but in a general way they arranged, for a fee, business deals between various large concerns. In those days of depression, everybody was looking for a way to increase his volume of business and it was Nelson's idea that Turck & Company would figure out deals in which several concerns might participate with mutually beneficial results and then sell them on the idea. Since the Chase National Bank was in a position to do business on a large scale and since Rockefeller Center was at that time the biggest construction job in the country—and was also wide open for tenants—Nelson's connections opened up many interesting possibilities for the new firm of brokers. They apparently made the most of the situation and, after a couple of years of profitable endeavor, Nelson bought out his partners and shifted the business to a part of the Rockefeller Center setup under the title of Special Work, Inc.

In his task as renting agent for Rockefeller Center, Nelson took a busy role in a kind of super job of selling space in a skyscraper development at a time when business was terrible and most owners of real estate in New York were fighting to hang on to any tenants who could keep up payments on the rent and resist the temptation to jump out of a window. Actually, Rockefeller Center, which was to become a monument to the clan in the heart of the nation's greatest city, was not the result of careful planning but an accident—the result of a chain of events that began in the late 1920's and developed through a number of surprising stages into an unparalleled private real estate adventure. It soaked up a great deal of Rockefeller money, around $125,000,000 in all, and it was later to represent one of the biggest chunks of the wealth of the five brothers.

But at the time Nelson plunged brashly into the affairs of the Center in 1932 there were many experts on real estate who freely predicted that it would be the biggest flop in history, and there must have been many times when Mr. Rockefeller, Jr., feared that the experts would turn out to be right. For Nelson, however, it offered an unlimited field in which to exercise his love of competition and for the better part of a decade he was competing for all he and the Rockefeller prestige were worth. If anybody had been under the impression that the third generation of Rockefellers was going soft in the business field there was plenty of opportunity to correct that misunderstanding during the building of the Center.

✖ VI ✖

ROCKEFELLER CENTER WAS BUILT IN THE PERIOD IN which the five Rockefeller brothers were completing their education and beginning their careers; a time when they were, perhaps, most likely to form vivid impressions, to be subject to deep doubts and high hopes. Some two decades later when they became owners of the world's most fabulous real estate enterprise the impression they retained most strongly was of their father's courage and vision in building the Center in the depths of the great depression.

There was, of course, more involved than just courage and vision, although Mr. Rockefeller had to display a good deal of both in order to get through the job. He was spurred by a multiplicity of economic and human factors but there was no question that he rode them through to the end and that the result can hardly be called anything less than magnificent. Rockefeller Center became not only a vast economic asset to New York but one of the most spectacular sights in America, a huge irregular mass of limestone, steel, glass and masonry set snugly into a dozen acres of solid rock. Its foundations are anchored sixty-eight feet below the surface and its towers rise 850 feet toward—and frequently into—the clouds, and it is actually a city within the city of New York.

Inside the brass lines that mark the Center's boundaries on the sidewalks, there are all of the material requirements for a secure and pleasant existence from babyhood to old age, except

61

for a place to sleep. Nobody lives in Rockefeller Center; not even a janitor. The Center's big plaza, however, is about as close as New York can come to a village green and the public not only takes an interest in what goes on there but assumes the right to criticize in a loud voice. This attitude is largely the result of a series of outdoor community events staged in the plaza and, for quite a period, featuring Nelson as master of ceremonies and ambassador of good will to the public. Easter music and Christmas carols are sung there by a volunteer chorus of men and women who work in the Center in front of the most lavish seasonal decorations that can be devised by the mind of man. A Christmas wreath to be recognized as a Christmas wreath at Rockefeller Center should be sixteen feet across, and a Christmas tree should be ninety feet tall.

In the fifteen buildings of the Center itself, there are twenty-six restaurants, three radio broadcasting companies, a hospital, a six-story garage, a volunteer fire department, a police force and a post office. There are many scores of shops and stores along about two miles of outdoor streets, indoor streets, mezzanine streets and elaborate underground streets.

There are eight handsome gardens and an eighty-foot brook that babbles with professional happiness across a rooftop eleven stories above the street. There is the world's largest indoor theater, the Radio City Music Hall, atop which the famous Rockette precision dancers acquire a midsummer sun tan with professional indifference to the stares from hundreds of adjacent office windows. There is an outdoor skating pond that attracts a constantly changing audience ranging up to 1,000 persons at a time and many thousands in the course of a winter day. There is a private street and there are about a hundred heroic murals, sculptures and mosaics that may or may not be classed as works of art.

About 35,000 persons work at the Center, and it is estimated that some 130,000 others visit it daily on business or just to look around, so that the floating population is believed to be about 160,000. This is an important business statistic from the viewpoint of Rockefeller Center, Inc., which likes to point out that there are only fifty-five cities in the United States with a population of more than 160,000.

Pointing out statistics is a major activity at the Center, which produces them by the hundreds. They include such miscellaneous items as the 138,392 tons of structural steel used in the fifteen buildings, the 28,000 telephones in operation there, the 16,500 windows that form a remarkable geometric pattern above New York late on a winter afternoon. And they range right on up to one of the most useless facts ever recorded—the disclosure that the shafts of the 215 elevators in the Center, if stacked on top of each other, would reach ten miles into the sky.

This incredible mountain of incredible statistics grew out of an unhappy series of events back in the late 1920's when business was booming and Wall Street fortunes were being made, on paper at least, overnight. Mr. Rockefeller, who played a pretty good violin in his day, and a number of other wealthy citizens became interested in a project for building a new home for the Metropolitan Opera Company. It was decided that a real estate development with the opera house as its center would not only enhance the beauty of the run-down area between Fifth Avenue and Sixth Avenue (later the Avenue af the Americas) in the lower Fifties, but that the development could make the Opera Company more or less self-supporting in the future.

Mr. Rockefeller agreed to an arrangement whereby he would lease an area between Forty-eighth and Fifty-first streets as the first move toward the group's operations. This land had once been part of a public botanic garden which was operated by Dr. David Hosack of Columbia College, but he sold it to the state in 1811 and it was turned over to Columbia College three years later. In 1823, the college received rent of $125 a year from the land.

One hundred years later, conditions were somewhat changed and the best deal Mr. Rockefeller could make was to pay Columbia University a rental of $3,300,000 a year on the land under a lease which, with options, runs until 2015, at which time the land and the buildings on it revert to the university. This was one of the biggest real estate deals ever made and it was probably the most profitable—but only from the viewpoint of the university.

After the lease was signed, catastrophe in the form of the 1929 stock market collapse ended plans for the new opera house. The Metropolitan's Wall Street angels fled for cover and left Mr. Rockefeller holding a bag that contained some of the most expensive rock and 229 of the most dilapidated old brownstone houses in New York City. In the depression days that followed, most of the city's real estate brokers were looking for an Indian who would buy back Manhattan Island for the twenty-four dollars' worth of trinkets and three kegs of rum that his ancestors had originally received from the Dutch. But the Rockefellers were stuck with real estate on which they were paying almost twice the normal rent for that area and on which they were losing some $3,000,000 a year, plus taxes of more than $1,000,000.

Mr. Rockefeller had no intention of breaking the agreement which he had signed with the university, but he had to do something and almost the only thing he could do was to defy the depression. Laying grand opera gently away in moth balls, he arranged for the firms of Todd, Robertson, Todd Engineering Corporation and Todd and Brown, Inc., to construct and operate for him a strictly commercial office building development. It was a tremendous gamble, but it was also a remarkable expression of faith in the basic soundness of the national economy.

The Center's managers picked out radio as the fastest-growing industry in the country and decided to create a "radio city" as the keystone in the enterprise. An arrangement was made to lease 1,000,000 square feet of office space and four theaters to the Radio Corporation of America, the National Broadcasting Company and Radio-Keith-Orpheum Corporation for a total of $3,000,000 a year. This deal was later modified but it was enough to enable the builders to start excavation for the first four buildings of the Center in July of 1931.

At this point, Mr. Rockefeller got a couple of breaks. The depression brought building costs down to about half of what they had been before the stock market collapse. Furthermore, the architects were able to take advantage of many new ideas and mechanical developments that came along after the First World War and were being perfected in the late 1920's. Sixteen years later when a new building was added almost the only improvements available were in fluorescent lighting and air conditioning.

In addition to mechanical marvels, Mr. Rockefeller always kept firmly in mind the idea of providing a place in which to focus community activities and community attention—a sort of hang-over from the days when he had been interested in a new opera house. The managers also felt that it was essential to give the project a strong dash of character in order to lure tenants from other sections of the city. At one point, Hugh S. Robertson, then executive manager of the Center, developed the idea of a fashionable shopping center that would have prestige of the kind enjoyed by Bond Street in London or the Rue de la Paix in Paris.

To carry out his idea, Robertson created an entirely new street through the middle of the project—a privately owned street in the heart of New York—and, although it never became known for its shops, it did achieve fame as Rockefeller Plaza. Once every year, with proper ceremony, including the news photographers, the three-block-long street is closed to the public for twelve hours, and all doors—they are largely those of financial concerns—opening on it are locked. This is done to preserve the Plaza's status as a private street, in accordance with a special agreement between Columbia University and Rockefeller Center, Inc.

Such promotional stunts were apple pie for Nelson and one reporter remarked that his "easygoing charm . . . made him the logical man, as the Center's various buildings were completed to open bunny gardens in the Sunken Plaza, dedicate wisteria exhibits and skating rinks, present certificates and gold buttons to outstanding construction workers, and so on. On these occasions he made graceful little speeches with the manner of a particularly articulate and successful basketball coach." But when he wasn't displaying his charm in public, Nelson was very busy turning it on for potential tenants of the Center. Good public relations as well as Robertson's success in signing up a number of large European firms greatly aided the early job of renting the Center's floor space, which eventually totaled 5,500,000 square feet.

All kinds of deals were made to entice tenants and some of these led to angry criticism of the Center by other real estate operators. The main point of contention was the offering of below-market rates for a certain period and, in some cases, of offering to take over the unexpired leases of potential tenants if they would move at once to the Center. In 1934 the controversy was brought to a head by August Heckscher, who had lost some business from the Heckscher building to the Center, and who sued the directors of the Center on charges of unfair competition and coercion in obtaining tenants. The suit was for $10,000,000 and papers were served on the directors, including John D., 3rd, and Nelson, but the case was dropped before it was taken into court. Nelson always felt that the methods employed by the Center in getting tenants were merely the methods being used all over town at that time.

Rents in big office buildings normally vary from a low rate on the lower floors to high rates on the upper floors. At Rockefeller Center the rates in 1932 averaged out at around $2.50 per square foot. As building progressed in the 1930's the Center was operating at a deficit of about $4,000,000 a year, the huge skyscrapers were mortgaged for $45,000,000 and Nelson was gradually moving up to a position of greater importance in the management. In 1937, he became executive vice-president and in the following year, after several highly paid managerial jobs at the Center had been abolished, he stepped in as president.

Although he kept activity at a high peak, it could hardly be said that Nelson took over in a blaze of glory because in 1937 conditions generally were so bad in the business world that some timid souls at the Center discussed the possibility of abandoning plans to erect the last three scheduled buildings. Such a decision might have been advanced to "cut the losses" of the Rockefellers, but it was obvious that the only chance of ever making an operating profit on the enterprise was to complete it as originally planned. Mr. Rockefeller, Jr., never wavered from that goal. He just kept on signing checks and insisting that the work should be perfection down to the last detail.

The details—some of which were pretty big ones—weren't always easy to arrange, and Nelson frequently had his hands full. One of his biggest headaches turned out to be art, a subject in which he had long been interested. Furthermore, it was Latin American art, a field in which he considered himself a well-informed if amateur expert. He had known the famous

Mexican painter, Diego Rivera, for some years and admired his work. He owned some Rivera paintings and the artist had done portraits of the children of Nelson's sister, Abby. So it was not strange that the Mexican, then at the height of his fame, was engaged to do a huge fresco across the wall of the lobby in the RCA building, easily the choicest spot for a mural in all of Rockefeller Center.

The artist began work on the wall with considerable publicity, ably abetted by the Center's public relations staff. Crowds of art lovers sometimes gathered to watch Rivera and his assistants climbing along the scaffolding erected in the lobby and tracing a huge and complicated scene against the wall. And as the work progressed the crowds, and the newspapers, became still more interested because Rivera was obviously painting a picture of determined political significance. The artist's admiration for Soviet Russia was well known but obviously the management of Rockefeller Center had not foreseen that he would imbed in their most prominent wall a devastating attack on capitalistic society as well as an idealized portrait of Lenin.

Robertson talked to Rivera, protesting the political ideas expressed in the fresco, and Nelson had a long meeting with him. He thought that he could persuade the artist to get back on the track and when the session ended Rivera, according to Nelson, promised to make various changes. Nelson had argued that the painting was going to be part of a commercial building and that some of the characters portrayed—dissolute looking card-players and a girl with syphilitic ulcers—would be offensive to the tenants, regardless of the political theme of the painting. Rivera was, he added, taking unfair advantage of the opportunity in order to deliver a series of affronts to the very people who made construction of the Center possible. When the artist departed, Nelson felt that it was going to work out all right.

It didn't, however. Rivera went back to work and kept on working day and night at great speed in order to complete his original painting, including the prominent head of Lenin. A great controversy arose in the press and the Communist party began screaming that there was a move on to destroy a priceless work of art. The Rockefellers couldn't afford to wait any longer. Rivera was called in and, during an ugly scene created by the artist, he was paid the full $21,500 he had been promised and dismissed. He was advised that the reason for canceling his contract was that he had included in the painting subjects that had not been in the original sketches, including a group of four highly objectionable female figures supposedly depicting New York life and a portrait of Lenin. Nelson was present at the final showdown and Rivera left him in great anger. "It was," Nelson recalled later, "eight years before he would even speak to me again. But we're good friends now."

The painting was covered by canvas and then, without delay, chipped from the wall amid screams of vandalism from the Communist press, and another artist, José Maria Sert, was hired to do the job. This time the management made sure they got a few characters like Abe Lincoln and Thomas A. Edison into the painting, and no Lenins. The Rivera incident was hardly an ordinary detail of Nelson's working day but there were plenty of lesser incidents to keep him working long hours.

There was originally a company union setup in the operation of the Center but during the height of union expansion under the New Deal the Center was organized by the American Federation of Labor building maintenance union. This turned out to be a long and difficult job of negotiating because nine different unions were involved, but in the next dozen years the Center had only one strike—a wildcat affair during the war.

It was the war period, too, that brought about a tremendous change in the real estate situation in New York and enabled the

Center to break out of the red on an operating basis in 1940. A couple of years later it made a profit after depreciation— again on an operating basis—and in 1947 profits were sufficient to require payment by the corporation of a substantial sum in Federal income taxes, in addition to real estate taxes of about $3,000,000. In the next few years the Center, in which the Rockefellers are the only stockholders, had boosted its gross income to more than $20,000,000 a year and had lifted the mortgage on the old homestead. At that time, not only were the buildings fully occupied by around 1,100 tenants but there were some 1,500 names on a waiting list of firms that at one time or another had requested space. The average rate, by then, had been increased to $4.50 a square foot.

This situation reflected the general postwar space shortage and it enabled the Center to operate on the most favorable basis that could have been foreseen by its builders. It didn't, however, definitely answer the question whether such beautifully conceived office building developments could be constructed generally on a profitable basis. Making a profit on an operating basis is not the same as amortizing an investment—in this case a big investment by Mr. Rockefeller—and not every builder can count on building during a depression period of low costs and renting during a time of severe space shortage. Some of the architects of Rockefeller Center, however, are convinced that it has proved the wisdom and business advantage of such projects. And, in any event, no one will dispute the great advance in city planning that the Center achieved through the architectural contributions of Raymond Hood, Wallace Harrison, Andrew Reinhard, Harvey W. Corbett, J. André Fouilhoux and Henry Hofmeister.

For the first time a group of skyscrapers was built in a manner that created a sense of order in the relationship of one building to another and with 10 to 15 per cent of the land

—a tremendous extravagance in a crowded city—left vacant to permit proper spacing of the buildings for light and air. Even if Rockefeller Center remains architecturally unique its basic influence has been felt in municipal planning all over the country.

The British Empire Building and La Maison Française, adjacent to the International Building, were built only six stories high, the smallest in the Center. They face Fifth Avenue and a flower-lined promenade, popularly called The Channel and usually filled with tourists, runs between them to form a main entrance to the Center and give the visitor a striking first glimpse of the soaring RCA Building in the background. The Channel leads into the lower plaza, a huge rectangular pit 125 feet by ninety-five feet and some seventeen feet below the street level. This was originally supposed to become a fashionable shopping area that would lead on into an underground avenue of shops stretching entirely across the Center. It looked good on paper but in practice it flopped. Nobody wanted to put an expensive shop there because it seemed out of the way. There was considerable anguish about this costly waste of space that nobody wanted, and the management finally decided to get what they could out of it by putting in two restaurants and making the plaza into a colorful and quaint Skating Pond in the shadow of the skyscrapers.

The Pond started off rather calmly but ice-skating seemed to bring out the ham in everybody who tried it and the place soon became one of the Center's main attractions, albeit an expensive one. There are always a dozen skillful amateurs and instructors—the girls in colorful costume—competing for attention with fancy figure-skating exhibitions. And there is always a sprinkling of beginners who don't mind falling on their faces for the amusement of a big crowd of idlers staring down from the sidewalks. The Pond is crowded most of the time for six months or more each year and the management feels a fine bond of friendship for the thousands of skaters who happily contribute a yearly total of $80,000 for the privilege of putting on a free show and, to a certain extent, salvaging the Center's biggest architectural mishap.

Six times a day a little rubber-wheeled tractor shaves off the rough ice on the rink, which is sprinkled and resurfaced in thirty minutes by five miles of refrigerating pipes under the surface. It is not frozen too hard, however, because fancy skaters don't like slick ice. In cold weather, when the ice gets too hard, the process is reversed and the pipes carry warm brine to soften it to the correct degree.

One of the brightest spots in the Center is a display of the flags of the United Nations around the lower plaza. They are a permanent display, run up each morning and taken down at sunset, but The Channel and plaza are elaborately refurbished a number of times each year with floral displays in keeping with the seasonal changes. This normally calls for ten or a dozen complete changes of plantings between the lavish display of Easter lilies and the final sunburst of October's chrysanthemums. Sometimes the plantings are all from a particular area or country, perhaps featuring tropical flowers and bushes. During such an exhibition featuring the vegetation of Puerto Rico it was discovered that one spectacular hot weather plant which attracted the biggest crowds would not live more than a few days in New York. Since the plant was particularly popular, the Puerto Rican government solved an awkward problem by flying fresh ones up every third day to be planted at dawn in The Channel flower beds.

The flower displays are all planned six months or a year in advance and the gardeners spend a great deal of time worrying about bringing them to a bloom on exactly the right day. If necessary, the plants are put in cold storage to make sure that

Nature keeps in line with the Center's timetable. The greatest foe of the gardeners, however, is the wind, which whistles violently through the plaza much of the time because the tall buildings form a kind of chimney with a strong draft. Eight elm trees were planted along the Fifth Avenue side of the Center in 1939, but even when they were fed with injections of chemicals they lived only about ten years. Cost: about $200 each a year. Beginning in 1951, as the elms died, they were replaced by honey locusts in the hope the new variety would better withstand the rigors of city life.

Although the plaza draws crowds to everything from fashion shows to televised presentation of election returns on a mammoth screen, the big event is the annual raising of the Christmas tree—always so huge that many of the limbs have to be cut off to get it through the streets and then reattached after the trunk is erected. The origin of the Center's Yule tree is attributed to a group of workmen who set up a tiny pine and strung a few lights on it while they were excavating for the first buildings back in 1931. The management decided to carry on their sentimental gesture by putting up a handsome tree in the plaza each Christmas. The trees, however, kept getting bigger and bigger each year and the growth of the enterprise over the next fifteen years became more than a little frightening. In 1934, the tree was sixty feet tall and draped with 1,200 colored lights. In 1935, it was seventy feet tall and the lights numbered 1,700. Except for some lack of progress during the war, it zoomed upward steadily until the year 1948 when the tree was ninety feet tall and required seven miles of wiring to illuminate its 7,500 lights. That seemed to satisfy most people and thereafter there was an inclination to taper off.

Such things, of course, were merely the window dressing for Rockefeller Center in the days when it was first coming into fame as one of the nation's biggest tourist attractions. The real business in which Nelson was involved during the late 1930's was keeping the tenants happy, a task that required 1,500 hourly wage earners and an administrative and clerical staff of about 300. The nerve center of this setup is a huge and complicated switchboard on the second floor of the RCA Building, called the control room, which has never been closed since the first tenant moved in. Only a few staff members ever see the control board, but the men who run it know what goes on all the time almost everywhere in the Center. They "see" everything through an intricate arrangement of lights, bells, telephones and alarm systems.

The control board shows every time a watchman or guard turns his key in a time clock—or if he fails to turn the key at the proper time. It is the center of an elaborate fire-and-burglar alarm system, and it automatically records the presence of any person attempting to leave a building by the fire stairs in time to permit a guard to intercept him and determine whether he has merely lost his way or is trying to escape notice. The operator of the control board can establish a telephone connection with most of the 215 elevators in the Center or carry on a conversation with any of the 100 patrolmen and watchmen by summoning them to a phone by means of signal lights throughout each building. If there is a fire or a flood—and the Center has had both on a small scale—the warning sounds first in the control room, automatically starting a series of alarms designed to handle the emergency without help from the outside unless that is necessary.

The engineer in each building is also the fire chief, with plenty of the latest portable equipment handy and with employes assigned to specific emergency duties. The Center is rather proud of the fact that it can usually handle these emergencies on its own. They have avoided calling for outside help, for instance, in such emergencies as a break in the air-conditioning water pipes that deposited several feet of water in a basement area and a fire that sent a lot of smoke up an elevator shaft. The fire was sufficient to bring city trucks clanging up to the door but when the helmeted firemen rushed in with their axes the Center's engineering department already had broken through the elevator shaft and doused the blaze.

"They had a disappointed look on their faces," one of the engineers remarked. "We not only had put out the fire but we had beaten them to the most elegant chopping opportunity they'd had in weeks. Not a thing left for them to ax."

The control board and its related service department handle almost 300 calls a day. Seven girls take the calls during normal working hours and type out memos for everything from knocking down a partition to opening an office door for some tenant who forgets his key. They also try to take the first flush of anger off a tenant who has a loud and bitter complaint, a task that usually calls for a maximum of tact and patience. One woman, for example, called to complain that the rain was blowing in her window. The control board politely suggested that she close the window. She happily followed the suggestion. Another woman, working at night in her office, complained that a hall light on the thirty-eighth floor of a building across the street annoyed her. A worried wife called at one A.M. to say that her husband had failed to show up for dinner, and that the telephone in his office didn't answer. The control board found him in a quiet poker game in the next-door office.

Once the control board demonstrated its remarkable sensitivity to what is going on by coming to the aid of a girl whom a guard found sobbing in the lobby of the RCA Building. She had a date to meet a soldier in the lobby, but she couldn't find him. The control board merely queried the patrolmen in all the lobbies, described the soldier and produced him from another

lobby in time to save the day for romance and the United States
Army.

The nerve system of intricate wires that reaches out from the
control room shows only the outline of the mechanical and
human operation required to run Rockefeller Center. There
are four underground levels where men and machines work day
and night to provide water, heat, air conditioning, electricity
and all kinds of supplies for the offices, shops and twenty-six
restaurants on the upper floors.

At the very bottom of the RCA Building is the central trucking space. Every day some 700 delivery trucks circle down a
ramp into this huge underground parking space, check in at the
main gate and are directed to the platform nearest the building
to which their goods are consigned.

The exhaust fumes from the procession of trucks—it mounts
to more than 1,000 a day at Christmas time—would soon make
the trucking space a death chamber except for big pipes that
suck the air out through the grilles in the ceiling and at the base
of the big concrete columns, and finally release it harmlessly
several floors above the sidewalks. This system changes the
air once every three minutes, but if that should prove inadequate
in emergencies there is an elaborate automatic checking device
that constantly measures and records the amount of carbon
monoxide in the air, turns on reserve fans and rings an alarm
if danger arises. Up until 1952, the reserve fans had never been
required.

Along almost a dozen miles of passageways in the other basement levels of the Center are whole platoons of pumps, motors,
fans, generators, switchboards, refrigerators and recording devices that automatically go about the business of making tenants
comfortable. Here, too, are the great pipes through which steam
under tremendous pressure comes from the New York Steam
Corporation and is filtered down into smaller conduits, and

finally into the twisting network of water, steam, electric, sewage and air-conditioning pipes, each a different color, that reaches to every corner and spire of the Center.

All these automatic operations—many of them with only casual human attention—create a feeling that robots run the place, until you get a look at some of the 1,800 persons busily performing duties for Rockefeller Center, Inc. These include, besides engineers and electricians and carpenters, a number of specialists, such as the two porters who do nothing but clean chewing gum off the floors and sidewalks, the two who pick up cigarette butts, and a crew that was assigned to the specialized job of cleaning cuspidors after the regular cleaning women balked at it in 1948. At that time, the management was surprised to find that they had 1,000 cuspidors around the place, some in tobacco-company offices and some in the offices of oil-company big shots who acquired the tobacco-chewing habit during their early days, when they were not allowed to smoke while working around oil wells.

Among the service workers, the 700 cleaners and porters are the largest group, with the 400 elevator operators next. Some statistician has figured out that the job of cleaning done each workday night at Rockefeller Center is about equal to cleaning 2,750 six-room houses, but it should be added that the equipment available is considerably more than the housewife's mop and vacuum cleaner. More systematic too.

Covering the wall of the cleaning headquarters on one of the lower levels is a huge chart, sprinkled with floor numbers, firm names and gaily colored pins to show just what has been done to each office, lobby and corridor since the first of the month and what remains to be done before month's end. It also keeps track of the cleaning regiment while it is at work.

In adjoining rooms are batteries of huge vacuum cleaners, floor-washing machines, waxing machines, buffing machines and a tractor snow shovel for the sidewalks. There are also rows of ordinary mops, brooms and dustcloths. Together, these cover the 5,500,000 square feet of floor space, from the deep carpeting of executive offices to the travertine Italian marble of the lobbies, five nights a week, at speeds varying from 300 to 10,000 square feet an hour. At regular intervals most floors get special attention. The 2,000,000 square feet of cork, linoleum and rubber flooring, for instance, are given two or three coats of wax a month and buffed once each week.

The cleaners, who spread 2,800 pounds of soap, 500 gallons of wax and 110 gallons of brass polish over a period of one month, assemble each evening like a small army collecting equipment and rations. Each man and woman has two uniforms, which hang in long rows in the stock room. These are provided by the management, which faced a major crisis after World War II at the beginning of a new style era known as the New Look. Almost overnight they had to lengthen the skirts on 1,000 dresses. The old-length skirts weren't long enough to cover the new slips worn by the cleaning women.

The cleaning squads move out with timetable precision soon after seven o'clock each evening. There is no call for anyone to get down on hands and knees to scrub and polish. This is strictly a mechanized operation. Women known as the low-dusters move into each office and clean everything to a point as high as they can reach. The high-dusters, who are men with ladders and special vacuum-cleaning equipment, make the rounds once a month and cover the walls and ceilings which the low-dusters cannot reach.

There is also a special crew for bronze polishing, which covers certain spots each night and works over the bigger areas, such as the huge statue of Atlas on Fifth Avenue, once a month. The Center is very careful about preserving its works of art and at one time worked itself into a dither over the big wood statue of Man and Nature which Carl Milles carved for the lobby of the Time and Life Building. The statue shows a man on horseback listening to a singing bird perched on a tree above his head. The bird really moves its wings and sings once every hour, assisted by a concealed phonograph record of a Mexican nightingale.

The Center's experts are unusually proud of the result—if you ever tried to get a Mexican nightingale to sing for a re- cording machine you would understand why—and were dis- tressed when the statue began to acquire a coating of dust and dirt. They finally wrote to Milles at his Michigan home and asked him how to clean it. The return letter from the tempera- mental sculptor, by air mail and four pages long, threatened lawsuits and perhaps mayhem against any cleaning woman who dared remove the patina of age from his statue. He finally ended up by telling the Center's experts that, if they simply had to do something, they might try blowing the dust off with a bellows. They did.

The cleaning department also has learned to be careful about wastepaper baskets. All wastepaper is gathered into sacks that are tagged with the floor number and date, and the whole lot, amounting to some 1,200 bags, is withheld from final disposal for two days. That two days is a margin of safety for recovery of valuables that tenants are constantly losing on the floor or in the wastebasket. Jewelry, watches and documents can be and are regularly recovered from the tagged sacks or from the vacuum cleaners, which are also tagged and remain unemptied for twelve hours. The biggest recovery was $80,000 in diamonds which had been misplaced in the trash of a jewelry shop. On another occasion a porter sweeping out an elevator picked up $20,000 in negotiable bonds.

In addition to all of this concern about the welfare and property of tenants, the Center devotes a great deal of time and money to cultivating the good will of the public. This policy was established firmly during the period when Nelson was particularly active in the management—by 1950 he was less directly concerned in the daily operations—but it had actually been inaugurated by his father. Nelson once told how his father formed the famous Sidewalk Superintendents' Club for excavation watchers in 1938 and how more than 75,000 persons became members and eleven branch chapters were organized in the country.

"While work was at its busiest in the construction of the Center," Nelson related, "my father stopped on the sidewalk to gaze down into a deep excavation where a big steam shovel was at work. You know how it is—the impulse that makes a crowd gather and watch men doing jobs with ponderous machines like a big steam shovel. Father has more than the average interest in that sort of thing, and he was standing there entranced, watching the jaws of the shovel close over a huge mouthful of rock and earth. A watchman employed on the job walked up to him and said in no uncertain tone: 'Move along, buddy! You can't stand loafing here!' My father obediently moved along and didn't stand loafing there any more.

"But out of the incident came the idea of establishing a place where people could watch construction work at the Center in comfort and without being chased away." Mr. Rockefeller assumed that other passers-by didn't like to be moved on any more than he did and he had special openings cut in the board fences so that any one could watch without interference. The Center's public relations experts quickly developed the idea and began presenting pedestrians with cards certifying their membership in the Sidewalk Superintendents' Club.

The Center has remained sensitive ever since to the public attitude and, in turn, the public has taken a sort of proprietary interest in what goes on around Rockefeller Plaza. When architects published plans to erect an oval building on Fifth Avenue the public wrote so many letters of protest that the idea was dropped. When luncheon-hour idlers in The Channel complained that they had to stand up while loafing, benches were installed. When Italy entered the war on the Axis side, the coat of arms of the House of Savoy was quickly boarded over and the Italian Building suddenly became a part of the International Building.

Sometimes the Center will go a long way to avoid a little fuss. One day a plain-clothes detective saw a woman slyly leave a brown paper bag on one of the writing desks in the RCA building post office. He examined the package and found that it contained garbage. Without a word, he picked it up and followed the woman to her apartment in a nearby brownstone house, placed the sack against the door, rang the doorbell and departed quietly.

It is refreshing, however, to know that there is a limit to this attitude of tolerance. During the war, when Victory gardens were in vogue, tomatoes were planted around the wall of the lower plaza. They were a great success and everybody seemed pleased until one day when Mr. Rockefeller, Jr., received a letter complaining bitterly that no salt or pepper was provided to go with the tomatoes—which loafers apparently were stealing as they ripened. He dropped the letter into a wastebasket with a sigh that suggested there were times when even the public can carry things a little too far.

✖ VII ✖

THE MANAGEMENT OF ROCKEFELLER CENTER IS A MATTER of great concern to the five brothers who own it but they had no intention of devoting their careers to it. Nelson became chairman of the board as well as president and the others assumed their duties as directors in time but once it was a going enterprise their main attention shifted elsewhere. Even during the decade in which the building and operation of the Center was a tremendous task Nelson was keeping various other balls rolling in his spare time.

He became a director of the Creole Petroleum Corporation, for one thing, and for another he staunchly followed up his mother's interest in modern art and, in 1939, was elected president of the Museum of Modern Art, which Mrs. Rockefeller had helped establish. The museum, which had been headed by another founder, A. Conger Goodyear, was nine years old and had been housed in Rockefeller Center but after Nelson became president it was moved to its own spectacularly modern building on West Fifty-third Street. Nelson had been a hard worker in raising funds for the new building and he took an active role in promoting the museum with the public, boosting the membership from 3,000 to 14,980 and instituting various new policies which, at times, failed to raise the enthusiasm of some of the art experts with whom he was associated.

In an odd way, his interest in the Creole Petroleum Corporation and the museum were closely linked to the beginning of his interest in Latin America. His job with Creole took him south of the Rio Grande on occasional trips, and he promptly became enthusiastic about the people and the possibilities for business development there. It was, perhaps, only natural that once he had become a figure of importance in the museum he thought of having exhibitions of Latin American paintings and sculpture which, he felt, would arouse public interest in the countries to the south and bring the Americas closer together, both commercially and culturally. Among other things, he gave the museum $25,000 anonymously for the purchase of Latin American paintings and encouraged several exhibitions as "a contribution toward better understanding of the people (of Latin America) and their culture."

It will probably prove a bit difficult for future historians to estimate Nelson's contributions to art, and during this period there were some who were inclined to scoff. His qualifications as a critic—as he would be the first to admit—were not anything special. He had studied a bit in school, he painted his own Christmas cards for a while, he helped establish a company for selling two-bit hand-painted postcards at Rockefeller Center and he had been made, with no great enthusiasm on his part, a trustee of the Metropolitan Museum of Art. But as president of the Modern Museum he at least contributed a great deal of vigor and persistence and eventually he inaugurated an expanded educational program that brought the Metropolitan and the Whitney museums into an agreement to co-ordinate their modern collections in an effort to increase popular understanding of art. Nor can anyone deny that he has done his darnedest in behalf of Latin American art, despite his unhappy experience with Diego Rivera's mammoth fresco.

His enthusiasm about Latin America, however, was by no means confined to the art world. He had made several trips there for the Creole company, for the museum and for the International Division of The Rockefeller Foundation before he organized, in 1940, the *Compañía de Fomento Venezolana* (Venezuela Development Company) to undertake development projects in Venezuela. The main result of this organization was the construction of the million-dollar Avila Hotel in Caracas, but Nelson's travels had taken him to every country in South America, he had begun to speak poor Spanish as a result of a quick Berlitz course and he had definitely come to the conclusion that the land of opportunity lay south of the border. He was trying to make up his mind what to do about it when World War II started in Europe.

After the fall of France in the summer of 1940, it became far more likely that the United States would be drawn into the war and the position of Latin American countries became of increasing importance in plans being made at Washington. Nelson had repeatedly talked over the problem of hemispheric co-operation with a group of friends, businessmen and experts who had special interests in South America and some of whom had traveled with him on that continent. They included Wallace Harrison, one of the Rockefeller Center architects and a close friend of Nelson; Beardsley Ruml, then a director of the Spelman Fund; Joseph Rovensky, of the Chase National Bank; and Jay Crane, of Standard Oil of New Jersey.

"I'd seen the Nazi penetration in South America," Nelson said later. "I'd talked it over with several persons close to President Roosevelt. I felt there was a real lack of understanding between this country and Latin America. South America is important to us in peace or war. As long as a lack of mutual understanding existed, we were vulnerable in the situation arising from the European war."

In June of 1940 the group with which Nelson had frequently discussed Latin American problems prepared a joint memorandum exploring the reasons and the opportunities for integrating defense and economic affairs of the Western Hemisphere through specific action in the fields of raw materials, trade, investment and public administration. The problem was one that had already been talked about at the White House and word had been passed along that such a memorandum would be well received. Nelson took it down to Harry Hopkins, who found it interesting and passed it along. Within a short time, James Forrestal asked Nelson to return to Washington and talk over the ideas contained in the memorandum and eventually he was summoned to the White House.

Nelson was a little uncertain about his meeting with President Roosevelt. The Rockefellers, after all, were staunch Republicans and they moved in a world that represented the bitterest opposition to the New Deal. Furthermore, the memorandum that Nelson had presented was critical of the Department of State's operations in South America, suggesting that it had failed to take advantage of the opportunity afforded by the closing of European markets to draw the Latin countries closer into our orbit. It also proposed that Mr. Roosevelt establish a separate organization that would be in a better position than the State Department to make the most of this opportunity.

Such concern as he may have felt as he went to the White House disappeared, however, after a few minutes' talk with Mr. Roosevelt. The President was very much interested. He pointed out that this was a matter entirely outside the realm of politics; Nelson's republicanism was of no importance. He was attracted to the idea—the experiment—of an agency that would have greater freedom of action than the tradition-bound State Department; that could take over a large sphere in which government might co-operate with and facilitate the operation of private interests in the promotion of closer economic, social and cultural ties among the Americas.

The conference lasted for half an hour. "I agreed with his concept of the situation," Nelson said later. "We thought alike." In August of 1940, Mr. Roosevelt established the Office of the Co-ordinator of Commercial and Cultural Relations Between the American Republics, setting what may have been a record for jaw-breaking titles even in the New Deal. He named Nelson as head of the office, which promptly became known as the Rockefeller Office because nobody ever remembered its proper title or had time to say it if they did remember. Eventually, it became the Office of Inter-American Affairs but was, throughout the war, usually called the Rockefeller Office or the Rockefeller Committee. Nelson's job was, primarily, to spread good will and convince the other American nations that it was good business as well as morally right to be on our side in a world crisis that was soon to force the United States into World War II.

The creation of this new agency by the President, who, incidentally, was to give Nelson some firm backing in his struggles of the next few years, did little more than ripple the surface of bureaucratic Washington. For the most part, neither the bureaucrats nor the politicians knew anything about Latin America and the general assumption was that this outfit with the long name was a presidential whim and that both the job and the rich boy who was trying to fill it would soon vanish into the bog of governmental agencies. This merely proved that their ignorance was not confined to the problems of Latin America. They didn't know Nelson, either.

It is possible that there were other recruits to Washington in those days who were as ignorant of the methods for survival in the governmental wilderness as Nelson, but it is doubtful if there was any other co-ordinator who was as determined or as energetic. Here, suddenly, his penchant for "getting organized" was turned loose in virgin territory, with the Atlantic, the

Pacific and the far blue yonder as the only limits, or so it seemed at first. The maze of governmental red tape, the endless bureaucratic rivalries, the political pitfalls and the struggle against inertia were a stimulating challenge to Nelson from the beginning. Unlike many tired veterans of Washington, he had the strength and the willingness to keep pushing and he was in the unique position of having no axes to grind.

Not that he didn't make mistakes and false starts or get rocked back on his heels a few times. One of the big problems confronting the new co-ordinator was the network of Nazi influence that had been carefully woven throughout most of Latin America, and which was especially powerful through newspapers which played up German ideas and achievements and played down American affairs. The Office of Inter-American Affairs sought to counteract this situation by launching a $500,000 campaign of advertising in Latin American newspapers publicizing the United States efforts toward better hemispheric relations.

This turned out to be a considerable mess. The State Department and particularly Sumner Welles, its staunchest advocate of the Good Neighbor policy, had looked at the new co-ordinator's office with lifted eyebrows from the beginning and the newspaper campaign seemed to confirm their feeling that it was all a big mistake. They protested to the White House that the campaign—about which the Department heads had not been consulted or informed—was likely to do more harm than good, that the Latin Americans would consider it too flamboyant, that the advertisements were appearing in Nazi-owned newspapers and not in some pro-American papers and that the whole approach was wrong. Mr. Roosevelt took Nelson to task for failing to get together with the State Department prior to launching such a program and told him to keep in line in the future. Nelson agreed with the President—

they were still thinking alike—and quickly made his peace with the Department, establishing a system under which they would be consulted. This made a good impression on the Department, especially when it was later disclosed that Nelson actually had talked the whole scheme over in advance with a Department representative who for some reason had never passed the information on to top-ranking officials. At the time, however, Nelson chose to let the buck-passing end with him instead of stirring up a quarrel that might slow up his office's work.

At other times, he ran into conflicts with such formidable Washington figures as Milo Perkins, executive director of the Board of Economic Warfare, and Colonel Wild Bill Donovan, who had a variety of jobs that included supervision over short-wave broadcasting. Donovan felt that he should be the last word in broadcasts to Latin America, and this difference of opinion called for a high-level decision. When it became apparent that the President would support Nelson's position, however, the new co-ordinator quickly made an arrangement with Donovan's office for close collaboration and friendly but regular exchange of ideas.

This idea, completely new to Washington, of making friends instead of enemies out of rivals in the bureaucratic jungle was basic in Nelson's approach to his job, which he never forgot was one of doing something about Latin America instead of about his own career as a public servant. It usually paid off in the end. At first, for instance, Nelson had very little authority to carry out his program as co-ordinator. If he found that it was highly important for the United States to release a shipload of scarce material to a Latin American country in order to stave off an economic disaster there, it was necessary for him to persuade some other agency such as Perkins' Board of Economic Warfare to issue the proper orders for the shipment. This obviously was going to lead to clashes and it did. Nelson's solution for the problem, however, was to suggest that his Economic Division under Carl Spaeth be put under the authority of Perkins' board, as eventually was done, in a limited way, and Spaeth with a staff of some seventy experts thereafter worked for both outfits. Mr. Roosevelt also expanded Nelson's powers and he was appointed to the Board of Economic Warfare in order to facilitate closer collaboration between the two agencies.

These conflicts of authority, although they started occasional rumors that Nelson was on his way out, were merely the most discussed features of a great deal of hard work that the Inter-American Affairs Office was doing. As soon as he learned how to keep his guard up, Nelson began making progress. His boyish frankness and his knowledge of Latin American affairs made a good impression on skeptical Congressional committees before which he appeared, and his budget climbed up to $45,-000,000. His organizational talents set up in his office an array of divisions, and subdivisions such as Press, Motion Pictures and Radio, Commercial and Financial, Transportation, Export Priorities, Commodities, Social Science and Education, Music, Travel, Art and a number of others. He brought into this organization around five hundred persons, from office boys to advisers, including Walter P. Chrysler, Jr., as a part of the Commercial and Financial Division; Wallace K. Harrison, as an assistant co-ordinator; John Hay Whitney, as head of the Motion Pictures Division; Don Francisco, former big-time advertising man and head of Lord and Thomas; John Abbott, of the Museum of Modern Art; Joseph Rovensky, who had been his superior at the Chase National Bank; John Clark, a classmate of Nelson's at Dartmouth; Frank Jamieson, a former Associated Press bureau chief and a Pulitzer Prize winner; and Moe Berg, once a catcher for the Boston Red Sox, who holds an LL.D. from Princeton and speaks seven languages. Berg was given the job of bringing sports into the sphere of better inter-American relations.

With such backing almost anything could happen in the Rockefeller office and frequently did. Nelson and his staff mixed in the propaganda hopper a good deal of back-slapping, a measure of topnotch journalism and a high degree of up-to-date diplomatic enterprise, well seasoned with incentives to businessmen in Latin America. He became an entrepreneur of culture, a publicist who peddled everything from one-paragraph newspaper items to a four-color picture magazine, a sponsor of a $25,000,000 health program and a promoter with incomparable contacts in the business world. He knew everybody, or at least he had everybody's name handy in the extensive card-index files that he had kept during his visits to South America.

Some of these activities were occasionally overdone and some of the cultural gestures failed to hit the target at which they were aimed, but there was not much to back up the waggish remark heard around Washington to the effect that "the Brazilians have warned us that the next time we send a good will mission to Rio de Janeiro they will immediately declare that a state of war exists with the United States." One of the important contributions of the Rockefeller office was the assembly of a black list of pro-Nazi business outfits in Central and South American countries. There were 1,800 names on the black list when it was published after a long investigation that showed hundreds of American firms were doing business with South Americans who were actively supporting Germany's war effort. In addition, Nelson's assistants brought out by thorough investigation the German control of important air lines in Latin America and opened the way for local companies, with aid from the Reconstruction Finance Corporation, to buy out the lines and put them under local control.

To combat Nazi influence on the press, Nelson set up a staff of around sixty writers who produced a couple of hundred thousand words a week for a dozen short-wave radio stations, several hundred Latin American newspapers and various press associations. They handled everything from society items to important government declarations and concentrated special attention on counteracting German propaganda. In addition, American movies, paintings, magazines, books, musical groups, actors, actresses, technical advisers, sports teams, sculpture and countless other items were sent to the Latin American countries as contributions to culture and as a supplement to the economic contributions—from steel to ships—that Nelson could arrange for them during the war. One of the most popular contributions was the magazine *En Guardia,* an expensive and well-edited magazine of photographs and articles that became one of the most sought-after publications in Latin America, and was frequently sold for whatever the market would stand by unscrupulous dealers, although it was supposed to be distributed without cost. Latin culture in the form of musicians and art exhibitions also was brought to the United States, the teaching of Spanish was encouraged in schools, contests were held on the subject of friendship of the Americas and thousands of booklets on the same subject were distributed. Axis propaganda was soon overwhelmed, and Nelson was beginning to appear as a kind of economic Simón Bolívar in the eyes of Latin Americans.

He was doing pretty well in Washington, too, despite occasional irritation over the delays and frustrations that go with governmental affairs. His staff was one of the hardest working and the most enthusiastic in the capital and there were few staff members who failed to build up a genuine respect for the boss.

He looked after them in big things and small and he had a way of making them feel that they were part of a team that was doing something important. For a while, before his family moved to Washington, he lived in a big house in Georgetown and was in the habit of telling new members of his staff to "come out and stay" until they could find a place to live. This attitude had the advantage of keeping around him day and night some of the men who were vital to formulation of the co-ordinator's program and resulted in the formation of a kind of "coffee cabinet" to thresh out policy matters at breakfast. But it had the disadvantage of turning the place into a small hotel with anywhere from a dozen to a score of guests, a situation that was not solved until Mrs. Rockefeller and the children arrived for the duration.

In all of this period, Nelson's idea was to demonstrate that there exists a big area in which the government can co-operate with private groups in strengthening the ties among the American nations; an idea that he was to consider more important than ever after the war as the influence of Soviet Russia spread in Europe and the Far East. This never meant to him that the United States should travel down a one-way street to improve relations or that such efforts should be limited to a wartime emergency. Every move that we made to bolster the economy of our neighbors meant that in the future, and especially in an emergency, the whole of the Americas would be just that much stronger. The whole basis of our wartime efforts to win Latin America was that the program would be continued in peacetime and the theme of Nazi propaganda was that we would drop the whole thing like a hot potato as soon as the war emergency was ended. It was to Nelson's credit that, by the time the war ended, most observers agreed that his office had done as much and perhaps more to create good will in the Americas than any other effort in our history. But it was also true that Congressional reluctance to continue the program after the war tended to destroy a great deal of the progress that had been made, and caused some Latin American newspapers to suggest that there had, after all, been some truth behind the Nazi propaganda.

Throughout the war period Nelson had, in addition to his other duties, acted as chairman of the Inter-American Development Commission, a collective agency of the twenty-one American republics, and as various shiftings of offices took place late in the war he became an Assistant Secretary of State in charge of relations with these republics. His appointment took place in December of 1944 and he continued in that job until August of 1945, when Secretary of State Edward Stettinius resigned.

The State Department in 1945 was, perhaps, suffering from a heavy sprinkling of amateur statesmen in the top echelon, but at the same time it was engaged in some of the most significant international negotiations of our era. The war was ending, President Roosevelt died that spring, the challenge of tremendous peacetime problems was at hand and the United Nations was being born with great pain but also with great hopes and fine, righteous determination. In many ways, it seemed to open up just the kind of a career that Nelson had been looking for. His prestige was high, despite some pettifogging efforts to dismiss the work of the Rockefeller Office as wartime boondoggling. He had learned his way around Washington and he had acquired at least a preliminary degree of diplomatic experience. He was on the best of terms with most South American areas and political groups and his Berlitz school Spanish had turned into an ability to speak the language, and some dialects, with considerable fluency.

He went to Mexico City in February as an alternate delegate to the Inter-American Conference on Problems of War and Peace, and, on behalf of the United States, signed the Act of

Chapultepec. Regarded as the most significant resolution adopted by the conference, it was a reciprocal assistance pact providing guarantees of territorial integrity and political independence not only from aggression outside the Western Hemisphere but also from aggression within the continent. At the time the act was adopted it was specified that it would be one of the regional pacts to be integrated into a world organization such as the United Nations, which was then being created.

When the United Nations Conference on International Organization convened at San Francisco on April 25, Nelson was one of the Assistant Secretaries of State assigned to help work out the final details. He was still a slightly boyish figure among the world famous diplomatic representatives and their well-tailored staffs. He, too, was well tailored but he had not quite overcome a tendency to be a little rumpled by the time he got within range of the news photographers' cameras. On one occasion Nelson and a famous New York political figure, well known for his meticulous appearance, agreed to make a few remarks for the motion picture news cameras. The New Yorker appeared with his hair beautifully combed, his tie knotted perfectly and his suit uncreased; gave himself a final once-over and stepped up to the microphones. Nelson came in with everything about normal—that is, not too neat—except that his necktie had someway been shoved around until the knot had almost disappeared under his collar.

The New Yorker's public relations adviser was standing by to see that everything went properly and he quickly grabbed the elbow of an associate of Nelson's, pointing out the crooked tie. "You can't let him get in front of the cameras like that," he exclaimed. "He can't wear his tie that way!"

"Oh, yes I can," Nelson's associate replied, disengaging his elbow. "And he will."

At the San Francisco conference, there was a good deal of

opposition to the idea of including regional pacts, such as the Act of Chapultepec, in the United Nations charter, but to Nelson it seemed that such an arrangement was essential, especially to United States policy in Latin America. This was, of course, the Department's viewpoint, and Senator Arthur Vandenberg, Nelson and other firm believers in the wisdom of such a course led the fight for inclusion of the regional pacts. Their efforts were successful, although the full significance of the agreement was not easily realized at the time. Later, when the great struggle between the Communist and non-Communist worlds became intense, the importance of the victory was illustrated by the realization that without it there would have been no Atlantic Pact to enable the Western nations to unite in their own defense.

The most important point at the conference, however, as far as Nelson's immediate future was concerned centered around Argentina. The dictatorial Perón government at Buenos Aires had caused a lot of headaches and was highly unpopular with the public in the United States. To many Americans, admission of the Argentine to the United Nations under these conditions seemed immoral. We were dealing with other dictatorships— Soviet Russia, for instance—it was true, but Perón, after all, was more or less *our* dictator, if you looked at it from the viewpoint of the Americas, and we seemed to be patting him on the head instead of kicking him in the pants by bringing him into the United Nations. This was an emotional attitude, to be sure, and it was not the attitude of the Department of State, which had to consider a great many other and more logical factors.

Just what Nelson thought about the question was never brought out publicly. Considering all the factors involved, it may be legitimately suspected that he didn't feel right about admission of the Perón government, at least until it showed some signs of reform. It is also more than likely that a number of his advisers were opposed to admission and that there may have been some soul-searching conferences on the subject. But the State Department wanted Argentina admitted and, in the end, Nelson adopted that policy and as an Assistant Secretary it was his job, of course, to work for admission. This he did with his usual energy and with success as far as the Perón government was concerned. As far as Nelson was concerned the operation was not so successful. A campaign of criticism of the action broke out in the newspapers and the Department took a heavy beating in the following weeks. Stettinius resigned that summer and when James Byrnes took over the Department Nelson was permitted to resign.

He returned, a bit discouraged, to New York and to private life. But he had no intention of giving up his interest in Central and South America.

✖ VIII ✖

JUST ACROSS THE HALL FROM NELSON IN THE ULTRAMODERN and functionally designed offices of the Rockefeller family is the office of Laurance, who has been Nelson's partner in various deals since they made pocket money as boys raising and selling rabbits. On the surface, they're not too much alike. Laurance is tall, thin-faced and sharp-featured compared to Nelson's squarishness but they have the same drive and intense ambition and they complement each other in many ways.

Early in life both decided that their parents had made a serious error in selecting names for them which they regarded as "sissy." This was a matter that seemed easy to correct, however, and after culling over the names of the heroes in the juvenile adventure books they had been reading they decided to call each other "Dick" and "Bill." Nelson didn't last very long as "Dick" but the "Bill" stuck to Laurance; the other brothers began calling him by that name and finally the whole family took it up—a development that sometimes proves confusing today to visitors who are not familiar with the boys' childhood background.

In contrast to Nelson's boyish enthusiasm, Laurance has a dry, almost sardonic humor that tends to keep plans from floating off on global wings. "This idea," he said recently concerning a business project, "is just common sense when you stop to think." A half grin twisted the corner of his mouth. "Maybe the only reason common sense is rare is that so few people stop to think." When he was in the Navy during the war his promotion to the rank of lieutenant commander occurred on the day he and his wife had been invited to a rather large social function. Laurance told no one of the promotion but went to a tailor shop and had the authorized extra stripe sewed on his uniform before attending the party. He met his wife, but she paid no attention to the new stripe. At the party, nobody mentioned it although Laurance walked around feeling that his arm was practically glistening with gold braid. It wasn't until they were ready to leave that a friend said: "Say! don't you have more stripes on your sleeve than usual?"

Laurance shrugged in disgust. "Thank you," he said. "I've been waving it around all afternoon and until this moment nobody has noticed it—not even my wife."

Laurance sometimes refers to himself as a "gadgeteer" because he has always been interested in mechanics and especially interested in trying out new things. At the Lincoln School he became an ardent camera fan and, instead of writing a theme that was required in one class, he took photographs that told a complete story and submitted them to his instructor. He also built an entire automobile chassis of wood, lowered it out of the school workroom window and took it to Pocantico Hills where he installed a motorcycle engine—and the thing ran. Later, he had a Model A Ford automobile which he decorated with several fancy horns and many other gadgets and which he polished with great regularity.

In school he played a pretty good game of basketball and in his senior year he was business manager of the yearbook, an experience that demonstrated, as one classmate remarked later, his "coolness, his ability to assess a business situation and, most of all, his willingness to take a chance in order to get results." The Lincoln School yearbook had always been a major financial disaster, an enterprise that was continued from year to year on a sentimental basis and perhaps with the idea of losing no more money than was absolutely necessary. Thus the business manager's job was to cut corners and act as watchdog in seeing that the editor of the book didn't spend too much. Such a system seemed like arrant nonsense to Laurance and he promptly began hounding the amazed editor, Harmon Goldstone, to spend more money and develop a bigger and better book.

"But we're not supposed to spend much," Goldstone protested. "We haven't got the money."

"You do the planning," Laurance said. "I'll raise the money."

He then started a campaign that had Lincoln in a mild uproar for weeks. Everybody was persuaded or bullied into bringing something to school auctions which were run off with a great fanfare of excitement. Boys contributed sports equipment, old cameras, pups and anything else they could rake up out of the attic. Girls made fudge and cakes, which were auctioned to the highest bidder. The more Goldstone spent, the more Laurance agitated for extra funds. He also took the pictures for the yearbook. In the end, they came out with the most elaborate book the school had ever seen but, when all the reports were in, they also had a small surplus in the till.

It happened that the books were delayed in printing and could not be completed until about a week after the school term ended and summer vacation had started. Laurance and Goldstone therefore had to deliver them to the homes of their classmates in New York City. "Almost all members of the class had known each other for at least four years," Goldstone recalled later. "We had all worked together and gone to the same parties. We never thought much about whether our classmates were rich or poor or whatever, and I'll never forget our amazement when we began delivering those books. One day we were dealing with butlers in big Fifth Avenue apartments and the next day we were climbing five flights of tenement stairs to a cold-water flat. Until then I don't believe either one of us could have told you in most cases which of our classmates we would find at which address, but that's the kind of school Lincoln was."

The next year when Laurance went to Princeton University he discovered that his intense interest in gadgets and business had given way temporarily to an interest—just as intense—in what made people tick, to be more specific, what made Laurance Spelman Rockefeller tick. It was, he felt later, a period of conscious adjustment and orientation in which he tried to understand the world he lived in and the role he might play in it. None of the five Rockefeller brothers was as austerely and humbly religious as their father, but they had been brought up in a strict atmosphere and religion had always been a powerful part of their lives. John's naturally devout attitude fitted smoothly into his philanthropic work as he grew older. Nelson had no trouble with the practical reconciliation of religious training with everyday adult life. But for Laurance it wasn't as easy. He found himself facing the necessity of making a rational adjustment between religious ideals of his boyhood and the world of practical affairs. For a sincere and intelligent young man with an insatiable curiosity and an unlimited respect for his parents this period of adjustment posed a great many problems. He rather felt as if he lived "always with a Bible in one hand" but he also was able to recognize the necessity for bringing his thinking into line with the world in which he was going to exist.

Laurance's attack on this problem was rather typical. He decided to major in philosophy and he took in the next few years every philosophy course offered at the university—not just most of them but *all* of them—in an effort to round out and balance his personal philosophy.

"I'm not sure," he said long afterward, "but I probably set some kind of record for the Ivy League. I wanted to understand.

I had always wanted to understand machines and gadgets. Now I wanted to understand people. It is, I discovered, a long and difficult process. I'm still working at it."

By the time he had finished his education, Laurance had more or less decided that there were two main challenges he—and his brothers as well—would have to face. In the first place, they had to make good in the job of carrying on the family affairs and interests, an area of operations "in which we naturally had a running start" because of the Rockefeller position and wealth. But, since so much had been handed to the third generation, Laurance felt that it was all the more important to find a way in which to make an original contribution—to do something that was not an outgrowth of the family background. In view of his interest in gadgets and his enthusiasm for trying something new, it was fairly obvious from the time he began his business career that Laurance would be up to unusual things.

This showed up even in minor matters. Soon after his marriage, when he was getting ready to furnish a house, Laurance asked Harmon Goldstone, who was a fledgling architect, about new designs in furniture. Goldstone had been to Scandinavia and was interested in the modern furniture designed by Alvar Aalto, a noted Finnish architect, but he had only a few photographs to show Laurance. That was enough. Laurance ordered a houseful of it sent from Finland, saying that he would take a chance on it because he liked the photographs. It was a large order and Goldstone wasn't at all certain how it would work out, but one day Laurance called him at the Rockefeller Center office in which he worked and said: "The stuff's being unpacked down in the basement. Come on."

Goldstone, Laurance and Wallace K. Harrison, for whom Goldstone worked, met in the basement to watch the unpacking and were so pleased with the first pieces of furniture they saw that they were all soon pulling at the wrappings and talking about how they could set up a company to import Aalto's furniture for sale in the United States.

"We'll have to keep the price reasonable," Laurance pointed out, "so there won't be much profit in it."

They took the precaution of checking with several experts on modern furniture before going ahead with their plans. In each instance, the experts told them they would lose their shirts (a rather imaginative figure of speech in Laurance's case) but they were too enthusiastic to pay much attention. They also had several advantages. Mr. Rockefeller, Jr., gave them the use of an old house on Fifty-third Street. The Museum of Modern Art had an Aalto show and borrowed some of their stock, later buying it for the Museum. They had an exhibit at the World's Fair in New York that year. And of course they had a great many friends who passed the word around about the new designs.

One salesman was hired for the Fifty-third Street store, but their business grew so rapidly that Goldstone was soon spending all of his time being a furniture dealer and neglecting his work in the architect's office. They had to hire more personnel and none of the three is quite sure what might have happened had not the beginning of World War II suddenly cut off their imports from Finland. As a result they decided to liquidate New Furniture, Inc.—the company they had formed—and split up a modest profit.

Laurance had always been interested in speedboats and in the 1930's he began experimenting with hulls similar to those that were later used on wartime PT boats. He liked to commute down the Hudson River from Tarrytown by speedboat occasionally and, after having tried out four craft over a period of years, decided to design one that would be exactly what he wanted, combining speed, seaworthiness and cruisability. This turned out to be an aluminum hull built around two Packard engines. The boat is sixty-five feet long and seventeen and one-half feet wide and will do about forty miles an hour. Laurance and his family occasionally use it for long cruises, one of which thoroughly tested its seaworthiness during a stiff storm in the Caribbean.

Laurance's willingness to take a chance showed up in his first large business venture. In the 1930's he gravitated toward the field of aviation because of his mechanical turn of mind and because it was a comparatively new field that was wide open for vast future development. It also was a field that gave Laurance the opportunity he was seeking to do something on his own. The Rockefeller family had never had any interest in aviation and, in fact, Mr. Rockefeller, Jr., carefully avoided even so much as taking a ride in an airplane.

In the middle 1930's the American aviation industry was in an uncertain if not chaotic state. Captain Eddie Rickenbacker, a great believer in the future of commercial aviation, had been having his ups and downs in the field but the "downs" so heavily outweighed the "ups" that leading financial experts had decided Eddie was a great guy and a wonderful pilot but no business-man. Laurance formed a different idea about the financial future of the World War I ace and he and Rickenbacker bought into North American Aviation, a part of the General Motors setup at that time, and in 1938 turned it into Eastern Air Lines. Laurance's judgment, which he backed up with cash, turned out to be sound and in the next decade Eastern became almost unique among the country's air lines. In 1946 it was the only leading domestic air carrier to report a net profit for the March quarter and in many ways it became a leading example of financial success, using its planes in a manner that permitted operation with much the lowest overhead cost of any leading air carrier.

This experience with Eastern more or less set a pattern for

Laurance's future operations in commercial aviation. He did not start any new enterprises but he kept his interest focused on new industrial horizons where science was beginning to produce spectacular results in airplane design, electronics, helicopters and, eventually, rocket engines. These were the fields that would expand most rapidly in the coming years and they were fields that had already attracted the nation's finest engineering and creative brains. But, at the same time, they were fields in which there obviously was a lamentable shortage of certain elements essential to complete success. There was not, for example, an oversupply of managerial brains. All you had to do was to look at the bankruptcy records to see that most such operations suffered from mismanagement. This was only to be expected in new and untried enterprises and, with customary caution, conservative capital was holding back its support until time and experience had demonstrated the proper way to proceed and had lessened the risk of investment.

Laurance's temperament and talents were well tailored to take advantage of such an opportunity. In 1938, feeling that the United States was not keeping up with European aviation development, he had co-operated with his brother, Winthrop, in establishing an organization to train young men and women in aeronautics, called Air Youth of America. He was a member of the advisory council of the Inter-American Escadrille, set up just before World War II to promote interest in private flying. He was a trustee of *Air Affairs*, an international quarterly, and a director of the American Aeronautical Archives, which he helped establish in 1940 to provide the finest modern aeronautical library in the world. He was also a member of the Institute of Aeronautical Sciences and a member of the New York City Airport Authority.

These extracurricular activities and his participation in Eastern Air Lines had given Laurance a rather thorough background in the aviation field by 1939 when an aircraft designer from St. Louis named J. S. McDonnell, Jr., walked into his office one day with a briefcase full of blueprints and an unhappy story of past financial experiences. At the time he first talked to Laurance, McDonnell had only a small experimental shop in St. Louis and an idea for a new pursuit plane for the United States Army Air Force. He had no orders from the Army. He didn't have the money to build the new model. He had had very little successful experience with management or financing in the past. But he had outstanding creative and engineering skill and when he departed a few hours later he had $10,000 of Laurance's money and the promise of further assistance. The plane McDonnell built never got into production for a variety of complicated reasons, none of which reflected on his engineering skill; but in the meantime Laurance had co-operated in providing the managerial talent and financial aid that were needed and had interested his brothers in investing in McDonnell. The little experimental shop blossomed into the McDonnell Aircraft Corporation—in all, the Rockefellers backed it with $475,000, most of which was Laurance's money—and during the war it moved forward with long strides.

The war, however, was an interruption for Laurance's business career. In July of 1942 he resigned as a director of McDonnell and later entered the United States Navy, where he served in the Production Division of the Bureau of Aeronautics, concerned primarily with production of naval aircraft on the West Coast. Although he always had been and still is primarily interested in civil aviation, his work in the Navy broadened his knowledge of production matters and made him realize how heavily the development of all phases of aviation depended on the extensive and very costly experimental work carried on by the government. He visited England at the end of the war to investigate progress there in jet plane production and later in 1945 returned to civilian life.

By the time he got back to his desk in Rockefeller Center, he was eager to make up for lost time and had soon plunged hip-deep into enterprises that overflowed with the ideas, skills and boldness necessary for mastery of the Atomic Age, but which needed money and a firm hand on the reins until they were out of swaddling clothes. Laurance was ready with both the cash and a firm hand.

✻ IX ✻

THE FOURTH SON OF THE ROCKEFELLER CLAN IS WINTHROP, who is also the biggest, the most convivial and the most likely to employ a personal approach to a job or a problem. Because they operate on such a large scale, it is customary for the Rockefellers to think in broad, sometimes abstract terms about what might be done to solve the "housing problem" or to relieve the "minority problem." This is not to suggest that some other approach would be better. On the contrary, any other attitude would doubtless be much less effective under the circumstances.

Winthrop, however, is more likely to see and be interested in the human factors involved in any given situation and to look for a solution in terms of the individual. His career has been devoted, broadly, to human relations, both during office hours at Socony-Vacuum and in many outside activities such as the Urban League, where he has provided vigorous leadership in dealing with social and economic problems of Negroes in city areas. Perhaps only a psychologist could suggest whether his career has been affected subconsciously by the fact that his older brothers sometimes were inclined to push him around as a child—until he outgrew them all.

"It seems cruel to me," Mrs. Rockefeller once wrote to her older sons, "that you big boys should make Winthrop the goat all the time. . . . You know very well that the only way to help him is by being kind to him. Abuse only makes him angry and much worse, while for love and kind treatment he will do anything." And some years later Winthrop suggested how well she understood him by writing on Mother's Day that "it seems strange to me that anyone would need to have any particular day set aside in which to remember his mother, but then . . . everybody couldn't have a mother like you."

The Rockefellers had originally decided to name their fourth son Winthrop Aldrich Rockefeller for his maternal uncle but when Mrs. Rockefeller realized that his initials would spell WAR, the Aldrich was dropped. At school, Winthrop didn't set any marks for scholarship but he enjoyed making friends and he was as intensely industrious as his brothers. He waited tables and cleaned rooms to make extra money and at one time received seventy-five cents an hour as a student supervisor in the school workshop. On another occasion he reported to his mother that he was picking up some change by cutting the hair of his classmates, an enterprise that apparently was short-lived. He was one of three boys in the graduating class at Loomis, where he went after Lincoln, to receive a prize for industry, loyalty and manliness.

All of the Rockefeller boys felt that their parents were much too conservative about the age at which they were permitted to learn to drive an automobile, and not all of them observed the letter of the law as laid down by Mr. Rockefeller. Winthrop began learning how to drive on the sly at least two years before his father felt that he was qualified. He started out driving a Ford car and later graduated to a White truck that was operated by one of the men who worked on the Tarrytown estate. When Mr. Rockefeller finally agreed that he might take his first driving lesson the employe who was to be his teacher knew that Winthrop could drive and, in fact, had ridden with him in secret on a number of occasions. Mr. Rockefeller probably knew it, too, or at least suspected the circumstances because after watching Winthrop steer the car once around a big circle on the estate, he remarked: "My, it is wonderful how quickly you and the other boys seem to take up driving." Winthrop had to agree that he learned quickly.

Later, at Yale, he was an indifferent student in the class of 1935, so indifferent in fact that he was dropped back to the class of 1936 and finally decided that it was not worth while; that he should quit his studies and go to work. "I just wasn't getting anywhere in college," he explained later. "When I was asked why, I said that I couldn't seem to study properly and maybe my eyes were bothering me. I went to a doctor who listened to my story about my inability to study, examined my eyes and then remarked: 'I don't believe the trouble is in your eyes. Did you, by the way, ever try opening a book in order to study?' "

With some hesitation, he informed his parents of his desire to quit school. They offered no reproaches and it was arranged for him to go to work for the Humble Oil Refining Company in Texas. Winthrop liked the idea. He had worked briefly in the Texas oil fields during his summer vacation in 1933 and at that time had gotten himself into the newspapers through no fault of his own. The inside story of that affair was never officially disclosed but it arose from an apparent threat to kidnap the young oil scion. Two agents were sent to act as bodyguards and stories appeared in the Texas newspapers to the effect that a kidnap threat had been received.

This was never confirmed but Winthrop left his summer job and flew back East, arriving at Newark on August 20, sitting next to a "Mr. Wedlich," who promptly denied that he was a government agent or a bodyguard. Dispatches from Texas said that bodyguards with a submachine gun accompanied Winthrop to the plane, however, and "Mr. Wedlich" carried a covered golf bag which might easily have contained a weapon. Actually it was Winthrop's bag and contained only golf clubs.

So effective were the Rockefeller efforts to avoid publicity that the newspapers never did learn any more about the affair. When Winthrop returned to Texas after leaving Yale in 1936, however, he got a commission as a deputy sheriff at a cost of one dollar and with it permission to carry a gun, if he desired, to protect himself against "fanatics." That was apparently the end of his association with law enforcement agencies, except for an incident at Houston when a motorcycle cop stopped him for speeding at forty miles an hour. When he gave his name, the cop asked him if he was a grandson of the oil billionaire and Winthrop said yes. The cop went right on writing the ticket.

"I have a courtesy card from the police chief here," Winthrop said. "Will that do me any good?"

"No," the cop said, handing him the ticket. Cost: ten dollars.

The great depression of the 1930's was at a low point when Winthrop started learning the oil business from the ground up by going into the fields as a "roughneck" laborer. It wasn't a time of pleasant relationships between labor and management and there wasn't any way in which Winthrop could avoid being regarded as management, no matter what kind of job he undertook. He wasn't, however, particularly disturbed by this fact. He had always been interested in all kinds of people and especially in the Baywater Community Center which his mother had founded in a predominantly oil worker town in New Jersey. The Center was established to provide a place where workers and their families could enjoy their leisure time and also engage in educational as well as recreational activities under a "group work" program. Winthrop also had been interested in Hampton Institute since he had visited that Negro educational center with his parents while still in high school, and he had since then made it a practice to assist some student attending Hampton. He felt that as long as he was interested in what they were doing he could get along with workers in the Texas oil field.

It wasn't, however, that easy. Oil-field workers are an independent and hard-fisted crowd by tradition and when they discovered that one of THE Rockefellers had moved into their midst they were not particularly pleased. When they saw that he was a big guy with an easy smile and a tendency to be friendly and considerate they thought he might be spying on them and, anyway, it would be a good idea to give him the works. One of Winthrop's first assignments was to work with the "cellar gang" which meant that he was given a shovel and told to start digging. The cellar gang did nothing but dig eleven-foot-square holes in the ground as a preliminary step to drilling an oil well.

"I knew when I showed up the first morning that all of the crew were watching me," Winthrop recalled later. "It was a kind of test to see what the hell I was doing in the field anyway. We divided up into teams of four men to a hole, each team having a mule and a scraper to haul the dirt away."

There was usually considerable competition among the teams over which could dig the fastest, and this morning the veteran diggers set a fast pace, although Winthrop's team figured they were working under a handicap. That, of course, compelled Winthrop to work as hard as he could and in a couple of hours the dirt was piling up faster than it could be hauled away. Finally, another mule and scraper was assigned to his team and when they knocked off for noon the hole was five feet deep, establishing some kind of local record. It also created a crisis of considerable importance in Winthrop's oil-field career. When it was time to eat lunch he discovered that he was so exhausted by his labors that he couldn't climb out of the hole. For a few seconds he felt that his efforts to prove that he could keep up with the team were going to end in failure because they would have to lift him bodily over the five-foot wall and the prestige that he had built up during the morning would vanish in ridicule.

But after the others had crawled out and started for the truck where their lunch boxes were piled, Winthrop called to the man who had been working at his side. "Hey, Pete! Toss me my lunch box, will you? I think I'll eat right here. It's cooler."

It *was* cooler in a shady corner of the hole than in the sun-baked oil field and by the time Winthrop had eaten his lunch he was feeling better. He got his second wind and managed to work on through the afternoon. It was the hardest way he ever discovered to earn seventy-five cents an hour, but he had passed inspection by his teammates and thereafter got along well with all of them. When he later moved on to another field his boss offered to write him a special recommendation.

Winthrop had a $4.50-a-week room and lived the life of an ordinary worker in the field except that on his days off he didn't get a chance to rest. Instead, he went into the local oil offices to consult with company officials and to pick up as much information as possible about the industry. After moving through several fields, he studied the problems of the researchers, producing and maintenance sections, cost accounting, sales, drilling and refining. He made a great many friends and most of them called him Rocky. A few of them exhibited an unrestrained curiosity about the Rockefeller family affairs, asking in great detail about members of his family, his home, the number of automobiles in the family garage and the number of yachts at the family dock.

Winthrop usually managed to evade these questions but he seldom resented them because they were so obviously asked by men who were honestly interested and frankly curious and who usually had a distorted Hollywood impression of how a wealthy man lived, or at least of how the Rockefellers lived. "I like people," Winthrop remarked once in reference to his friends in various strata of society. "I usually get along with them. Sure, I've always noticed that people look up sharply when they hear the name Rockefeller but you get used to that and you can tell which ones are interested in you and which ones are merely curious about the family name. Sometimes people take a cynical attitude about the friends I've made in various strange places; but I'm not cynical about them. Occasionally, I find that it is a pleasant feeling to prove to somebody that such friends aren't out for something. Just as it is sometimes pleasant to prove that not all rich people are stuck-up so-and-so's."

When Winthrop returned to New York City he went to work as a trainee in the Chase National Bank and a year later joined Socony-Vacuum Oil Company's foreign trade department. He exhibited a great interest in the company's human relations problem. His business career, he felt, was going to be devoted mainly to "trying to find out more and more about the individual worker and his relation to his work, his family and his community."

"That's a bit indefinite," he explained at one time, "but my objectives aren't easy to define. In a vague way, I suppose you could say that I'd like to contribute to a better, happier use of manpower. In industry, we spend millions of dollars on equipment but the greatest cost is labor. We know everything about the equipment, yet we haven't scratched the surface in our efforts to understand the relation of the worker to the machine. About all we know is negative—that there are a lot of round pegs in square holes. A great many questions are still to be solved before we can say that the human machine is being used in the best way and for the greatest benefit of everybody."

Winthrop's efforts along these lines were not confined to his working hours in the office. He became an industrial relations consultant for Rockefeller Center, Inc. He formed and became chairman of Air Youth of America upon the urging of a noted flier, Frank Hawks. He became, in 1940, a director of the executive board of the National Urban League to deal with social problems of Negroes in urban areas. And in 1938 he took a leave of absence to become executive vice-chairman of the Greater New York Fund in its initial year.

The beginning of the Greater New York Fund illustrated a rather typical Rockefeller attitude. It was customary each year to have charitable drives to raise money for various funds, some of which were sponsored by Jewish organizations, some by Catholic or Protestant groups, and so on. The result was a great deal of lost motion, extra expense and, not infrequently, lack of public interest in certain causes. Nelson Rockefeller was approached with the idea that everybody, including the public, would fare better if the various groups united in a single campaign for public donations which would then be properly divided among the groups sponsoring health and social work. He was asked to serve as vice-chairman of such a drive, but being unable to accept, he suggested Winthrop for the job.

The amount of money contributed had been decreasing during the depression and had caused an acute financial situation for some city charities. The Greater New York Fund was organized to handle the financing and planning of private health and social work in the city by a co-ordinated appeal to business and employee groups. It was the first united philanthropic movement of its kind and included all faiths and all races in its charitable appeal. Winthrop devoted full time to administration work during the first campaign and established a pattern that has since become a fixture for New York City.

These activities, his office work and a mild participation in New York night life kept Winthrop busy enough up to the beginning of World War II. Almost a year prior to Pearl Harbor, he enlisted in the Army as a private, and began making a lot of new acquaintances as well as a few new friends. He also got a "break." The Socony-Vacuum Company, for one year, made up the difference between his twenty-one dollars per month Army pay and the eighty-eight dollars a week he had been receiving on his job, a practice that it had previously instituted for the benefit of all employees going into the service. Some of Winthrop's acquaintances at the Twenty One Club and El Morocco expressed doubt that he was going to be able to make ends meet even under Army restrictions, but Winthrop took the company's differential pay and buckled down to work at Plattsburg.

He had originally tried to enlist without any publicity but some of his friends leaked the news to a Broadway reporter and most of the newspapers carried stories about his induction at Fort Dix and his transfer to Plattsburg in January of 1941. One inductee, talking to a reporter, referred to him as Mr. Rockefeller and was promptly bawled out by an Army major who overheard the conversation and snapped: "He's Private Rockefeller from now on." Winthrop talked briefly to reporters, explaining that he had enlisted because his number in the draft was one that would not be called for a long time. Actually, he felt that the family should be represented in the defense forces and, being the only bachelor, it was logical that he should be the one to volunteer. He grinned for a lot of news photographers and then, after a day or two, he was swallowed up in the vast routine of Army life. The following October he was a sergeant in the First Division, and early in 1942, after officers training school at Fort Benning, he became a second lieutenant. The next year, when he had moved up to first lieutenant and was "H" Company commander in the 305th Infantry, 77th Division, he gave every man in his company a "good luck" silver dollar for Christmas and his mother sent wristlets, a scarf and a sweater—most of them knitted by her and her friends— to each of them. By 1944, when he went overseas with the 77th

Division, Winthrop was a major in the supply section and had developed a lot of ideas of his own about the Army, the conduct of the war and the political situation at home. Occasionally, he got these ideas off his chest in letters to his parents and friends, with whom he kept in close touch. On one sea voyage in the Pacific he wrote eighty-five letters and still felt that he hadn't properly kept up his correspondence.

"I learned that our Regiment had received an opening for one student to the Command and General Staff School at Fort Leavenworth and . . . the Colonel forgot that I wanted to go and turned it down," he wrote to his parents on one occasion before going overseas. "I went to him again and told him first how anxious I was to go. He [again the Colonel] seemed pleased that I had pulled no wires and agreed to see if the wrong might be righted. . . . I should know tomorrow."

Sometimes he reminisced: "The other day . . . I was reminded of the day in 1934 when Grandfather was getting over that spell of pneumonia and you and I, Father, went up to see him. During the course of the conversation you told him how fine and uncomplaining you thought he had been through it all. . . . He smiled and said, 'John, it has really been a blessing for I have had an opportunity to think over all the wonderful things that have happened in my life and remember the fine people that I have known. Had it not been for this confinement, I would have missed all this.' Not that I can in any way compare my life with his, but these quiet days of rest and letter writing have been a true source of pleasure to me."

In 1944, on a Pacific Island, he became tremendously interested in building an Officers' Club, which he had to plan and for which he had to scrounge the material. "We have been piecing [it] together for the past weeks. I . . . had to beg, borrow and steal to get the materials to make it but now that it is all finished it has turned out to be most attractive. Last Saturday night we had a very gay party attended by most of the biggies and they, too, seemed pleased. . . . I have appointed myself chief landscape architect and am having much fun with it."

In August of 1944, Major Rockefeller's outfit supported the landing on Guam and on August 30, he wrote: "This time I am writing from my foxhole on the island of Guam. . . . Our Marine friends have already started to refer to us as the 305th Marines—a compliment that I have never heard them pay any Infantry unit before! . . . All in all it has been hectic . . . and this has been complicated by the rainy season." Winthrop's letters didn't tell all of the story of his combat experience. On one occasion when the 305th was wading ashore from landing boats that could not reach the beach because of coral reefs, he found himself in water up to his neck alongside a comrade who couldn't swim. It was nighttime and they had about 1,000 feet to go to the beach and the water was full of craters that had been made by bombs dropped earlier in the air force assault on Japanese defenses. The boy beside Winthrop was, like everyone else, carrying a heavy pack and when he fell into a bomb crater he sank like a rock. Winthrop staggered over and pulled him out. Two minutes later, he fell in another crater. When Winthrop tried to fish him out this time both of them sank straight down. Eventually, Winthrop managed to inflate his life preserver and they got to solid ground but the major had had enough. He made the boy take hold of his belt and follow him from there to the beach, figuring that if he had to dive for him once more neither one of them would make it.

A month or so later, when things had been stabilized somewhat on Guam, Winthrop wrote something about his difficulties in the service of supply. "If I were the Commanding General of the U.S. Army one of the first things that I would require is that all officers be given a very thorough training in the subject of logistics. One of the required assignments would be that each student be required to move on his own back the supplies for one company for one average day in combat over a distance of one-quarter mile. Then as a graduating present of the course, I would give them a multiplying machine so they can rapidly calculate the tonnage which we must move daily to support them. I can think of nothing that would do more to knock some of the headaches out of our life with so many people expecting us to do the impossible all along. For the civilian to appreciate this problem is just hopeless!"

Not long afterward, he commented on the "inevitable disintegration of the soldier's respect for property." "I know that you would not believe for a minute the degree to which stealing is carried on during and after a campaign such as we have been through. . . . If one complains about it you are looked at as though you were an obstructionist, to say the least. And as far as getting any backing at trying to discourage the practice, you are always told the same thing . . . 'Nothing can be done about it.' Each time that I am told that I can't help but think of the many hours that I spent burning Edgar Guest's poem ["It Couldn't Be Done"] into the board that now hangs in the Bayway Community Center, and just boil. . . . But the thing that concerns me is how are you going to be able to convince G.I. Joe that this practice should cease when he steps on the ship to go home."

After President Roosevelt's re-election in 1944, he wrote: "Again and again and again he comes back to the White House. Just think of it, you have not got one single grandchild that can remember any other President of this country with the possible exception of Mitzie. . . . They say that about 67% of the soldier vote went to Roosevelt. It is hard to believe that those of us who are fighting to make our country free for opportunity are willing at the same time to turn right around and vote for a fourth term."

Winthrop's outfit at one time was largely composed of Southerners and a period of considerable tension arose when they were on Leyte beachhead because a Negro unit was unexpectedly attached to them. He promptly recognized the danger of trouble between the veteran members of his outfit and the new Negro unit but there wasn't much he could do but wait. A few days later two officers from Georgia came to him and demanded that the Negro sergeant of the unit be broken because he had not quickly ceased the work he was doing to obey an order.

"I suppose I was expecting something of the sort," Winthrop recalled later. "We got the Negro unit—a duck platoon that operated those big amphibious trucks—because we were on the waterfront and had to supply our troops by water. I had not expected a Negro unit but the sergeant in charge was a splendid fellow and we talked over the question of where they would put up their tents and I told them to eat in the regular chow line. The sergeant obviously wanted to work things out as well as possible—as individuals—and avoid being aggressive or demanding. Then these officers of mine from Georgia complained."

Winthrop listened to the complaint and he felt that the trouble was largely due to prejudice. He also decided that it was vital to make his own position unmistakably clear at once to avoid a lot of future trouble. He told the two white officers to stand by and then he called in the Negro sergeant and asked for his side of the story. With the complaining officers present, the sergeant said that he was engaged in an important task and that he had delayed in obeying the order.

"Your outfit is new here," Winthrop then told the sergeant. "Perhaps you don't understand exactly how we operate in the infantry. When a superior officer gives you an order, you carry it out immediately. You don't use your own judgment as to whether it would be better to delay. However, I should have explained that to you when your outfit first arrived, so I believe this misunderstanding has been my fault instead of yours. Now that it is cleared up, you make certain that all of your men understand and don't let me hear of it happening again."

The two complaining officers were angered because the offender was not punished and for the next few days Winthrop waited nervously for trouble. Everything, however, went along with reasonable smoothness.

"They knew," the major said later, "that I was going to back up the new unit just as if it had been a white unit or any other unit. And from that time on, we never had one unpleasant word or unpleasant experience. I think that experience is a valuable one to many people in business and industry. If the management is going to back up a fair deal everybody goes along. If the management is wishy-washy, you're going to have trouble."

On April 2, 1945, during the invasion of Okinawa, the 77th Division had just finished clearing out a small force of Japanese in the Kerama Retto islands which are part of the Okinawa group. Winthrop was on a ship off the shore when a Japanese suicide bomber recognized the vessel as a headquarters ship and dived into it. There was a tremendous flash of flames.

Winthrop's next letter to his parents was written from a hospital ship. "I am hoping against hope that you haven't received one of *those* telegrams from the War Dept., and if so that this letter follows soon after. Yes, I have been slightly wounded. The facts as censorship allows are that I received third degree burns of both hands and my face was scorched. We have been receiving excellent and most conservative care aboard this hospital ship and already my face is well enough to be shaved. My hands are coming along beautifully and the doctor promises that I will be as good as new, with no scars, in about two weeks. The reason my writing is so poor is that I do have 'boxing glove' bandages. The bark is worse than the bite! My general condition is excellent and my spirits couldn't be better."

The hard fighting of the Okinawa invasion was not yet over by the time Winthrop got out of the hospital and back on duty. Then in August he suffered a severe attack of jaundice—his second—and after V-J Day was returned to the United States for further hospitalization. He had made a lot of new friends in the Army and he has since kept in touch with many of them in all stations of life. Like a boy of Italian parentage named Jimmy, who had Winthrop up for a spaghetti dinner at his house in the Bronx. Eventually, Jimmy went into business for himself in a town about a hundred miles from New York and Winthrop didn't hear much from him until one day in 1949 when Jimmy called him at his office.

"I'm in town, Brother Rock," he said, using the name by which many in the outfit knew Winthrop.

"I'm sorry, Jimmy," Winthrop replied, "but I can't see you today. My wife is ill and I have to go home."

"But, Brother Rock, that's why I'm here! I read about it in the paper and drove down to ask if there's anything I can do."

Winthrop likes to tell that story because he believes good human relations are a two-way street and that mutual respect and co-operation will flourish under any conditions if given a fair chance.

Toward the end of the war, Winthrop had had plenty of time in the hospital to think about what was going to happen to the boys in the Army when the fighting was over and they returned to their homes. There had been half a dozen illiterates in his outfit and quite a few others with so little education that he felt they would have great difficulty in readjusting them-

selves to civilian life after the violence and recklessness of war.
Once back in the United States for recuperation, he decided that
the most important contribution he could make to the postwar
era was a study of how veterans fared when they got home.

He had hardly started looking into the problem when Secretary of War Robert P. Patterson heard about his plans and
asked him to make such a survey in behalf of the War Department. Winthrop agreed and decided to see for himself what was
happening to veterans in every part of the country. As a result
he spent six months of 1946 roaming by automobile all over the
United States, accompanied only by his "assistant," Jimmy Hudson. Winthrop calls Hudson his assistant because he has never
been able to think of any other title for the young Negro who has
been with him since 1937. Hudson had been working for the
Police Juvenile League in Harlem and had come to know of the
Rockefellers through his efforts to raise money to buy baseball
equipment for youngsters. He has worked at various times for
Nelson and David but mostly for Winthrop, doing everything
from cleaning and chauffeuring to taking part in the veterans
survey. "I couldn't cook, but Mr. Winthrop taught me," Hudson explains. "He likes good sauces, cream soups and roast
chicken and he can still do them all better than I can. Some
people used to think that because he likes to have a good time
he wasn't conscientious about other things. But very few people
know how hard he works or how much he can get done in a day
and an evening—and he's usually working evenings, too."

Winthrop and Hudson traveled 18,000 miles on their veterans survey. They talked to local officials in hundreds of towns,
met with Chambers of Commerce and newspapermen and civic
groups. Hudson made a thorough check with the Negro leaders
in scores of communities. When they ended the tour neither
of them was much impressed by the efforts that were being
made to ease veterans back into civilian life. "I felt that the

G. I. Bill was an effort to buy off the veterans with cash but without really giving them a helping hand," Winthrop said later. "Not even giving them a college education could do the job without something else.

"I urged in my report the formation of a central organizing committee that would go to the bankers or the Chamber of Commerce in each community and establish citizen committees to work out the veterans' problems on an individual basis. Such a committee in each community could assay the qualifications of each veteran and reach some decision about how much help he needed. They could give advice and assistance in the light of local conditions. The veterans' problem, unfortunately, was handled from the top instead of from the bottom level where the community might have taken an interest and done a better job."

These ideas and a great deal more went into Winthrop's report to the War Department, which apparently filed it in one of the Pentagon's deepest and darkest pigeonholes. Shortly thereafter the author of the report was separated from the service after six years in which he had risen from private through the ranks to be a lieutenant colonel on the General Staff. He has continued in the active reserve after his discharge and took an active part in the 77th Division Association, which was set up after World War I to serve veterans of the Division.

Winthrop went back to a desk at the Socony-Vacuum Oil Company—he remained there in the Production Department until 1951—appeared occasionally in night spots frequented by Café Society and, in 1948, married a striking blonde divorcee, Mrs. Barbara Sears, better known to Broadway columnists as Bobo. Their wedding at the home of polo-playing Winston Guest near Palm Beach, Florida, was a headline event for many newspapers which insisted on describing Mrs. Sears, without much regard for accuracy, as a "Cinderella Girl." This was based on the fact that her parents were farmers of very modest means and that at the time of her romance with Winthrop she was living in a walk-up flat adjacent to the Third Avenue Elevated on New York's East Side. It was, however, a very comfortable flat and Mrs. Sears was a familiar figure in Café Society. The newspaper excitement was intensified by an accident that occurred on the airplane that was carrying Winthrop to Florida. The hub of a propeller disintegrated while the craft was over the ocean about 140 miles off Jacksonville. One blade of the propeller crashed through the plane and killed a steward but Dick Merrill, a famous figure in aviation, managed to keep the craft aloft and brought it in to a safe landing.

There was also a mixup in Florida in regard to the date of the wedding because of the delay, required by law, after issuance of a license. Winthrop and Mrs. Sears were finally married a minute after midnight on February 14, amid considerable newspaper fanfare. A son, Winthrop Paul, was born to them, but the marriage was not a happy one. Late in 1949 they were separated and Mrs. Rockefeller took her son to the Midwest to live with her mother on a farm. All of this, of course, was worth a great many thousands of words over a considerable period in the less dignified newspapers of the nation. It was a new experience for the Rockefellers but there wasn't anything they could do about it except to rally around, sit tight and wait for the storm to blow itself out.

✖ X ✖

WHEN DAVID, THE YOUNGEST OF THE ROCKEFELLER brothers, was a small and chubby boy there was nothing he enjoyed more than entertaining his playmates and, on occasion, his schoolteachers. There was plenty of opportunity for such activities in the big Rockefeller mansion on Fifty-fourth Street and especially at Pocantico Hills and Mrs. Rockefeller encouraged her youngest son, although sometimes she felt he was inclined to overplay his hand. When David planned a picnic in the woods he apparently was unable to stop issuing invitations until his entire class was included and the young guests were likely to arrive by the score, all of them ravenously hungry. And once his mother remarked that he obviously would not be satisfied until she had invited every teacher in his school to dinner.

This inclination diminished only slightly if at all with the passage of years and after he had established his own home David still enjoyed collecting several score assorted guests for dinner on the terrace around his swimming pool high on the hills above the Hudson River. Such a gathering might start out as an affair in honor of some dignitary, say the Prime Minister of Pakistan. From there on it would be anybody's guess as to who would be invited. There would certainly be a sprinkling of internationally famous names on such an occasion. But it would also be probable that David would remember some hard-working stenographer in an organization interested in Indian affairs. She would be invited. He would know at least half a dozen scholarship students from distant parts of the world and ask them with the idea of promoting their knowledge of and interest in India. In the end, there would be as diverse a gathering as could be imagined around the swimming pool and the host would get along fine with all of them.

David has a happy faculty of finding something in common with any guest. This is a trifle baffling to strangers at first, because he is a quiet man and gives the impression of personifying Wall Street dignity to the point of stuffiness. On second glance, the sense of dignity remains, but the idea of stuffiness disappears. He likes to talk about a wide variety of things, from beetles to bulldozers—one of which he maneuvers skillfully around his place—and on to high finance and international affairs, in which he is intensely interested. He likes political give-and-take and is particularly pleased when he can maneuver distinguished acquaintances of radically different opinions into an impromptu debate across the coffee cups.

Basically a political economist and a banker, David more than any of his brothers has a casual, almost academic air of assurance that arises from an easy sense of humor, a deep enjoyment of life and a broad educational background. In a quiet manner, he gives the impression of knowing what he wants to do and why he wants to do it, and of taking most things in his stride— whether it is a matter of international banking or the arrival of his wife in the front driveway with a small, newly purchased burro named Cleopatra ensconced in the back seat of her automobile. On the latter occasion, incidentally, there was reason for confusion because Mrs. Rockefeller had set out enthusiastically to buy a thoroughbred saddle horse, which Cleopatra definitely wasn't.

This casualness, however, covers an ability to absorb detail and sustain an intense interest in many things. There is nothing hit-or-miss about David. When he was a small boy at Lincoln School in New York City, one of his teachers interested him in collecting beetles. He learned to classify them and mount them on pins. He suddenly discovered that there was an immense and fascinating insect world right at his feet, hidden in the grass and the rocks and the old tree stumps. With most boys beetle-catching would have been a passing hobby, but once David's attention was caught he began learning all he could about the insects, discovered that his studies were in a field of great agricultural importance and carried through to the logical entomological end. A bottle in which to cage his finds became a regular part of his boyish equipment and he was likely to break off play at any moment to pick up a new specimen in an odd spot.

As he grew older he went on several expeditions of the Museum of Natural History and, later, financed a notable expedition to Mexico where some 100,000 specimens were collected for vital agricultural research work. The Mexican expedition was credited with collecting more varieties of insects than had ever before been obtained in that region. David's own collection is one of the finest private collections in the world, numbering about 40,000 beetles that range from pin-point size to some that are as large as a mouse and marked in brilliant colors. The collection, mounted on pins and carefully indexed, is housed in cabinets that cover one wall of his study and he still adds to it when the opportunity arises. In the course of his ordinary travels to out-of-the-way places, he sometimes still amazes new acquaintances by suddenly pulling a small bottle out of his pocket and making a quick dash to collect a new specimen that he has spotted in the grass or on a tree.

From Lincoln School, David went to Harvard and graduated in 1936 with a B.S. degree. He did postgraduate work in economics and then attended the London School of Economics, which had been aided by Rockefeller money. He finished up at another Rockefeller-favored school, the University of Chicago, where he received his Ph.D. in August of 1940.

In Chicago, David decided that the time had come to break out of the strictly academic atmosphere and rub elbows with life. At that time, life in the United States was dominated by the great depression of the 1930's, the New Deal and the forward surge of labor organizations such as had bitterly fought the Rockefellers in the past. The whole trend of economic and political affairs, the Rooseveltian revolution that was then in progress in the United States, interested David strongly and he wanted to try his own hand in the political arena. His first thought was that he had better find out whether he could make a public speech and he promptly enrolled in the University bureau that provided speakers for all kinds of meetings, including rallies that were often dominated by a strictly left-wing audience. There were various occasions on which David was sent to address groups that were eager to give any capitalist a going-over and that were delighted by the opportunity to heckle a Rockefeller. But they discovered that this Rockefeller knew his economics and was aware that the world was changing. David got along pretty well.

David's doctoral thesis in economic theory was published in 1940 under the title *Unused Resources and Economic Waste.* He was greatly influenced by Professor Frank H. Knight at the University, and the purposes of the thesis were to discover why fixed resources are sometimes used in production and at other times left idle as well as to find the meaning and cause of economic waste. David's final product was difficult reading for any amateur in the field, but he demonstrated an ability to wrestle with the technicalities of broad problems of production and monopoly and, in attacking several theories that were popular at the time, he showed that he also could take off the gloves and fight bare-fisted when the occasion arose. The ordinary reader probably would conclude that the book revealed an unusual talent for analysis and argument, although a psychologist might easily fit David's examination of monopoly and his search for the causes of waste into the Rockefeller background of money-making, public service and frugality.

After his marriage to Margaret McGrath in 1940, David's political interests continued and that year he waded into the field of New York City as one of the secretaries of Mayor Fiorello La Guardia. The Mayor was more or less a maverick as far as party organization was concerned but various aspects of his "reform" administration fitted in with David's ideas at the time and he kept busy at a number of jobs during the eighteen months he was connected with City Hall. One job was a special fact-finding survey for the Mayor of facilities at La Guardia Field, then the city's main airport, for the purpose of turning some of the waste space into property that would bring in an income. He also represented La Guardia on the committee that helped select a site for an airport in nearby Westchester, where problems of encroachment on the city's watershed were involved. He accompanied the Mayor on various public occasions and, in between times, spent a great deal of time answering the avalanche of letters that poured in to the office—usually complaints—or talking on the telephone with indignant citizens who demanded to be put through at once to the Mayor.

It was an exciting and interesting time for David and he liked the life so well that he might easily have stayed with it had he not come to a considered decision that he needed more experience in other fields if he was going to be in a position to make any contribution of his own to government. "I liked politics," he said later, "but I wanted to have something to offer other than just a knowledge of politics. The danger in that field is that you spend all of your time running for office."

Another factor that may have influenced him was that the war was coming closer and closer to the United States and he didn't feel that there would be much time for any kind of career before he was confronted by the prospect of military service. At that time, the city's Department of Health was organizing the first medical research bureau to be established by any municipality in the country, known as the Public Health Research Institute of New York. When it was ready to start operations, David became a trustee, a post he held until April of 1942. Meantime, in October of 1941, he became New York state assistant regional director of the United States Office of Defense Health and Welfare Service, devoting most of his efforts to the task of working out a co-ordinated housing program for defense plants in New York state.

This lasted until the spring of 1942. In May, he enlisted in the Army as a private but later went to the Engineer Officer Candidate School at Fort Belvoir, Virginia, and became a second lieutenant in March of 1943. He also attended the Engineering School at Camp Ritchie, Maryland, until June of 1943. The next two years he spent in the service in North Africa, mostly in intelligence work. About the time the war ended, he was made Assistant Military Attaché in Paris and continued in the Army, as a captain, until December of 1945. He was awarded the Legion of Merit and the French Legion of Honor.

Upon his return home and separation from the service, David resumed a number of activities that had started before the war and also went to work at one of a number of desks "on the floor" in the Foreign Department of the Chase National Bank. Like Nelson, he had been much interested in Latin America before the war and in 1941 he was one of the original members of the New York City Committee for Latin American Scholarships. This committee co-operated with the Office of the Co-ordinator of Inter-American Affairs in giving scholarships in New York City colleges to South Americans. He had also served as a director of International House in New York after 1940. After the war he became chairman of the executive committee and undertook an important expansion of the program that enabled many students who attended universities in the United States to continue their association with International House.

David's immediate interest in a political career had faded when he returned from the war but he displayed a progressive attitude in community and organizational affairs. At one time there was a serious labor dispute in connection with International House, where the workers in the cafeteria demanded a vote on recognition of a union. International House is a philanthropic institution and the Board of Directors was composed largely of men of considerable wealth and of rather reactionary views toward labor organizations. A few of the more extreme right-wingers came to the conclusion that the demand for a union vote could be legally refused and the Board was on the point of doing so when David and John intervened and were able to force a change of policy that permitted the election.

There were a number of David's classmates at Harvard whom he assisted in getting started on careers after their graduation and he continued a close interest in the University and in Chicago University as well. He served as a member of the Visiting Committee in the Department of Economics at Harvard even before the war and, later, he became a trustee of the University of Chicago.

Immediately after the war, however, his main attention was given to his job at the Chase National Bank of which his uncle, Winthrop Aldrich, is chairman of the board. He was an assistant manager in the Foreign Department and then an assistant cashier and at the end of four years he moved up to the grade of vice-president—the last of the Rockefeller brothers to graduate to a private office. As vice-president, David supervised the bank's business in Latin America and, under his direction, several new branches were opened in Cuba, Puerto Rico and Panama. He also founded in 1950 a new Chase quarterly economic publication called *Latin-American Business Highlights*.

Despite his early penchant for politics, David rapidly became more and more absorbed in the business of banking. In 1952 he was promoted to be a senior vice-president responsible for supervision of customer relations and in charge of all branches in the New York area, with general supervision of the economic research department.

A LMOST ALL THE ACTIVITIES OF THE THIRD GENERATION
of Rockefellers are influenced, directly or indirectly, by
their family background. It is important, therefore, to pause
before examining their postwar activities in order to look briefly
at the origin of the family's philanthropic and related affairs.
The manner in which their grandfather began the tremendous
task of giving away substantial parts of the world's greatest
fortune and the way in which their father expanded the business of philanthropy had a significant role in guiding the five
brothers into new ventures intended to help make the world a
better place in which to live.

The greatest and most successful endeavor of the family in
this field is The Rockefeller Foundation. Its vast enterprises in
all parts of the world have been closely studied by the brothers
and have greatly influenced their own activities, but it is interesting to note that the Foundation is an autonomous organization
outside the family's control and that the only Rockefeller now
directly connected with it is John D., 3rd, who is a member of
the twenty-one-man Board of Trustees. On December 2, 1952,
he was elected chairman.

The Foundation grew out of the charitable activities of the
original John D. Rockefeller, who had always had on his mind
the job of saving souls. As a boy earning four dollars a week
at his first job, he still managed to squeeze out twenty-seven
cents every Sunday for the Baptist Church. He taught Sunday
School for many years and liked to remind his classes: "Seest

thou a man diligent in his business, he shall stand before kings."
As his wealth increased and his business empire grew he urged
his employees to be virtuous and moderate and not to drink or
gamble. His own piety seemed to increase with the years.

This did not, of course, mean that all was peace and good
will in his business affairs. Beginning in the late 1870's, the oil
magnate and his associates faced various angry Congressional
and state investigators looking into their monopolistic methods.
Twice they were involved in sensational criminal conspiracy
trials. They were the target repeatedly of attacks by newspapers,
government officials, preachers and social reformers. Occasionally John D. had to barricade himself in the shabby old Rockefeller building at 140 Pearl Street in downtown New York—
then the center of his powerful empire—to avoid subpoenas
and other harassments. The great Farmers' Alliance of 4,000,-
000 members whipped up opposition to the "trusts" and, by
its influence over state legislatures and members of Congress,
forced enactment of strong new restrictive laws against
monopoly.

In all of this, John D.'s smooth business organization forged
ahead, keeping its eye on the ball. The oil magnate himself was
an impressive figure then, tallish, slightly stooping, impeccably
dressed. He had a handsomely shaped head and a lean jaw, and
his birdlike eyes were set well apart under narrowed, drooping
lids. In public, on the witness stand, he gave a convincing appearance of eagerness to please and help, but he foiled his
questioners by adroit answers, by cleverly taking advantage of
every mistake or loophole while remaining within the frame-
work of complete legal and personal truth. By the late 1880's
his position was fully consolidated, his great fortune was made
and still growing rapidly. But his public relations were getting
worse. He was faced with the wrath and distrust, not to mention
the envy, of many of his fellow citizens. He had little peace.

In all of the incessant fights in the business world and against official authority, he seemed hardly to have rested for years. "How often," he once said, "I had not an unbroken night's sleep. Work by day and worry by night, week in and week out, month after month."

He had another problem, too, concerning his charities. His wealth was increasing so rapidly that the whole question of what to do with it was getting out of hand. It was at this time, in the late 1880's, that he came into contact with Frederick T. Gates, head of the American Baptist Education Society. Gates was fifteen years younger but, like John D., he had grown up in upstate New York and in a strict Baptist family, exposed to the same fire and brimstone philosophy. Gates had turned his hand to many jobs and, after working his way through the University of Rochester, became a preacher. In this role, he turned out to be a remarkable money raiser and a man with some new ideas.

In view of late Rockefeller experiences, it is interesting to note Gates' connection with George A. Pillsbury, the famous flour king of the Northwest. When Gates was preaching in Minneapolis, Pillsbury asked him to help draw up his will, which included a gift of several hundred thousand dollars to a Baptist school.

"Give them only $50,000 on condition that they raise a like amount," Gates advised. "That way they'll take care of your money properly."

Pillsbury agreed but the Baptists were dismayed. They believed it was impossible to raise the matching fund, but Gates rolled up his sleeves and raised $60,000 for the Pillsbury Academy. He was promptly made head of the new American Baptist Education Society, which had as its chief goal the establishment of a great university in New York or Chicago. The Society naturally turned to the richest Baptist in the world for help in founding the university and John D. eventually invited Gates to spend a week end with him.

Gates went but he didn't do much talking. Mostly he listened. The oil man became interested in him, especially when he learned that Gates was acquainted with the Merritt family in Minneapolis which owned the vast Mesabi Range iron ore deposits. John D. knew that if he could buy Mesabi Range and develop it under the techniques he had developed in the oil business he could become the master of American steel and iron. Furthermore, the Merritts needed money.

Not long afterward Gates was instrumental in getting a large loan for the Merritts, who pledged the key railroad into the iron field as security. It was Rockefeller money, although the Merritts didn't know it, and in time John D. had the railroad, and forced the Merritt family to sell out to him at his own price. The steel men immediately took alarm when they saw the Mesabi Range fall into Rockefeller hands, but John D. apparently did not want a knockdown fight and he later leased the deposit to Carnegie for fifty years.

Meanwhile, Gates had achieved his goal. In May of 1888, he was able to stand before the general convention of the Baptist Education Society in Boston, strike a theatrical pose and say: "I hold in my hand a letter from our great patron of education, John D. Rockefeller, that he will give six hun-n-dred thous-s-and dol-lars. . . ." The audience drowned out the rest with cheers.

In view of the general public hostility to Rockefeller at the time, the praise that now came from the Baptists and other denominations hoping for similar gifts must have been soothing to John D. Many religious publications praised him extravagantly and the pastor of the fashionable Euclid Avenue Baptist church in Cleveland said: "People charge Mr. Rockefeller with stealing the money he gave to the church but he has laid it on the altar and sanctified it."

The Rockefeller gift, at Gates' suggestion, had strings on it: the church must raise $400,000 before it got the money. Gates took charge of the campaign and made the goal with the help of other denominations and a gift of land worth $125,000 by Marshall Field. Thus the languishing Chicago College of 1856 was started on its way to become one of the nation's great universities—one that eventually received some $80,000,000 of Rockefeller money. Critics and politicians were later to criticize Rockefeller gifts in bitter fashion, charging that he sought to rule religion and education in America as he ruled oil. This attitude did a great deal at the time to spur the various states in building up their own universities which would not be answerable to wealthy donors but to the taxpayers. The result was a great educational revival in the land. Later, there were times when ignorant and prejudiced taxpayers exerted damaging pressure on state institutions of learning but, on the other hand, the University of Chicago came to enjoy a reputation as perhaps the most liberal and progressive school in America.

When he made his first contribution to the University, John D. remarked as he handed the check to Gates that "perhaps this is an indication we can work together to help the world." The former preacher was willing to try and he moved into the handsome new offices of the Rockefeller empire at 26 Broadway, New York, to preside over the Rockefeller philanthropic expenditures. Gates turned out to be a careful guardian of the Rockefeller conscience and the Rockefeller money. Once he had his feet up firmly on his desk—his usual posture—he scrutinized requests for aid through a perpetual haze of cigar smoke and let no goats in with the sheep to graze in the happy pasture of Rockefeller support.

He was not a narrow man and, as the years rolled by, his

ideas about philanthropy broadened steadily. At first he opened the purse for modest undertakings, chiefly religious—a new church or a mission, now and then a park or a public building, a hospital, school or university project. It was no easy task. Requests came in by the bushel. In one month, he had 50,000 new appeals for aid from institutions, clergymen, inventors, crusaders, crackpots and the poor, sick and hungry. All of them had to be screened and many had to be studied. But he was establishing a policy. It was more or less a traditional policy of giving to enterprises that would be lasting and of help to the community. He had to turn a deaf ear to many pathetic personal appeals. But still the Rockefeller money was piling up faster than it could be given away and, after ten years, the situation had become impossible.

That summer Gates went on a vacation in the Catskills and there he read *The Principles and Practice of Medicine* by Sir William Osler. It fired him with a great idea and he rushed back to New York's mid-summer heat and dictated a note to John D. In it, he pointed out that America lagged far behind Europe in medical research. We had nothing to compare with the Pasteur Institute in Paris or the Koch Institute in Berlin. Here was an opportunity for a vast service to all mankind: establish a great research institute to delve into new medical fields and to relieve "appalling unremedied suffering and fatality."

"Your fortune," he told John D. later, "is rolling up like an avalanche and unless you distribute it faster than it grows it will crush you and your children and your children's children."

The oil magnate listened with a wry smile. But it was an idea that interested him and that he didn't forget—nor did his son or his son's sons forget it—and Gates kept on pressing. So did John D., Jr., who was then starting his business career. He believed that men's souls could be better saved if they had healthy bodies and he supported Gates. It was surprising, however, that few prominent doctors shared their enthusiasm. Many of them looked upon large scale research as impractical if not a waste of time and a foolish dream.

Such a discouraging attitude on the part of men who were best qualified to judge and who stood to profit most by the research would normally have stopped any philanthropist. But it was significant, and it has probably strongly influenced the Rockefellers of a later generation, that John D. had a bold imagination and believed that the road to progress could be followed only by striking out in new directions. "Probably the greatest single obstacle to the progress and happiness of the American people," he said later, "lies in the willingness of so many men to invest their time and money in multiplying competitive industries instead of opening up new fields. . . . It requires a better type of mind to seek out and to support or to create the new."

Once he was convinced that Gates was on the right road, John D. went even farther than the former preacher had dared hope. He decided to attack boldly on the two broad fronts of education and medicine and to do it on a massive scale. In 1901 the Rockefeller Institute for Medical Research—of which David Rockefeller became president in 1950—was established with $8,000,000 as a starter. Later gifts to the Institute totaled $60,000,000 and its present portfolio represents a much larger amount. The next year, the General Education Board was set up to promote advanced education. And probably most important of all, Gates voluntarily relinquished his own power over Rockefeller spending. Both new enterprises were autonomous organizations and the work was put on an organized and scientific basis.

The General Education Board in the coming years assisted university building programs, provided laboratories, aided in setting up new institutions and backed many new lines of education in all fields of learning. The Medical Institute began a program of intensive scientific investigation and experimentation, in the field of medicine. Then came a chance occurrence that was to lead eventually to a world-wide program of disease eradication and the extensive development and improvement of public health practices. It began with the chance meeting of two men on a train traveling through the South.

One of the men was Dr. Charles W. Stiles, an employee of the embryo United States Health Service, which then amounted to little. He had long been interested in the fact that many poor families in the Southern states were afflicted with yellowish skin and a lazy disposition, that they dragged themselves about as if they were more dead than alive. The children could make little progress in school and all were subject to tuberculosis. Most doctors and health officials took the view that they were just lazy and worthless people, but Stiles had some different ideas about it. One day while chatting with a man he had met on a train, Stiles pointed to a shambling, listless man on a station platform.

"See that fellow?" he remarked. "Fifty cents' worth of drugs would make that man a useful citizen in a few weeks."

His companion asked for an explanation.

"He's got hookworm," Stiles explained. "He goes barefoot and parasites worm into the soles of his feet and keep on multiplying in the intestines. There are thousands and thousands like him and all they need is a few cents' worth of drugs. A few million dollars would restore the South to health, but who is going to provide it?"

By chance, the man Stiles was talking to knew the answer. He was Walter Hines Page, future Ambassador to Great Britain but then a member of the board of the Medical Institute. When they got to New York, he took Stiles directly from Pennsylvania Station to the Rockefeller offices. Gates promptly saw what might be done and called in the experts, including Simon Flexner, head of the Medical Institute. Hookworm, the "germ of laziness," Stiles told them, had chained eleven Southern states to sloth and despair, sickness and poverty for decades, with cumulative deterioration of the population in entire regions. The cause was known, however, and a simple, inexpensive cure was available. If there could be a general clean up of pigsties, privies and back yards in combination with medical efforts permanent results were easily possible. It would take money, intelligent planning and concerted effort but the evil could be abolished entirely.

Mr. Rockefeller was immediately interested. Experts were sent out to gather all possible data and they confirmed everything Stiles had said. By 1909 the plans were ready and the Rockefeller Sanitary Commission, under Wickliffe Rose, a Southern educator, was set up in Washington to handle the campaign. It took a great deal of diplomacy and occasionally it took some straight talking and a lot of persistence but in time the co-operation of local authorities was fully enlisted and the campaign became one of the most dramatic achievements in the history of medicine and public health. Today hookworm is almost unknown in the South.

But the campaign could not be halted within the boundaries of the United States. Experts estimated that a third of the human race was infected. The same methods were extended to the American tropics and within a few years some 7,000,000 persons had been restored to health.

Results of the hookworm campaign made apparent the lamentable state of medical education in the United States, and in 1910 this was emphasized by a report of the Carnegie Corporation stating that there were very few good schools among the 155 medical institutions in the United States and Canada. Most of them were described as paper-diploma mills that should be closed and dozens of them, thus exposed, did close. Gates read the report and promptly got hold of Abraham Flexner, younger brother of the head of the Rockefeller Medical Institute, who had conducted the investigation.

"What would you do," he asked Flexner, "if you had a million dollars to use in reorganizing medical education?"

"I'd give it all to Dr. William H. Welch of Johns Hopkins," Flexner replied. "Look what he's done with an endowment of only $400,000. He's created the finest school in America. Think what he'd do with a million more."

Flexner said that he believed about thirty strong nonprofit medical colleges should be built up, each with a well-equipped hospital and each located so that it could serve various parts of the country in an adequate manner. Dr. Wallace Buttrick, head of the General Education Board, was brought into the discussion and agreed with Flexner's ideas. So did Mr. Rockefeller, Jr., and an inquiry revealed that Welch was in full agreement. The discussions continued for some time as the possibilities were explored with a view to meeting the needs of students, the medical profession and the public.

Up to this time, the Rockefeller endeavors had followed three main lines—education, medicine and health and public sanitation, represented by the General Education Board, the Medical Institute and the Sanitary Commission. In many ways, the work of the three groups overlapped but, despite some remarkable accomplishments, the over-all effort was not well coordinated. The work needed to be put into a broad pattern. It was necessary to eliminate competition and wasteful duplication. Why not a super organization to make a concerted drive on the major evils of poverty, ignorance and disease everywhere?

On May 14, 1913, The Rockefeller Foundation was established with an initial endowment of $100,000,000.

✶ XII ✶

JOHN D. ROCKEFELLER, 3RD, WAS ONLY SEVEN YEARS OLD and David was not yet born when The Rockefeller Foundation was established by their grandfather "with the sole motive of devoting a portion of my fortune to the service of my fellow men."

Not everybody took the elder Rockefeller's words at their face value and a federal investigation of such Foundations was undertaken by the United States Commission on Industrial Relations, which reported that "the funds for these foundations are largely invested in securities of corporations dominant in American industry and are derived from payment of low wages" or by "exploitation of the public through the exaction of high prices." The Commission contended that the big corporations would inevitably influence or control the educational policy of the Foundation and that this would constitute "a most serious menace."

Just what would have happened to the plans of Gates and Flexner for improved medical schools is uncertain because the program was halted by World War I. But the large number of draft rejections, the sickness among troops and civilians and the great influenza epidemic brought home to everybody the dire need for better basic medical training and proper facilities. After the war, the elder Rockefeller, through Gates, put into Flexner's hands about $50,000,000—and later another $25,000,-000—to start the program, with no strings attached.

Flexner promptly gave Johns Hopkins almost half a million dollars but his efforts to build up a fine medical school in New York City were frustrated. Both Columbia and Cornell universities had reasonably good medical schools for those days and were associated with New York hospitals but they fell short of the Flexner requirements and declined to undergo thorough reorganization along lines prescribed by the General Education Board to make them eligible for Rockefeller support.

Flexner decided on a flank attack. The University of Rochester, which had a wealthy benefactor in George Eastman, the camera manufacturer, was without a medical school. He believed that, if he could start from scratch, a new institution could be built there to provide the best in everything for medical education. Gates suggested that he get Eastman interested and proposed that the camera magnate, who had already provided Rochester with a dental school, should put up half of the money for the new medical school. The Rockefellers would put up the other half, but it would really be Eastman's project.

When Flexner outlined his plans to Eastman and told him it would cost $10,000,000, the industrialist was interested but the most he would offer was $2,500,000. Flexner returned to New York. Eastman sent word that he would make it $3,500,-000. "That," Flexner replied, "would make it a Rockefeller school, not yours. It must be yours." A few weeks later Eastman summoned Flexner, shook his finger under the visitor's nose and shouted: "I'll put up five million—then I don't want ever to see your face again!"

Welch was summoned to lay out plans for the new school and hospital and the results built a fire under educational institutions all over the country, particularly in New York. Cornell and Columbia, seeing they would be left behind, got busy on improvements and wealthy New Yorkers—Morgan,

Harkness, Payne Whitney—opened their purses. Out of this came such great schools as the Columbia and Cornell medical centers in Manhattan.

Nor was the forward march confined to the East. Iowa educators were disturbed by Flexner's original criticism of medical training at their state university and the state was further upset by the high percentage of farm boys rejected in the draft. The Legislature increased appropriations for the medical school and a member of the Board of Regents went to New York to ask Flexner for funds for a modern pathological laboratory. Flexner turned him down. Nothing, he said, would be done piecemeal. If Iowa wanted such a laboratory it would have to spend $5,000,000 to modernize the University equipment, improve teaching methods and provide a better staff.

The cautious farmers in the Legislature were not used to that kind of big money talk and they balked, but when Flexner offered to match local funds with Rockefeller money they couldn't resist it. Once in the mood they went on to vote $1,000,000 a year for operations and a great medical center arose in Iowa City. This development spread the fire to many other states. Many of them got the benefit of Rockefeller funds. Modern schools and medical centers rose at Vanderbilt in Nashville and Washington University at St. Louis. Eighty outmoded medical schools closed, but those that survived had to get in line by modernizing their equipment and methods. Thus the $75,000,-000 that the Rockefellers distributed stimulated a great wave of improvements for which private benefactors, state legislators and city governments spent probably a half billion dollars. In a few years, the country was started on the road to leadership in health, sanitation and medicine.

Again, the momentum was too great to limit this progress to the United States. The Foundation gave funds to institutions in Canada on a big scale and it kept on spreading its assistance until it had provided important aid in twenty-two countries. Nor was there any end to the fields of scientific research in which it has pioneered or given assistance: studies of amino acids, vitamins, nutrition, metabolism, enzymes, sex habits and pathology, venereal diseases, influenza, tuberculosis, typhus, rabies, yaws, senescence, hormones, radium treatments and blood composition. Besides its famous yellow fever serum, the Foundation and the Medical Institute have been interested in better smallpox vaccine, a special brain syphilis test, improved Wassermann test, and new serums for diphtheria, typhoid, pneumonia, Rocky Mountain spotted fever and trachoma. The new wonder drugs, especially penicillin, owe something to the Foundation. In connection with modern high altitude aviation, its scientists have undertaken studies of the effect of altitude on human and animal organisms by establishing laboratories some 15,000 feet above sea level in the high peaks of the Andes.

The story of the Foundation's fight against yellow fever, which cost the lives of six of its outstanding scientists, has often been told but the sequel to that struggle—the discovery of eleven hitherto unidentified diseases caused by viruses—is less well known. The yellow fever campaign had been extended from America early this century to countries in distant parts of the world. A vaccine developed by the Foundation has protected many millions of persons, and the "galloping death" has been brought to bay everywhere except in the remote African and American jungles.

This great achievement, however, led to perhaps an even more exciting discovery of viruses that caused diseases, opening up an entirely new avenue of medical investigation. The Bwamba and West Nile viruses were found in fevered natives. The Ilheus virus, which thwarts embryo brain development, was discovered in Brazil. Other viruses were found, more or less accidentally, in lizards, monkeys, mosquitoes and a dead mongoose. The Foundation started an intensive study of virology, which as a science was about where bacteriology was in 1900, in the hope of quickly bringing knowledge in the field up to a high level. The virus infections are responsible for a wide range of illnesses, ranging from the common cold to infantile paralysis, and the development of vaccines is a difficult and costly task.

Another Foundation campaign, on almost a world-wide scale, has been directed against malaria, which still brings sickness to some 300,000,000 persons and takes 3,000,000 lives annually. At one time it was estimated that it would require perhaps fifty billion dollars to eliminate malaria everywhere, but new drugs and insecticides that have been developed in recent years indicate that the figure may have been too high. The Foundation already has acquired wide experience in the field and won some notable victories.

Many kinds of Anopheles mosquitoes carry the disease, but the most pernicious is the Anopheles gambia of Africa, which spreads an exceedingly virulent and deadly type of malaria. In 1930 this mosquito crossed from Africa to the New World probably by boat and, before control measures were introduced, spread over some 12,000 square miles of Brazil, bringing illness or death to many thousands. In the Jaguaribe Valley in Ceará alone almost every human was stricken, the fields lay uncultivated and starvation threatened the region. Such a large area was affected that it seemed hopeless to attempt the only solution—the eradication of every mosquito. The Foundation and the Brazilian government, nevertheless, mapped out a campaign and, under direction of Dr. Fred L. Soper, an army of men armed with insecticides and sprayers was organized to launch the attack. They were entirely successful, wiping out the gambiae down "to the last mosquito."

The knowledge that this could be done on such a large scale

and in such difficult territory was highly encouraging and it paved the way for similar operations in Egypt in 1945 when the gambiae moved into the Nile country, causing the worst epidemic in Egyptian history in which many thousands of persons died.

But perhaps the most remarkable phase in the Foundation's fight against malaria developed in Sardinia, once the seat of empire and great wealth but in modern times so ridden by malaria that almost none of its 800,000 inhabitants was free of illness. In Brazil and Egypt, the gambiae had been an invader, a newcomer, not yet adapted to its environment. But in Sardinia the tough, indigenous Anopheles labranchiae were entrenched centuries ago in every rock, cranny and pool and at every altitude. A campaign to free the island of the malady was started after World War II, a joint undertaking by the Italian health authorities, the UNRRA and the ECA, with the Foundation providing technical experts and part of the funds necessary. Foundation doctors, with less than a dozen trained men available, built up a fighting army of 33,000 Sards, armed with picks, shovels, dynamite, hand sprayers, power sprayers, airplanes, fog machines, powerboats, oil and insecticides. Practically every inch of the island was covered and, in 1949, not a single case of malaria was reported.

House flies also perished in the drive. Intestinal diseases decreased. So did infant mortality. The general health level started an upward climb and the draining of great swamps, as well as the clearing of brush and woods that had harbored mosquitoes, made it possible for the farmers to cultivate large areas that had been unproductive in the past. Until 1949 Sardinia had been an economic liability. Today it is becoming an asset. Its fields and industries are flourishing again; its workers are healthier and more efficient. The island so profited by the anti-malaria campaign that it soon was calling for immigrants from the crowded Italian mainland.

The Foundation's war against disease has not been confined to human ailments. It has vigorously fought the viruses, bacteria and pests that afflict plants and livestock in many parts of the world, as part of an over-all effort to increase food supplies. Perhaps the most extensive and successful work in this regard was done in Mexico at the request of the Mexican government. Mexico's population is increasing—it will be around 50,000,-000 in another two decades—but in recent years its corn yield had been dropping. The average was as low as ten bushels to an acre and the amount of land available was limited. In an effort to correct this decrease in yield, the Foundation in co-operation with the Mexican government established a 300-acre experimental station at the National Agricultural School at Chapingo and set up smaller stations in nine other states to test the needs of different regions. The soil was studied scientifically and fertilizers were tried out. More than a thousand varieties of Mexican corn were tested for nutritional value, yield and disease resistance and then the best strains were crossbred to produce fine new strains called Rocamex corn.

But merely producing the new strains was not enough. The natives were unaccustomed to modern farming and were suspicious of change. A campaign of education, including celebrations, ceremonies and speech-making, was necessary to inform them of what had been done. The new seed was distributed at fiestas and dances in order to spur interest in improvement, and prizes were offered for the best harvest. The winner of the first prize—a tractor—demonstrated how successful the experiments were by growing 125 bushels per acre. By 1949, for the first time in thirty-five years, Mexico did not have to import any corn. In five years of intensive effort, a country with serious agricultural handicaps got itself off the list of lands unable to grow enough basic food to support the population. The work was later extended to wheat, beans and other nutritious crops, and the government subsidized new training schools to increase the number of experts available for such work.

In addition to education, health and food, a major interest of the Foundation is in the field of the social sciences and humanities, work that ranges from studies of economics and government to the writing of plays in Ohio and in Dublin. New libraries have been built in the Orient, Latin America, London and war-devastated areas. The Pekin man, a fragment of skeleton dating back 500,000 years, was discovered by a Foundation expert, as were traces of the fabled human giants of antiquity in Indonesia. The Foundation financed work in developing the date of prehistoric remains by carbon radiation.

In the humanities, the Foundation has kept pace with trends in the modern world, with special grants for studies of international relations and for cultural studies in China, Japan, Turkey and the Arabic countries. Special emphasis has been placed on the Russian Institute at Columbia University, which has been given about half a million dollars, to train specialists and promote knowledge about Russia and the Russian people. Many of the State Department's experts and advisers on Russia have come from the Institute.

One of the great difficulties in carrying on Foundation work in recent years has been the problem of penetrating the Iron Curtain that was erected around Soviet Russia and its satellites after World War II. Many Foundation enterprises in these areas were brought to a halt and a large number of students financed by the Foundation were cut off, prevented from continuing their research and sometimes singled out for special persecution by Communist governments. Occasionally letters are received in roundabout fashion from some of these students. One from Hungary said: "Seven years have passed away since I came home from America. Seven terrible years full of unspeakable sufferings . . ." He asked whether all of the Foundation's work would be in vain and added: "I could remark that between all Hungarian Rockefeller fellows there was an unspoken but obvious spiritual connection that remained solid among the ruins and on which the future of mankind can be reorganized. So the work was not and will not be in vain."

In all the Foundation has directly or indirectly granted more than 10,000 fellowships at a total cost of more than $25,000,-000, investments in intellectual capacity, imagination and character. There are no strings attached to the work of these students and researchers. They are not even required to make reports of what they are doing, although many of them do so. In recent years, many fellowships have gone to scientists and educators whose work had been interrupted by the war and subsequent turmoil. Some of them came from crowded, lice-filled concentration camps to join faculties and research laboratories in America, their vast knowledge and talents preserved for the future of mankind.

Implicit in the over-all efforts of the Foundation is a new concept of the social sciences, an effort to make them a positive tool for solving human problems rather than mere fields of research for facts and phenomena and the fabrication of theories. This goes far beyond the original ideas of the elder Rockefeller whose purpose was to save souls. He believed that therein lay the force to eradicate most of the world's evils. He wanted to strengthen individual character, in the belief that any man living virtuously and modestly and working with energy, integrity and knowledge could maintain himself and his family in comfortable circumstances. If one widened the number of persons thus endowed, poverty would disappear from the world. This concept was gradually expanded to include the goal of a sound mind in a sound body and to recognize that, through public sanitation, environment had to be changed to assist rather than hinder man.

Out of the Foundation's work in the humanities and social sciences eventually came a still broader idea. This was to take man's social and economic problems out of the realm of prejudices, emotions, political interests and racial antagonisms and put them into the hands of trained experts utilizing scientific methods of investigation and applying scientific conclusions. The time had passed, the Foundation declared, when natural science, medical science, social science and humanism could exist "in separate and self-contained spheres." They had to be organized for a large-scale attack on all problems of human relations, government, politics, crime, juvenile delinquency, sex relations, family life, and so on.

Studying a more positive approach to child and adult welfare, the Foundation in 1929 put $4,500,000 behind a new Yale Institute of Human Relations intended to bring representatives of all the social sciences together in a combined attack on human and social problems, eradicating the old artificial divisions between anthropology, psychology, psychiatry, economics, sociology and political science. A new building of 166 rooms, including 130 laboratories, was erected at Yale and scholars in all phases of instruction pertaining to man—from medical specialists to theologians—were centered there. The experiment didn't work out quite as well as had been hoped and the Foundation gradually withdrew its support. There was too much of melding the old and the new; of trying to fit the old patterns into the new scheme and purpose. But the Yale Institute accomplished much in the form of contributions to psychiatry, psychology and anthropology, and, more important, it had a healthy influence elsewhere. Some years later, fifteen well-rounded centers of social-science research had been started in various countries, some of them aided by Rockefeller money.

Of these one of the most notable is the Harvard University Laboratory for Social Relations, which has received grants from the Foundation.

Throughout the years, the Foundation has kept firmly in mind that the causes of war are rooted in human misery, disease and poverty; and that only by eradicating these evils can the basic conditions that will make war unnecessary be established. It is beside the point that, in seeking this objective, the Foundation contributed heavily to the development of nuclear fission and, unhappily, the atomic bomb. Twenty-three scientific leaders in atom research—such men as Oppenheimer, Fermi, Allison, Smyth and Compton—were trained with the aid of Foundation fellowships. Direct support in atomic research was given to Niels Bohr in Copenhagen, Harold Urey at Columbia University and others, and liberal support went to the physics and chemistry departments at such key institutions as Princeton and Chicago universities. The Foundation also financed the 184-inch cyclotron at the University of California and other cyclotrons that were vital to the development of atomic power. It was, said Raymond B. Fosdick, then president of the Foundation, "an adventure in pure discovery motivated by the unconquerable exploring spirit in the mind of man . . . a token of man's hunger for knowledge."

It was also the fire that dropped on Hiroshima just before the end of World War II. The making of an atom bomb was unforeseen when the original research began and the officials of the Foundation have since been gravely concerned over this unexpected outcome of experiments that might have been—and presumably will be in time—of incalculable value to mankind. But at the same time they know and emphasize that no solution can be found by curbing science in its search for knowledge; that the only real solution to war is to uproot the causes of conflict by creating conditions "which will foster peace, education, tolerance, understanding and creative intelligence."

Today the Foundation is under the control of a twenty-one man Board of Trustees, who direct the expenditure of a dozen or more million dollars each year. At the end of 1949, for example, the Foundation had assets of $153,471,555 and an income during 1949 of $10,984,524. Since it is possible under the terms of the Charter of the Foundation to draw on capital, $12,903,380 was spent to carry on the Foundation's work in 1949.

Statesmen, scientists, doctors, editors, philanthropists and businessmen make up the Board. They include such people as Karl T. Compton, Dr. Thomas Parran, John Foster Dulles, Arthur Hays Sulzberger and Henry Allen Moe. Only John D., 3rd, could be said directly to represent Rockefeller interests, and, in fact, there is a familiar quip that "if you want to be sure that the Foundation rejects an idea all you have to do is to get somebody in the Rockefeller family to propose it." The Board of Trustees acts in establishing the broad policies of the Foundation but the actual operations are in charge of trained experts under direction of the president, a post that was taken over in 1952 by Dean Rusk, formerly of the Department of State.

Thus the Foundation represents a tremendous change from the days when the Reverend Gates pored over bushel baskets full of letters and parceled out the Rockefeller money. Nor has the effect of the change been lost on the third generation of Rockefellers. All the brothers have been profoundly influenced by the Foundation's broad, international character as well as by the methods that its experts have developed in an effort to make dollars achieve the greatest possible permanent good for mankind.

❉ XIII ❉

SOON AFTER THE END OF WORLD WAR II ALL OF THE ROCKE-feller brothers were back in New York, picking up the threads of their varied careers and working out a system under which they could work together without unnecessary conflict. The war had been an interruption. It had changed some of them considerably; others not so much. But it had brought about a definite change in their collective status. By the time it had ended they were all adults with at least the beginnings of careers behind them; yet they were still of an age at which they could plunge enthusiastically into new enterprises that would demonstrate what the third generation of Rockefellers was going to stand for.

The problem of what they were going to stand for as well as more immediate business concerns was frequently discussed at meetings of the brothers on the upper floors of Rockefeller Center, where the vista of a great metropolis stretches out on every side, laced by glistening rivers, bordered by the ocean and with the horizon limited only by the majestic curve of the earth's surface. The topics of conversation at such gatherings often cover an even wider horizon. Sometimes they discuss the effect of drought on the corn crop in Brazil; sometimes it is the best building material for workers' homes in the Belgian Congo; again it may be the latest development in the field of electronics and not infrequently it is rocket motors that may one day fly to the moon. These things and many more have been—and still are—of vital everyday concern to the Rockefellers.

The brothers meet, sometimes as often as once a week, not only in their sleekly modern skyscraper but at the home of one brother or another, whenever one of them has a problem or an idea or a proposal that impinges on the interests of all. They may talk about business or investments or philanthropy or civic affairs or modern art. Very rarely there is a sixth man present and when he is they listen carefully to what he has to say and they argue with him only when they're sure of their ground, for the alchemy of the years has increased rather than diminished their respect for their father.

While sessions to co-ordinate activities and thresh out differences of opinion are an old custom in the family it was largely after the five brothers returned to New York after the war that they were able to focus their joint and individual endeavors in a workable pattern. Rockefeller Center as an office and Tarrytown as home have contributed to the ties that bind them together.

Even so, it was not a simple matter to establish a broad pattern of operations. Each of the five is a distinct individualist with his own interests and ideas and, on occasion, the family sessions have displayed a lack of harmony comparable only to a chance meeting of the Hatfields and McCoys.

One basic disagreement that even a casual visitor to their headquarters sees immediately is in the appearance of their offices. Outside the elevator doors is a short hall marked only by a small directory of offices on that floor, in this case a simple designation: "Rockefeller—Office of the Messrs." At the end of the hall, a clerk presides at a desk equipped with a complicated array of push buttons and switches and inter-office communication boxes and a device for automatically unlocking certain doors.

The visitor who is escorted to the right toward the southwest corner of the floor enters a series of richly furnished offices in the traditional manner—softly gleaming wood, comfortable leather chairs, handsomely carved desks and paneled walls on which are hung etchings and colored ship paintings and a few portraits. There are fireplaces with bright brass pokers and tongs. The carpeting is deep and subdued and the rooms are pleasantly large. Visitors and clerks and secretaries go sedately and firmly about their business in an atmosphere reminiscent of the good old days. These are the offices of Mr. Rockefeller, Jr., and his closest associates. In the northwest corner the office of John D., 3rd, is furnished in authentic Colonial style.

But the visitor who turns to the left from the lobby enters almost another world, the world of the briskly modern interior decorator. A long hall angles sharply into a maze of offices surrounding an irregular lobby, leading the visitor past smooth blank walls decorated with vivid modern paintings. There are glimpses of glass brick walls and big, low circular tables and comfortable sectional furniture and of blank doors like blank faces fitted snugly into walls. Many of the paintings are South American, a reflection of Nelson's enthusiasm, and all the furniture is severely functional, in small offices designed to make the best use of every inch of space. Here, in a breezily modern atmosphere, are the offices of Nelson and Laurance. David's office, on the north side of the building, is middle-of-the-road, decoratively speaking.

But if the offices are miles and years apart in atmosphere, the Rockefellers manage to keep fairly close together in ideas and actions. They argue to let off steam; they talk and plan and work to carry on the "stewardship" of the fortune.

This sense of endeavor and responsibility they express as individuals, as a family and as a corporation. In one way, they form a sort of self-contained molecular cosmos, but one which enters into chemical composition with almost every new and exciting undertaking of the modern world. Into their cosmos come ideas and projects of every shape and size; affecting everything from local affairs to the state of the nation and reaching on out across the seas. Out of this stream they select the ideas and projects that interest them particularly and in which they think perhaps they can play a part.

No operation is undertaken haphazardly. Expert advice on almost anything that might be of interest is close at hand, and they have no hesitancy in going far afield for technical assistance when necessary. One close associate in many affairs is Wallace K. Harrison, architect of some of the country's best-known modern skyscrapers and director of planning of the United Nations ensemble in New York. Another is Norwegian-born Berent Friele, an expert on coffee, among other things, and an authority on Brazil. Still another is Philip Keebler, the family's principal tax advisor. Dana Creel is a philanthropic advisor; Frank Jamieson is public relations advisor and John E. Lockwood is legal advisor. If they need financial advice they are likely to call on Lewis Strauss or Richard Mansfield, while Belgian-born Joseph Jennen is suave, charming and expert with advice on investment and development problems. Lawrence Levy is secretary for a number of the Rockefellers' joint enterprises, and Robert W. Gumbel is an authority, past and present, on the activities in general of the Rockefeller family. And there is sedate Thomas M. Debevoise, close confidant and right-hand man of Mr. Rockefeller, Jr., and a man to whom the brothers still say "sir" with both respect and admiration.

This group is a nucleus that, to a great extent, holds together many of the brothers' activities and permits a kind of continuity and co-operation without putting a severe brake on their individualistic operations. "Each of us puts something in," one of the Rockefellers explained. "At the same time, we multiply our individual effort by five. That way you can paddle your own canoe while working together. The basic idea is to stick together as a unit, despite our disagreements."

Thus, by a kind of trial and error method, they have shaped their general objectives along similar lines and evolved a solid working basis. In the broadest sense, what they want to do is to use their talents, energies and wealth in a manner that will contribute most effectively to the progress of society and to vitalization of the democratic capitalist system in this era of totalitarian-made crises.

The world-wide dislocation brought on by World War II and the period of vast upheaval that began immediately after the war taxed the strength of the democratic capitalistic system as never before and confronted the United States with both a challenge and an opportunity. The challenge of a new and dynamic system backed by the vastly increased power of Soviet Russia was soon easy enough for everybody to see. But the opportunity for the United States to assume world leadership, to work in a new and generous spirit, to use its technological skill to help restore stability in a more just and a more enduring world—these possibilities were less easily seen and there were many Americans who did not want to see them.

"Someone said shortly after the war ended," John pointed out in 1948, "that it was terrifying the way the world was looking to the United States for leadership. . . . This country faces a very challenging opportunity in the years which lie ahead. World leadership is ours if we will assume it." But, he added, to meet that challenge the country must be "strong—mentally, morally and physically."

This broad idea, this "chance to be of service" was very much in the Rockefellers' minds after the war. "The third generation of Rockefellers," an associate remarked, "is still exporting the missionary idea, just as their grandfather did through his large contributions to foreign missions of the church." It is true that there is a strong missionary motivation behind some of their operations, but their methods can hardly be compared to the technique of saving souls in earlier days. Times have changed and so have the Rockefeller objectives. "Grandfather's idea was to save souls," one of the brothers commented. "Father said you have to do something to keep people healthy as well as to save their souls. Perhaps my generation agrees with both ideas but adds that people also must have security."

Those words, almost painfully simple, go far toward summing up an idea that dominated much of the Rockefeller thinking in their approach to postwar problems. Security was obviously not easy to achieve for countless millions in a world seething with expanding populations that had long since overstrained its facilities to provide even such an elementary necessity as food. But science and modern technology could provide new powers of production and, teamed with greater social justice, might enable the world to alleviate much of the existing misery and to avoid at least in part the threat of a great, chaotic upheaval that could only affect every land on earth.

In line with these broad ideas, the Rockefellers believed that there was an important role for private capital to play, particularly in connection with the government's efforts in behalf of the democratic capitalistic system. They felt, for instance, that private capital could do a great deal to help America extend technological knowledge and sociological methods to underdeveloped parts of the world. In this way, health conditions and living standards could be improved as a bulwark against totalitarianism. On the other hand, if private capital should abdicate and leave such undertakings wholly up to the government it would be an admission of impotence, an acknowledgment that the spirit of initiative and enterprise no longer existed. Furthermore, such an abdication might eventually leave the United States as merely an island of free enterprise in a world of statism and force; a world in which our own freedoms would soon wither or die.

Thus, in a practical rather than merely a philosophical sense, the Rockefellers decided that they should try to prove by example that private business, co-operating with government as may be necessary, could make a fair profit and still achieve major social objectives, particularly in helping low-income groups in the United States and abroad. This was a goal they regarded not as idealistic but as logical and essential if our way of life was to be maintained and if the United States was to meet its world responsibilities in the latter half of the twentieth century.

These are broad, stereotyped phrases that could be as meaningless as a political oration. The test was: What, if anything, were the Rockefellers going to do about it?

"You have big thoughts and big ideas," Nelson once remarked with a characteristic inclination to look at the facts, "but when it comes to doing you usually feel that you are dealing only with little things." He paused and shrugged. "Well, little things can take you a little way forward if you're headed in the right direction."

The brothers' search for the right direction began officially in 1946 when they first gave their united efforts a formal existence, an event which the raucous New York *Daily News* greeted with the headline: "The Rock Mob Incorporates!" The accompanying article announced the formation of Rockefeller Brothers, Inc., a limited partnership company which was later reshaped as a service agency to provide research and management, with Laurance as president. Although it sounds as if it were a big and wealthy corporation, the truth is that Rockefeller Brothers, Inc., is mainly a holding company for the ideas and ambitions, instead of money, of the five brothers and their sister, Mrs. Abby Rockefeller Pardee. It has offices and a staff, but the staff is only seventeen persons—fewer employees than are needed in a good-sized grocery store. It has capital and can command more but it is only nominal capital. Thus it merely symbolizes and implements an over-all united front within which each brother operates independently, with assistance from the others in whatever degree each desires to participate.

Basically, the organization is an outlet for the Rockefellers' "risk" or venture capital and it represents an effort "to achieve social and economic progress as well as a fair profit on investment." Actually, the six children, acting as individuals, put, less than four million dollars into ventures directly sponsored by Rockefeller Brothers, Inc., in the first five years of its existence, whereas their over-all investments of venture capital in that period totaled almost fifteen million dollars.

Investments through Rockefeller Brothers, Inc., may be described as using venture capital to build up businesses—preferably in a new field—that are a gamble but which pay off handsomely if successful and which contribute importantly to technological progress. The key idea here is an important one—the encouragement of technological progress. Such investments normally are of a temporary nature—perhaps five to ten years—and when the new enterprise is on its feet (or has definitely failed) the Rockefellers withdraw their original capital and profits (or take a loss) for reinvestment in another venture.

A way to combine money and managerial ability with good engineering skill is sought in order to promote an enterprise that, while new and struggling, has a bright and expanding future. The emphasis on technological advance, the development of something new overshadows the old business attitude that the important point is to dominate or gain control. The old way was the way the great oil, steel and railroad and other empires were built up and consolidated. Most modern venture capital operations are primarily concerned with helping industry to develop in new directions, to get something different going, put it on a sound and profitable footing and then gradually pull out to undertake another similar enterprise. This calls for more than just money. It requires energy, time and, what is often more important, enthusiasm.

Laurance's shrewd business judgment and his flair for gadgets—meaning anything from a motorcycle to a rocket plane—have played a role in such enterprises. He believes that flexibility rather than rigidity is essential to new concerns in new fields. Perhaps the most satisfactory arrangement, he feels, is a three-way control divided among the management directly in charge of operation, a block of stockholders interested in profits and a third party, such as himself, who is interested both in profits and the success of a "new idea" business. Such an arrangement tends to prevent any one of the three from going off at a tangent or trying unwisely to speed up or hold back; yet it does not stifle initiative or inventiveness, or close teamwork.

Laurance's chief passion, as has been said, is aviation, a field in which he has done considerable business pioneering. One of his early air-minded investments, in addition to Eastern Air Lines, was in the Platt le Page company, a pioneer in the building of helicopters. But it was his connection with the J. S. McDonnell Aircraft Corporation that perhaps best illustrated the successful application of Laurance's ideas about use of venture capital. As noted earlier, McDonnell was a man far above the ordinary in the world of aviation engineering, yet he had not achieved financial success. He had been educated at Princeton, the Massachusetts Institute of Technology and at an Army Air Corps flying school. Starting in 1924, he worked for several airplane companies and, in 1928, branched out on his own by forming the engineering firm of J. S. McDonnell and Associates. The firm turned out a low-cost monoplane that

McDonnell had designed, called the "Doodlebug." The design was good but there were various "bugs" to be worked out and in the course of these experiments bad luck in the form of accidents plagued McDonnell. There were also problems of management and financing and, when the depression of 1929 came along, the whole enterprise went under.

McDonnell went to work for the Glenn L. Martin Company for the next six years but he kept plugging away at his own ideas and designs and in 1937 his brother, a St. Louis banker, helped him to get money for a small shop where he perfected his blueprints for a new Army pursuit plane. At this point McDonnell had well demonstrated his ability as an engineer and his ideas as a designer. Technologically speaking, here were the seeds of future progress in a field that was comparatively new and sure to expand vastly in the future. Yet the line of future progress was not yet stabilized; nobody could be sure that McDonnell was on precisely the right track. He was a risk, and he needed capital and the means to establish managerial efficiency. That was when he spread his blueprints out on Laurance's desk and, in return, received $10,000 to build a fighter plane that the Army hadn't yet contracted for.

The contract came through in 1941, a $14,000,000 deal to build the XP67. McDonnell built it and it was a good plane, but his luck was still bad. The plane burned in flight, not because of any construction defects so far as could be determined but just because of an unhappy chance. The contract was canceled. Laurance had, of course, put more money into the firm in the meantime and, with the threat of war coming always closer to America, the company turned to subcontracting in the aviation industry as a part of the rearmament program. It soon had more business than it could handle, doing about $60,000,-000 worth of subcontracting and experimental development in the course of the war period. McDonnell also built another experimental plane in 1944, this time a five-ton twin-engine helicopter for the Navy.

When Laurance went into the Navy he had to make a temporary end to his active connection with the McDonnell operations because he was busy on aircraft production problems for the service. His wartime work, however, kept him closely in touch with aviation affairs and, late in the war, he was greatly excited by the work being done on jets by the British. After he was discharged, he was delighted that McDonnell also was enthusiastic about the new craft and that the McDonnell company, which was not tied up by production contracts as was almost every other well-established airplane company in the country, was able to get to work on them in a hurry.

The Rockefellers after the war put an additional $400,000 into the McDonnell company, assuming control of 20 per cent of the outstanding common stock, and Laurance resumed his active role as a director. They soon had one of the first American jet planes, the Phantom, streaking through the skies and, in 1946, it made the first successful landing by an all-jet plane on the deck of an airplane carrier. Sixty Phantoms were built, the first time the company had turned out a multiple product, and then all the backlog of careful preparation began to pay off. By 1948 the company's sales were $21,000,000 and its gross profits $2,700,000.

Early in 1949, the company got an order for a secret "very advanced . . . new type fighter" and the Navy ordered a more advanced model jet, the high-flying Banshee fighter. By that time the concern had piled up a $90,000,000 backlog of orders and was installed in a huge war-built plant near the St. Louis airport, for which it paid the city $480,000 a year and in which it employed 6,000 workers. In the next year or so, Laurance began reducing his holdings in the McDonnell corporation. It was a firmly established concern that had contributed importantly to the development of jets as well as other aircraft in the United States and plenty of capital was available. The cycle that began with Laurance's $10,000 a decade earlier had been completed and the Rockefellers felt that their venture capital could now be used elsewhere to help promote some other similar technological advance. This time they had made some money on their investment and their labors—mostly Laurance's labors in this case, as far as the family was concerned—but without discounting the importance of returning a profit they regarded the technical contribution to the aviation industry as far more important. The United States had been far behind various other nations in jet plane development when the war ended, but in a few years it had moved forward at a tremendous pace. Had that not happened the consequences might have been far-reaching. The American-manned air force, for instance, might have been driven out of the air early in the United Nations effort to halt Communist aggression in Korea.

Laurance's great interest is in civil aviation rather than production for the military, but it is recognized that in the vast transitional stage that now confronts airplane experimentation only the government can afford the huge costs of rapid progress. Thus the pioneering in military plane design must produce the advances that will later be of benefit to civil aviation. In this connection, Laurance has had a deep faith in the future of helicopters and the McDonnell company has made twin-engine types as well as a small ram-jet helicopter for liaison and artillery spotting, known affectionately as "Little Henry." The early Platt le Page company, in which Laurance was interested, had not turned out well and an attempt had been made to merge it with McDonnell. This failed, costing McDonnell some $350,-000, but he came out with blueprints of new helicopter designs that proved invaluable.

Another of Laurance's ventures was in the Piasecki Helicopter

Company of Philadelphia, which also represented a salvage from the Platt le Page outfit. While working with that concern, Piasecki hit upon a revolutionary principle. One day he observed that a le Page helicopter seemed to fly better sideways than forward. This gave him a new idea about balance, maneuverability and efficiency. He put rotors fore and aft, tilted up the fuselage and built a machine that did away with the need to balance the payload pendulum fashion as had been necessary in the past. The new Piasecki company soon secured important Navy contracts.

All of the efforts devoted to helicopter development paid off in the Korean fighting when the machine became an all-round work horse for almost all units, and prompted the Army to announce that it would place "vast expenditures behind helicopter development" with the intention of simplifying and improving the machine and adapting it to general use by the public. This was right in line with Laurance's belief that the helicopter will one day be of great importance in civilian life where it will be used for shuttle work, for taxicab trips from a hotel roof to the airport, for rapid movement of mail to suburban areas, delivery of local freight, sowing and dusting of crops for pest control and many other similar tasks. With this in mind, Laurance and David became important minority stockholders in New York Airways, Inc., which in 1952 was designated as the operator for helicopter service in New York City and in the adjacent suburban area. The company, which believes that helicopter passenger fares can soon be almost as cheap as taxicab fares, expects to start mail service in the area in 1953 and later develop passenger service on a large scale.

In future airplanes, Laurance believes that the turbo-jet will be the main power plant. The ram-jet, which is midway between the turbo and the rocket-jet, is ideal for extreme speed and altitude and for guided missiles. It has quick power and thrust and incredibly little weight in relation to power output. Under optimum operating conditions, which means a guided missile moving at three times the speed of sound and at about 50,000 feet altitude, the ram-jet is probably the most efficient power plant ever designed.

A third important line of development, in Laurance's opinion, is rocket engines, and it was this reasoning that led him into a floundering New Jersey concern called Reaction Motors, Inc. The company had developed a remarkable liquid-fuel rocket engine and the Navy was much interested in its future. "It was," Laurance noted, "as big a creative achievement as that of the Germans, whose development of wartime rockets was along parallel lines." The engineering geniuses of Reaction Motors, however, were completely absorbed in their technical work; they had little time for business affairs and they ran out of money.

Navy people were very much concerned about what was going to happen to Reaction Motors, Inc. They hoped it would not be merged with any older company. Security problems were involved. There was also the danger that a merger might put a brake on the inventiveness and initiative of the engineers. It was perhaps only natural that Laurance, who had served in the Navy, was urged to take an interest, which he happily did. Today the company has a plus value and a good financial backlog and is in production with new models. Reaction Motors turned out the Viking Rocket and a rocket engine for the Bell XS1 airplane, which broke through to supersonic speed for the first time. They also built a plant for the Douglas Skyrocket turbo-jet plane, equipped with an auxiliary motor of the liquid-fuel rocket type. In 1951, the Skyrocket flew higher and faster than any plane ever built—probably at the speed of 1,500 miles an hour.

Aviation has provided an obvious and natural field for the Rockefellers' venture capital, and especially for Laurance's activities. In the postwar years, he continued a steady expansion of his interests until he and his brothers have pretty well blanketed all major phases of aviation development. In 1950 they invested about $250,000 in the Marquardt Aircraft Company of Los Angeles, which is now developing and manufacturing ram-jet and pulse-jet engines as well as electronic devices for air navigation and controls. The company increased sales about 55 per cent in 1951 to $3,900,000 and sales for the six months ending June 30, 1952, were $2,700,000. Other interests include the Laboratory for Electronics, Inc., of Boston, which makes cyclotron equipment and radar components as well as electronic flight control and guidance systems and in which David has a special interest; the Airborne Instruments Laboratory at Mineola, Long Island, which is developing advanced radar and electronic devices including a moving target indicator that eliminates everything from the radar screen except moving targets; and the Aircraft Radio Corporation of New Jersey, which produces radar and other similar instruments. In 1952, Laurance also put almost $1,000,000 into the Glenn L. Martin airplane company, makers of some of the outstanding passenger craft in America, to help tide the company, which is vital to American defense efforts, through a financial crisis.

Outside of the aviation field, Laurance and David each acquired a 20-per-cent interest in Horizons, Inc., a development engineering concern interested in a number of research projects, including a new and much cheaper process for making titanium, a metal twice as heavy as aluminum but half as strong as steel. The metal, which is not corrosive and stands up well in salt water or heat, has cost about $6.50 a pound in the past but, if the new process is successful in final tests, it can be produced for less than a dollar a pound and will be in great demand.

Laurance likes to call such discoveries "new horizon products." He believes it is good business to put risk money into such enterprises for a limited time to determine whether they can be developed into solid and profit-making operations. If a reasonable time does not produce results—and he has been in a number that did not—he takes a loss and withdraws. "What we want to do," he emphasizes, "is the opposite of the old system of holding back capital until a field or an idea is proved completely safe. We are undertaking pioneering projects that, with proper backing, will encourage sound scientific and economic progress in new fields—fields that hold the promise of tremendous future development."

❈ XIV ❈

THE IDEA OF MAKING MONEY, OF CONDUCTING SUCCESSFUL business and financial affairs as described in the preceding chapter is important in the lives of the Rockefeller brothers. Yet, accumulating money, as did their grandfather, is definitely less important in their scheme of things than contributing to the progress of our time and, in another grouping of enterprises, the brothers have boldly risked considerable sums to carry through long-range experimental projects of broad social importance. In this category, they have sponsored and invested in undertakings that may be very slow to show even a modest profit but which, if successful, fill an important gap in the capitalistic democratic system.

Such enterprises, although operated on a businesslike basis, are designed to establish a trend of action, to prove a theory that may be of major economic or technological or social significance in the future. "We're really setting up pilot plants," Nelson explained when this phase of activity got underway after the war. "Our way of life is confronted with a lot of big problems that have to be solved. We hope that our pilot plant operations will demonstrate some of the things that American enterprise can do to help solve these problems that are vital to our everyday life and to our position in world affairs. Because we've got to master such problems if our system is going to survive."

Needless to say, the element of risk is greatly magnified in such a broad and vaguely charted field of human affairs, but all of the brothers have become interested, in varying degrees, in undertakings of this nature, designed to show that businessmen can help promote economic and social progress and, at the same time, make a profit. These twin goals have been approached in various ways and with varying results, ranging from downright failure to substantial success.

An enterprise known as Island Packers, Inc., was initiated in 1948, for example, with the idea of bolstering the economy of two underdeveloped areas in the South Seas. The plan was to aid the Fiji Islands by employing native labor to catch tuna and to aid American Samoa by erecting there a tuna-canning plant, which would employ native workers. Both areas would benefit economically by these activities, the standard of living generally would be given a slight boost and, in time, other enterprises backed by other capital might come into the area. Meantime, the tuna catching and processing company would be making a fair return on its investment by selling on the American market. On this basis, a company was formed with a score of investors putting up some $2,000,000 in capital, fishing boats were acquired and converted for use in tropical waters and a processing plant was erected. Only then was it discovered that something had gone wrong—there weren't enough tuna in the area in which the boats could operate. The South Seas bubble collapsed with a bang that blew up a million and a half dollars of which about $500,000 was Rockefeller money.

But if tuna catching in the Fiji Islands turned out to be a poor method of working toward an objective it did not necessarily prove that the objective couldn't be reached. In another underdeveloped part of the world, the Rockefellers became interested in a somewhat similar project known informally as Filtisaf (Filatures and Tissages Africains). This was a company formed jointly with 60 per cent Belgian capital to manufacture textiles in the Belgian Congo on the shores of Lake Tanganyika. Several Belgian companies capable of contributing technically and otherwise to the enterprise became partners in the new venture. The Filtisaf factory as well as housing for native labor had to be built from scratch. Machinery and many materials were imported from the United States, including a North Carolina textile mill that was shipped to Africa lock, stock and barrel.

The village-grown cotton in the Congo was of good quality, but some 1,000 natives, with no industrial experience, had to be trained to operate the textile machines. All of this took time, but with good management and with introduction of an incentive system for workers, the unit production in the mill soon was raised to a ratio of six to ten as compared with that of a southern mill worker and it is still going up. In all, profits were made much sooner than had been anticipated by the sponsors of the enterprise.

But profits, from the viewpoint of the Rockefellers, were only a part of the design. The mill has contributed significantly to the economic development of a part of the world that, since the war, has assumed more and more importance in the future of western civilization. The entire output of the textile mill is for local consumption, reducing the need for foreign exchange, attracting other new industries to the area and providing the people, in addition to better wages, a cheaper and better home product.

It provided the women of the region with something else, too—a consciousness of style—which had not been in the minds of the sponsors of the project, but which they regard as of more than passing significance. In the past, the native women had worn cloth of whatever color or design happened to be sent into the Congo. But now that they make their own cloth they are also able to influence the design, and it was probably only natural that their first patterns reflected the advent of machinery in their land. A print known as the "four cylinder" pattern quickly became popular. Then, as was to be expected, the leaders of local fashion switched to a "six cylinder" print, presumably just to be different. "It was," remarked one of the Rockefeller experts, "interesting to watch the changes as the women became style conscious. It seemed just like Fifth Avenue."

These isolated examples suggest the idea behind the efforts of the Rockefellers. They had to take risks; they had to feel their way in new areas of endeavor. A great many theories had been expounded about what could be done in such fields, but they had very little in the way of practical experimentation to guide them. The idea, however, that the future of international trade is closely linked to the ability of businessmen to assist in the self-improvement of underdeveloped areas was firmly planted in the minds of the Rockefeller brothers and they were moving toward a far more ambitious effort to demonstrate their theories.

Not all of their efforts were directed abroad by any means. One of the biggest postwar problems in the United States was housing and it was a problem that the Rockefellers—and particularly Mr. Rockefeller, Jr.—had been interested in since before the war. These early efforts were not particularly successful for a series of complicated reasons and as a result of unhappy political developments in Washington, which undermined the program in which Mr. Rockefeller was involved. But after the war the housing problem came up again in quite a different way as a result of the brothers' close association with Architect Wallace Harrison, who married the sister of Abby Rockefeller's first husband, David Milton.

Harrison had long been an important figure in Rockefeller affairs, an associate in many enterprises and a director of various business and charitable projects that the family had participated in. He has been perhaps as influential as any person outside the family in the undertakings of the five brothers and he has shared in shaping their ideas because of his tremendous vitality and enthusiasm. He is a big, brown-eyed man, six feet two and weighing over two hundred pounds, genial and breezy but intense and something of a perfectionist.

After wartime service in Washington, both Harrison and Nelson returned to New York and did some hard thinking about what was going on in the world, and particularly in the United States. One of the things Harrison was thinking about was an old dream, a conviction that "the advantages of modern American technology should be made available for one of humanity's basic needs—low-cost shelter." And, as a result of the mechanical miracles he had witnessed during the war, he began to get an idea. Why, he reasoned, couldn't a new method be developed for building low-cost concrete houses at high speed by applying the techniques of modern road building to mass production of houses?

Following up this thought Harrison reversed the procedure of mass producing houses in sections at a factory from which they had to be moved, at high cost, to sites. He began working out a system which in effect moved the factory to the site, cutting out heavy transportation and labor costs. He believed it could be done by building the houses of concrete. As the method finally evolved, steel forms were made to replace the conventional wooden forms, which required much carpentry and were nondurable. A giant thirty-ton crane of great mobility, such as was devised during the war for air-strip work and for handling heavy airplanes, was purchased and, in December of 1947, land was cleared on a site next to Harrison's potato field near Huntington, New York, for the experiment.

First, big mixers poured a concrete house floor. Then the crane moved up the special steel wall forms, which could be locked or unlocked in a few minutes. Concrete mixers, elevated above the forms, poured concrete through prefabricated chutes and four hours later the forms were filled, making the roofless walls of a complete house. It consisted of a living room, two bedrooms, bathroom and kitchenette with plumbing and electrical outlets all ready for the attaching of fixtures. When the concrete had set the next morning, the steel forms were unlocked and moved away for use on the next house.

Meanwhile, a single pre-cast concrete slab weighing thirteen tons had been prepared on the ground as a roof and the big crane, using a patented vacuum lifting device, moved it into place over the walls, setting it down with an accuracy that varies only a fraction of an inch. Thus the shell of a house was set up in a manner that eliminated much of the ordinary work of construction, and much of the ordinary cost of materials.

The first experiment in Harrison's potato field didn't go that smoothly, of course. There were a great many bugs to be ironed out, but the experiment did show that a low-cost house could be built in a series of simple operations that would become economical when a large number of structures were put up on one site, as in a housing development. At this time Nelson was hard at work on plans for his most ambitious venture, aimed toward Latin America, and one of the problems involved was housing. He was enthusiastic about the possibility of employing Harrison's method in building houses in warm climates and, with this in mind, a housing corporation was set up as part of the International Basic Economy Corporation—the name that was to become familiar in Latin America as the Rockefellers extended their activities there in the next few years. Winthrop Rockefeller later became chairman of the board of the IBEC Housing Corporation.

To round out the new company, Roger and Louis Corbetta of the Corbetta Construction Company were brought into IBEC Housing Corporation, and Louis Corbetta accompanied

Nelson and several associates on a trip to the site of a proposed housing development. Corbetta is a big name in construction work but Louis, like his brother, was a rough-and-ready self-made man and, outside of business hours, he may have been a bit skeptical of the bright young sons of millionaires. In any event, on the first night of their stay at a plush hotel, Corbetta came into the dining room by himself after the others were seated at a table and, after a quick look around, took a place at a single table some distance away. Nelson spotted him and motioned him to the party's table but Corbetta, apparently believing it was merely a polite gesture, declined. Nelson is seldom declined so easily. He got up and escorted Corbetta to the table, got a chair for him before the eager waiter could perform that duty and snatched a plate and silverware off another table to set a place for the newcomer. By the time the evening ended, Corbetta was feeling just fine about the energetic young sons of millionaires and the foundations of a firm friendship were laid.

The first big job of IBEC Housing Corporation, under direction of George Dudley, a young architect from Harrison's office, was not in Latin America but near Norfolk, Virginia. The company contracted to build 204 small four-room houses on a landscaped sixteen-acre tract that was being developed by a local real estate man in behalf of the Norfolk housing authority. The houses, under the contract, were to cost less than six dollars a square foot as compared to a normal cost at that time of about ten dollars. Over-all cost for each house was $4,000, including preparation of the site, a gas range, electric refrigeration, hot water heater, oil space heater—and a large living room picture window. At this price, the developer was able to sell them at not more than $5,000 or to rent them for $45 a month, as stipulated by the housing authority. And, to its surprise, the Rockefeller corporation quickly began reducing the time required—the whole job outside of foundations, etc., now can be done in about eight hours—and made a profit of about 12 per cent on the 204 houses. Thus the price could be reduced on future jobs in the United States but the saving also meant that such housing could be erected cheaply enough to make it feasible to transport the heavy forms and equipment to foreign lands—such as Israel and South America—and still compete successfully in building low-cost houses.

The opening ceremonies at the Norfolk project were a big day for Nelson, and he showed a number of officials and friends the equipment that had been developed by the company. The big crane was particularly impressive and prompted somebody to remark that it must take a lot of skill to operate it.

"Nothing to it," Nelson replied. "A child could run it. The whole thing is electrically controlled and works with push buttons just like an automatic elevator. . . . Look, I'll show you!"

He scrambled up into the lofty control house and began pushing buttons. The huge machinery whirred and the crane moved smoothly. Nelson pushed some more buttons. The crane was still smooth but somewhere a mistake had been made. It swung too far around and banged against the side of the partly constructed house, nudged a workman off his perch and knocked a concrete mixer to the ground. Nobody was hurt, however, and Nelson's enthusiasm was undiminished.

In 1952, Winthrop Rockefeller, as chairman of the housing corporation, announced that preliminary plans for three major developments in El Salvador were being completed. The projects are for rebuilding five towns in Valle de la Esperanza, which was rocked by a disastrous quake in May of 1951; a 1,000-bed hospital in San Salvador, and a master plan for civic improvements, especially in roads and utilities, in San Miguel, the third largest city in El Salvador.

The Rockefellers' venture into low-cost housing—like the African textile mill and other similar projects—represented only a facet of their long-range planning. This planning centered on the problem of what private business could accomplish, particularly in South America, in harmony with what later became President Truman's Point Four program for aid to underdeveloped areas of the world. They were looking for a progressive method of operations that would promote good will, enlist the aid of the peoples—and the capital—of Latin American countries and encourage self-improvement. They also wanted something that would return a profit and would thus gain the support of American capital. In view of the tangle of trade and exchange regulations after the war and the difficult situations created by militant economic nationalism in backward countries it was obvious that a new type of foreign investment had to be evolved in tune with the changing times.

Needless to say, nobody suddenly turned up with the answer. What did happen was that a broad experimental pattern finally began to emerge out of the ideas of a large number of experts on various phases of the problem. The experiences of governmental agencies, particularly the early New Deal agencies formed during the depression, were examined and modified and adjusted to the new pattern. The successes and failures of The Rockefeller Foundation provided guidance, particularly the policy of making foreign governments responsible participants in medical and scientific projects in order to assure permanence of the projects despite changing political regimes. But above all the operations had to set a pattern, to establish a mechanism based on practical business experience that would demonstrate increasing value of and necessity for international co-operation in underdeveloped areas.

ONE OF THE TENETS OF THE ROCKEFELLER PHILOSOPHY is that the United States can continue to grow and realize its future productive possibilities only if there is parallel economic and social development in other countries, and especially in the underdeveloped areas of the Western Hemisphere. Just for example, this country is increasingly dependent upon vital imports for industry—and at a time when it is emerging into leadership of the defense of the free world. Thus American business as well as government has a responsibility as well as a mounting self-interest in helping underdeveloped regions to increase productive capacity and to create greater economic and social stability by raising living standards.

"In the last century capital went where it could make the greatest profit," Nelson Rockefeller pointed out in a discussion of foreign trade shortly after the war. "In this century, it must go where it can render the greatest service."

That was more or less the idea that the Rockefeller brothers agreed on when they launched their major experiment in international co-operation by setting up two separate organizations to operate in underdeveloped areas of Latin America. The organizations were the International Basic Economy Corporation, which was promptly nicknamed IBEC, and the American International Association for Economic and Social Development, known as AIA. Nelson became president of both.

IBEC, in which the Rockefellers and others invested, was to

provide financing and management for an indefinite number of enterprises intended to help raise the standard of living in the localities involved—chiefly Latin America—and to return a profit, if possible, to the investors. It was started in January of 1947 with initial capital of $2,000,000, which was later increased to $10,824,000.

But even before the corporation was formally inaugurated the Rockefellers recognized that other measures would be necessary. IBEC operations would be in areas where standards of living were low and often primitive. Facilities for guarding the health of the people, normally provided by government in modern times, would be lacking in some instances. So would educational facilities which are so essential to modern farming and manufacturing. So would credit establishments.

The answer which the Rockefellers devised was the AIA. Actually established in July of 1946, in advance of IBEC, the AIA was a nonprofit philanthropic agency with the broad purpose of giving people in underdeveloped regions the tools—education, health, farm training, roads, supervised credit—that they need to improve their standard of living.

Thus the AIA became a pioneer in a new postwar approach to international co-operation and progress. Two fundamental concepts were set forth in its charter: "First, a faith in the inherent dignity and worth of the individual and in the capacity and desire for self-improvement of human beings of whatever nationality, race, creed or color. Second, a conviction that the welfare of each nation and person in the modern world is closely related to the welfare and opportunities for advancement of all people of the world."

Starting in Brazil and Venezuela, after expert surveys were made, AIA was designed to work in contractual association with local government, which agreed to match AIA funds and to contribute personnel to carry out a three-year program of training, educating and assisting rural workers and farmers to better production and better living. It was financed by the Rockefellers, the leading Venezuelan oil companies and the Brazilian subsidiary of the Corn Products Refining Company— a total in the first three years of around $3,500,000—in addition to the local government funds devoted to the program.

It would have been difficult to find two countries for the Rockefellers' experiment that offered more similarities and more contrasts than Venezuela and Brazil. Brazil is a vast country, larger than the United States. Venezuela, although six times the size of England, is a tenth as large as Brazil. There are 50,000,-000 persons in Brazil, most of them speaking Portuguese. The 5,000,000 inhabitants of Venezuela speak Spanish.

In both countries the bulk of the population lives near the coast or in the temperate highland areas nearby. The great industrial center of Brazil is São Paulo, capital of the coffee state of São Paulo, but cities of considerable size also are found in the mining states of Minas Gerais and Goiáz. In addition to Rio de Janeiro, often called the most beautiful city in the world, Brazil has many important ports from Rio Grande do Sul in the far south to Belém at the mouth of the Amazon. Venezuela, on the other hand, has few cities. Caracas, the capital, which lies on a high plateau about an hour by highway from the coast, is the largest. Maracaibo, at the mouth of a great sea-lake of the same name, is the principal oil-shipping center. Ciudad Bolívar on the Orinoco River is deep in the hinterland of plain and jungle.

Beyond the fairly narrow strip of settled and civilized city and farm land along the coasts, both countries have vast jungles in the interior as well as great empires of open grazing land. There are regions in both Brazil and Venezuela that have never been successfully explored. Only recently two great iron deposits were discovered in Venezuela, and one of the greatest waterfalls was found. Although ocean liners can go a thousand miles up the Amazon to the old-time Brazilian rubber city of Manaos, and smaller vessels can go several thousand miles farther, little of the country lying back from the river has been opened up. Thus both countries offer tremendous opportunities for future expansion and development.

During and since World War II, Brazil was rapidly industrialized in limited areas by construction of enormous steel mills, rubber, metal, cement, paper, chemical and machine factories. No country in South America has been industrializing so rapidly. São Paulo, one of the fastest growing cities in the world, has tossed its skyscrapers against the sky with the exuberance of a new Chicago. Venezuela has few modern industries although it produces vast quantities of oil. Only recently has it acquired oil refineries and, despite its large ore deposits, plans for its first steel mill were drawn up only in 1951.

It was perhaps to be expected that the Rockefellers would select these two countries for inauguration of their experiment. Nelson had become greatly interested in Brazil, during his government service and he had collected and helped to promote through the Museum of Modern Art the paintings of Candido Portinari. One of his advisers, Berent Friele, was closely associated with private business in Brazil for years and had married a prominent Brazilian girl, Jenny Muller Camps. "Probably no country in the world, undeveloped or otherwise," Friele remarked, "offers for the long range more fruitful possibilities for creative enterprise. This means creative enterprise in the application of machines, electric power transport, science and management to the natural resources of the Brazilian earth."

But, Friele added: "If Brazil is to realize her industrial aspirations, she must find ways of increasing the productivity of the workers, releasing workers from the land and expanding her unit farm output to feed the increasing population in the cities.

That can be achieved in part through the mechanization of agriculture, supplemented by improved seeds, fertilizers, insecticides and other advances in farming techniques."

The Rockefellers also had a special interest in Venezuela because of the Creole Petroleum Corporation, a family interest in which Nelson and Winthrop had been active. It is a subsidiary of Standard Oil of New Jersey and the biggest producing company in the world. Several of the brothers had been to Venezuela at various times on Creole business as well as in connection with another of their enterprises, the building of the handsome and successful Hotel Avila in Caracas.

Venezuela was particularly in need of help. Prior to World War I it had been an underdeveloped agricultural country, isolated, largely self-sufficient. The start of the oil industry in 1914 had changed that. As oil production rose and cities grew in size, the traditional economy of the country did not expand at the same rate. More and more eggs were put into the petroleum basket, till Venezuela became the second largest oil producer in the world. Thereby it became almost a one-product land, its entire well-being dependent on the price of oil over which it had little control. "The richer we are, the poorer we get," became a stock Venezuelan saying. "Venezuela is a poorhouse, built on a gold foundation"—the gold being oil. From 21 to 93 per cent of such staples as rice, corn, sugar, wheat flour came to be imported, though Venezuela has much rich unused agricultural land, and therefore sold at very high prices. Venezuela has one of the highest cost-of-living indexes of any country on earth. Of the masses, only some 45,000 oil workers —1 per cent of the population—lived in relative comfort. As a result, says one AIA report:

"Venezuela presented the paradox of a nation with one of the highest per capita government revenues in the world, while two-thirds of its population had a low level of living. The government's income is almost exclusively from taxes and royalties on oil. While national wealth from oil has increased, agricultural productivity has failed to keep pace with population increases, thereby placing greater dependence upon imported food."

Venezuela was in need of a more rounded economy, particularly a greater farm output. In this effort, the new Rockefeller enterprises could be of great help. But there was one big stumbling block: a President who had once strongly advocated nationalization of oil and who had once attacked Nelson personally in the most violent and bitter language.

In *Ahora* of March 23, 1939, President Rómulo Betancourt, at that time merely the leader of the minority Democratic Action party and editor of the paper, had commented sarcastically about the current visit of Nelson on a Pan American clipper, saying he was immediately surrounded and entertained by oil company managers and lawyers who were getting the oil companies exempted from the wage and profit-sharing provisions of the new constitution. Betancourt made many charges. One of them concerned eviction of poor tenants from recently acquired oil lands, and concluded that Nelson's maxim as stated to the press on his arrival that "the star that guided him in the proper use of money is: the well-being of humanity in the entire world" was "specious and hypocritical."

"After looking over his vast oil properties . . ." wrote Betancourt, "in the West . . . and in the East . . . he will return to his office atop Rockefeller Center, to the warm shelter of his home, to resume his responsibilities as a philanthropist and Art Maecenas.

"Behind him will remain Venezuela producing 180 million barrels of oil for the Rockefellers. . . . Behind him will remain Venezuela with its half million children without schools, its workers without adequate diets . . . its 20,000 oil workers mostly living in houses that the Department of Fomento [Development] states should better be called 'over-grown match-boxes'; Venezuela, with its three million pauper inhabitants, victims of frightful epidemics. . . . Such is the meaning of Rockefeller's exploiting our country with his specious hypocritical maxim."

Acute misery had indeed brought Betancourt into office by a military coup during the war. The oil tankers could take out oil, but could not bring in food, and vessels that customarily touched at Venezuelan ports, since nearly all belonged to United States companies, had been commandeered by the American government to help in the war effort. Here was the odd phenomenon of a country booming with activity, its oil never in such demand, the price never higher, yet the people unable to obtain enough to eat. Acute starvation stalked the land, and the people rioted and finally put Betancourt into office.

At once Betancourt started an independent shipping company with Ecuador and Colombia and pried better terms out of the oil companies, and through the government-owned Venezuelan Development Corporation worked hard to develop agriculture and small industries to make Venezuela less dependent on outside food and give it a more rounded economy. This policy Betancourt called *"sembrando el petroleo"*—sowing the oil, *i.e.,* plowing it back into benefits for the people and the country, to make Venezuela stronger when the day came that all the black gold would be pumped out and gone forever.

The New Jersey Standard Oil Company publication, *The Lamp,* praised this policy, which it described as "oil-produced government revenue . . . being stoked into a forced-draft effort to give everyone a living more in keeping with national income" —more schools, doctors, roads, sewers, irrigation, electric plants, food, airports, health and literature.

But in spite of Venezuela's grand financial position, thanks to oil, and though Betancourt was putting 40 per cent of the country's revenues—about a quarter of a billion dollars—into basic capital expansion, he needed more capital badly; even more he needed expert technical help. The Rockefeller plans were in line with his policy of making Venezuela more productive in new fields, so he put aside his early harsh attitude and invited both corporations to Venezuela.

He sent a cabinet minister to greet Nelson at the airport and saw him within a few hours and immediately gave him the green light on everything proposed. The humor of Betancourt's about-face was not lost on the public. *U. R. D.*, a famous anti-government weekly, wrote that though Betancourt had once demanded that Venezuela "liberate itself from the asphyxiating yoke of foreign capitalism, now it is required that we open our doors to the Messiah . . . and grant him the exploitation of hundreds of thousands of hectares of Venezuelan lands. God forbid that we think of Mr. Rockefeller as a bird of prey or a gangster—as he was called eight years ago [by Betancourt]— for he has come to our country to make us bigger and raise us up. . . .

"Mr. Rockefeller has been received by Señor Rómulo Betancourt, and amidst the clinking of crystal goblets and before the cleanest linen of Lucullus' table, the furious enemy of the cheerful descendant of old John D. renders homage to the new Standard Oil called IBEC. . . . The people—though humorous about it—are confused and do not understand the changeover."

At any rate, the Rockefeller experiment got off to a good start and, even when the inevitable criticism arose later, Betancourt ardently defended the enterprises in the press and before Congress.

Aside from getting the backing of the governments involved, the Rockefellers had also to enlist the interest and financial support of private business, such as the big oil companies in

Venezuela. This, to put it mildly, was not an easy task regardless of the fact that Nelson Rockefeller's name gave him an inside track when it came to dealing with oil men. After some negotiation, the companies agreed to make contributions but Nelson felt that they were not fully sold on the idea and he arranged to go to Venezuela for a conference at which the plans would be explained in detail. For this occasion, he took with him a man named Robert W. Hudgens, who had been selected to direct the activities of AIA.

Hudgens and Nelson had met several years earlier in Washington where the former was in the Farm Security Administration. He had at one time been a banker in South Carolina and, when the depression hit that state's textile industries, he became interested in the first rural rehabilitation program. Farmers needed loans to keep going but interest rates at the banks were high and many mortgages were forfeited. "Our idea was that the community, the home and the farm had to be rehabilitated as a single operating unit," Hudgens said later. "We started with a new concept of the farm credit system. We tied credit to education—education in efficient farming—so that the farmer would run his affairs better and be able to pay back what he had borrowed.

"We found that we also had to inaugurate a health and sanitation program because good health was essential, too, if the farmer was to avoid disaster. All of this was designed to take people off the relief rolls and get the farms on a sound working basis. And we found that those people paid back more on their loans than the banks had ever been able to recover."

The brain trust in the New Deal administration at Washington got word of what was happening in South Carolina and Rex Tugwell later asked Hudgens to go to Washington in the Resettlement Administration, which eventually became Farm Security. Some of the ideas that had been developed in South

Carolina were carried on into the national efforts of the Farm Security Administration and the success of those practices had interested Nelson in Hudgens. He felt that AIA would encounter many of the same problems in South America and one day he sent a telegram to Hudgens, asking him to luncheon. Over the luncheon table, Nelson talked about the AIA, which had been set up the year before.

"I'm looking for a director," he finally said. "What would you think about taking over?"

Hudgens said he'd like a little time to think about it. He had several important points to think about. One was the argument, not infrequently advanced, that by setting up both IBEC and AIA the Rockefellers were indulging in a kind of double-standard bookkeeping not enjoyed by ordinary business. In other words, IBEC was getting a break as a result of the philanthropic work of AIA.

The Rockefellers believe, however, that AIA is merely trying to take up a cultural lag where there are inadequate governmental institutions. Governments in various Latin American countries, for example, have lacked resources to establish such institutions and AIA is intended to give them a lift in the right direction as well as to facilitate the work of putting IBEC enterprises on a sound basis. "If a business is to succeed," Nelson points out, "you have to get the people who are participating on their feet by educational, medical and other aid. That normally is a philanthropic or governmental job and, in effect, AIA is a pioneer operation that the governments one day can take over in whole or part."

What probably was most important in Hudgens' mind, however, was the charge that was made then and later in Venezuela and Brazil that the whole AIA and IBEC program was merely a false front for the greater glory and the greater profits of the oil companies. This is a point that has frequently been argued by important Brazilian newspapers, which have contended that the Rockefellers actually were not interested in promoting bona fide farming or welfare activities but were setting up a false front in order to get hold of potentially rich oil lands.

When Hudgens met with Nelson at a later date, he summed up his own feelings this way: "I'm intensely interested in the idea behind the AIA and I've always wanted to try it out in the international field. But I don't want to try it if the main idea is to promote business for the oil companies."

Nelson quickly reassured him. The oil companies, he said, would be solicited for funds but the nature of their contribution would leave them no voice in the management of AIA or IBEC.

"Well," Hudgens said, "it seems to me that the most important thing is to get the right kind of a credit system—a kind that will encourage the people to do things for themselves."

Nelson told him he would have a completely free hand. "In other words," Hudgens said later, "I could not have had a freer hand if I had written my own ticket. Nelson has always backed me up."

On their trip to Venezuela to explain the AIA plans in detail to the oil companies, Hudgens was constantly impressed by Nelson's methods. He seemed to know everybody and to spend all of his waking hours at work. On the airplane he met two Venezuelan labor leaders and spent hours talking about their problems. His Spanish was getting better all the time and he talked easily with the local newspapermen.

Nevertheless, the big job was to sell the oil-company executives and it couldn't be done by mere talk. They were staunch foes of the New Deal and they had no use for "do-gooders" who ran around wanting to save the world. They were "sharp pencil guys" who wanted facts and figures and a balance sheet, very much as Nelson's grandfather had wanted to know "what the figures show" when his young grandsons had told him of their business dreams. Nelson explained to the executives the general purposes of AIA and later Hudgens talked to them as a banker who had had considerable experience with loans to poor farmers as well as with government credit agencies.

Hudgens had been impressed in Venezuela with the fact that the oil-company towns were neat and pleasant inside the cyclone fences which surrounded company property. But just outside the fences were all of the signs of abject poverty. He began explaining what supervised credit methods had been able to do in the rehabilitation of farming areas in the United States. He knew he was on the right track when one company president remarked: "Well, something is going to have to be done here to close the gap between extreme poverty and those who are well off." In the end the various oil companies confirmed that they would put up $3,000,000 to run AIA for three years without any strings attached.

In the next few years, eight AIA programs were launched in Brazil and Venezuela, and each of these tended to branch out into other allied activities covering a wide field. "We are trying to take the world's organized, technical knowledge," Hudgens explains, "and step it down and apply it to the lives of people who need help. If such a program had been started in the Balkans thirty years ago it might have prevented the Second World War."

Most of the work of AIA is in simple fundamentals. In the summer of 1950, for example, a case of smallpox was discovered in a village in Carabobo state, far back in the hills of Venezuela. Such a discovery at one time might have meant anything from panic to a plague in a countryside that was remote, backward and superstitious. In the old days, if the government did anything at all it moved in troops to vaccinate the people by force. Sometimes the frightened villagers believed they were deliberately being inoculated with the dread disease and their terror occasionally ended in rioting and bloodshed.

But what happened in 1950 was quite different. Within a few hours a bright yellow station wagon dashed into the town and began touring the streets, broadcasting through a loud-speaker a message that seemed far removed from either plague or panic.

"Free movies tonight!" the driver cried into the microphone. "Come to the plaza at dusk for free movies."

Dusk is the usual time for the plaza promenade, a custom in all Latin American countries, and on this occasion the promise of entertainment drew almost everybody in town. A projector and loud-speaker had been set up and a motion picture comedy was shown on the white-washed wall of the church. The plaza was filled with appreciative laughter. Next came an animated cartoon that amusingly but clearly told the story of how contagious diseases, such as smallpox, spread and how vaccination could protect the individual, the family and the community.

Even the children could understand that vaccination was harmless and that it was important to their welfare. At the end of the show, the townsfolk were informed that a case of smallpox had been discovered in the village and that the local clinic would be open the following morning. Early the next day there was a crowd of men, women and children at the door of an improvised clinic and the village was soon past all danger of epidemic.

The yellow station wagon, the movies and the clinic merely suggest the methods employed by the AIA in a broad program being carried out in association with government agencies in Venezuela and in the Brazilian states of Minas Gerais and São Paulo. By 1952, four programs were in operation in Venezuela —a rural development program, a farm-to-market road building program, a nutrition information program and an advanced

training program in farm operation and management for qualified Venezuelan youths at the Inter-American Institution of
Agricultural Sciences at Turrialba in Costa Rica. Farm credit,
rural rehabilitation and health programs are in effect in Brazil.
All of these activities are intended to be taken over by official
agencies as soon as possible.

Meanwhile, families of low-income farmers have begun to
learn how to assist themselves to better living conditions. At
the little town of Yagua in Venezuela, for instance, a community center was operated for a time by the government and
the AIA through an autonomous agency known as the Council
for Rural Welfare. Every morning about eighty children hurried
through the streets to the center where they played a game that
might be called "tooth-brushing and hand-washing." The reward for this ordeal was a meal of fresh milk, bread and cereal.
AIA personnel, with Venezuelan assistants, ran the center. The
state provided the milk. The bread was given by the Venezuelan
Children's Council. The house was donated by a local resident
and mothers of the children took turns helping with the work,
at the same time learning about nutrition, hygiene and similar
subjects. Eight such breakfast stations were in operation by 1951.

In addition, another autonomous agency known as CIDEA
operated five station wagons that toured an area from the Andes
down to the coastal region to promote an information program
devoted mainly to health and nutrition. Each wagon was
equipped with a 16-mm. sound projector, turntable, loud-
speaker and generator. The wagon crew tried to arrive in a town
about noon. Then the driver, a Venezuelan, would call on the
mayor and other local leaders and get them to record short
speeches. They would also enlist volunteers to distribute leaflets
around town and at the time the movie was shown. Anywhere
from 200 to 3,000 persons would attend the show, usually in
the village plaza, and be exposed to some visual education as

well as a bit of movie entertainment. The movies usually include a sports film, a comedy, and several reels carrying simple lessons in sanitation, balanced diet or child care. One film might show what happens when impure water is not boiled. Another shows the effects of different kinds of food on the body. The listeners also hear recorded talks by nurses, doctors and local leaders.

About 200,000 persons saw such shows in 1951 and the program was so successful that the government in 1952 turned over to CIDEA twenty-two additional station wagon units to carry on the nutrition information program. Forty-six radio stations in Venezuela also broadcast about 10,000 AIA programs in a year and press releases on similar subjects appeared in 1951 on an average of eighty-three times a month in more than fifty newspapers. Overall, the experts estimated that the program was reaching an average monthly audience of 1,500,000 out of a population of about 5,000,000.

Though AIA is a joint effort with the government authorities, its technicians work directly with community groups, farmers' clubs, educational societies, local committees and children's organizations. In Venezuela, 13,000 young people have enrolled in eighty-five nutrition clubs. In some instances such groups have made their own special direct deals to match AIA funds in order to get desired projects; if not with money they may go on a barter basis, putting up corn, milk and other products AIA can use.

A slightly different operation was set up on beautiful Isla Margarita off the north coast, quite a tourist mecca, but otherwise sadly neglected because of its remoteness from the mainland. Though a small tropical island, it has 70,000 inhabitants engaged chiefly in self-supporting farming, pearl-fishing and the weaving of unusually beautiful hammocks. Some divi-divi for rotenone fertilizer is grown: another minor local industry is the making of coconut oil.

Here AIA set up a farm center with two United States technicians and two Venezuelan trainees. Some three hundred types of service were performed for those who applied at the center, which was visited by more than 4,000 people the first year. But its most popular effort was the free milk station, where some 8,000 servings a year are made. Short courses on health, hygiene and recreational activity are given. Girls and farm wives are enrolled in ten courses on sewing, nutrition, carpentry, etc., and demonstrations are given by mobile units throughout the island on canning, poultry-raising, vaccination, tree grafting and seed selection.

Another example of AIA work—this one in Brazil—is a traveling clinic, manned by a doctor from the Department of Health, and a nurse provided by AIA. Enter again the station wagon, this time painted black, with the white words, *Departamento de Saúde*. Each day it bounces up the dusty road to some village "Municipal Palace" or to the porch of a fazenda or plantation house. The doctor and his assistant set up a table, perhaps under some large shade tree in the plaza and pile it with medical supplies and literature and begin to check the health of the men, women and children who gather around, usually from thirty to a hundred each time. The doctor and nurse test blood pressure and look for evidence of internal parasite infections which in some areas afflict 85% of the population. Maybe thirty people are vaccinated.

The folk are urged to wear shoes against hookworm and similar infections and are given vermicides to fight parasites. For their home gardens, the children are given plants, some wholly new, such as broccoli, which have been grown in the AIA greenhouse.

The nurse tries to organize home clubs and personally visits farmer homes, teaching child diet and suggesting that the babies be kept off the floor and away from animals. Midwives are given proper instructions. Materials and medicines are distributed. It is not always easy to make the approach. Distrust and suspicion must be overcome, confidence must be won.

Ernesto Patrone fumbles with his straw hat, which he has removed from his matted black hair, and pulls his sickly ten-year-old girl, Dora, forward to the clinic table. She is barefoot, in a thin yellow calico dress. The doctor's quick eye observes the drawn yellow-gray complexion, the sores on face and hands, the definite symptoms that both are suffering from yaws, the dread disease nicknamed "tropical syphilis," for in time it rots away the flesh.

A few years ago it was considered almost incurable, at best a long, costly process. But the clinic gives a few shots of penicillin. Even one shot may suffice. The disease is contracted because of diet deficiency, and Ernesto, who is a widower, is told what foods he and the girl must eat, simple cheap foods easily obtainable. He soon believes what they tell him and nods his head vigorously; his black eyes shine, he looks at his little girl fondly. Distrust is ended and confidence is established.

These mobile clinics cover a regular route of about fourteen stations within a twenty-mile radius of the central laboratory every two weeks. Each time word of the visit gets around, timidity or fear grows less, more people show up. In several places health improvement has been so good that the stop has been dropped from the regular schedule except for a check-up every three months.

Much of this effort has centered around São Paulo, but in the highland Minas Gerais mining country, 5,320 persons were vaccinated and 1,312 treated, mostly for parasites in the first year. The work was backed up with a sanitary campaign of literature and public lectures.

Problems of health are only one phase of AIA activities. Many Venezuelan communities are isolated in the mountains or in jungles where it may be necessary to travel for hours over burro path to reach an automobile road. In the Andean region, for example, were four villages which had never seen a wheeled vehicle and the problem of transportation had to be solved before progress could be made in any other direction.

AIA experts felt that the quickest solution would be to build the type of mountain truck-trails that had been developed by the United States Forest Service, with some modifications in grading and drainage to make allowance for heavy tropical rains. A former governor of Tachira persuaded his state to put up enough money to bring a bulldozer and a Forest Service road engineer from the United States to do the job. To the people, the clattering, roaring road-making machine was like something out of this world. They were skeptical and a bit nervous at first, and the children looked on fearfully as the bulldozer was put into action by its American operator, who wore a cocked Western hat. The skepticism and uncertainty were brief. Soon crowds of people were gathering enthusiastically and kids were clambering over the machine, wanting to learn to operate it. Within a week every boy in the neighborhood wore something that resembled the American's cocked Western hat.

In fifty days a seven-kilometer road was put through. Seven young Venezuelans quickly learned the road-building knack. They were taught to sidecast, ditch, bulldoze, operate levelers and graders and keep the equipment in good order. They soon built another road sixty-five kilometers long. Four mountain jungle villages were given easy access to the outside world for the first time—and, most important, the people had discovered that they could do the job themselves next time. Other communities and states that had watched the experiment began putting up funds for similar work which was planned by the AIA experts and executed by the newly trained bulldozer crews.

A country road over the mountains to a small community may seem a minor achievement but actually the introduction of U.S. Forest Service technique was of major importance in a huge area that had always been held back by lack of transportation. In 1950 a road was pushed through to the jungle-bound community of San Nicolás where some 3,000 persons had always been so isolated that they lived mostly by barter, although the village was only twenty miles from a good road. A remarkable change immediately came about in San Nicolás and today the community does a steady and lively business with the outside world, selling rice, bananas, tobacco, coconuts, pineapples and lumber in the city markets and, in return, getting the products of distant factories for their own use. The difference is perhaps best illustrated by the fact that a Tachira farmer formerly had to allow a full day for the long, hard trip by burro to the market at San Cristóbal. Today he can make as many as four daily trips if necessary.

While such technological improvements were being put into effect the AIA also went about the business of spreading its basic gospel—the idea that once they are helped to get on their feet the people will be able to stand alone and, in time, to maintain these services for themselves. It is a gospel that Nelson spread everywhere he moved in Brazil and Venezuela, and he moved around a great deal on his visits to both countries. Winthrop, David and John D., 3rd, also made long and short visits to the scene of operations.

Nelson's greatest interest is people and, as he became familiar with the languages and the country, he spent many hours of many days talking with farmers and workers and housewives and children. He dislikes formality even when an occasion compels him to observe it, and he has no use for class distinctions. Latin Americans are likely to be very formal, especially in the presence of foreigners, and more than once he shocked local or governmental dignitaries by his disregard for the usual practices. He would insist upon visiting the lowly and often not very clean home of a peasant farmer to see what the AIA had done for the family, or what it might do. He would play with sticky-fingered babies and pose for a photograph with the family. He sometimes grabbed a hoe and worked in the garden beside a sandal-shod farmer in order to question him without interrupting his work. He would stop to chat with sweaty and dust-streaked workers, while his official companions waited uncomfortably in the hot sun.

"He goes a little like a mad man from daybreak until dusk and then he wants to talk things over with the experts until midnight," one associate said after a long trip to Venezuela with Nelson. "Only once in a period of several weeks did I see him show any sign of strain. We had been going hard all day and settled down in a hotel room after dinner for a talk with some of the local people. After a while, Nelson folded his arms on the table and put his head down on his arms. I thought, well, at last, I've seen him get tired. But about that time, he said: 'Just keep on talking. I'm listening.' It was pretty obvious though that he was all in and the session broke up early. As it turned out he was ill. He'd picked up a bug somewhere and he was pretty sick for several days."

On one occasion Nelson and a group of local officials were driving along a country road when their automobile ran over a pig and killed it. The chauffeur kept right on going. Nelson was furious. He ordered the driver to turn around and go back to the farmhouse. Then he made him go in and pay—with Nelson's money—for the pig they had killed. The driver protested that he had never heard of such a thing and intimated that Nelson must be "loco" to think of bothering to pay a peasant for the loss of a pig.

When Nelson and David made a three-weeks' trip to South America in 1948 they were interested in the same problems but they approached them in strikingly different ways. Nelson seemed always to be hurrying. David was deliberate and wanted to know the details. Nelson frequently seemed to get the feel of what was happening in a flash. David always kept on probing until he was satisfied that he had learned about all the angles; he could ask questions systematically all day and never repeat a query. Later, Nelson could talk eloquently about broad trends and wide open opportunities in South America. David liked to keep to a narrower track and deal with specific areas.

In Peru and Chile, David noted, "the desert is broken only by a few rivers flowing to the sea. The beds of green flanking some of the rivers have been widened very considerably by irrigation projects and the sight of them makes one realize how much more could be done."

In Chile: "Tendency toward overindustrialization."

In Ecuador: "It is all she can do to sell enough cocoa, coffee, bananas, rice and a few other agricultural commodities to enable her to purchase the basic necessities from abroad."

In Peru: "President Odriá is outspokenly interested in improving the lot of the Indians. . . . Through a series of drastic measures he has brought about a decided improvement in the economy of the country."

On this journey, Nelson and David had an opportunity to see the AIA program in its early stages and to study the conditions under which it would work. That program, as it picked up speed, went far beyond the problems of health and nutrition and rural rehabilitation. It soon became an attempt to find basic solutions for many farm problems, such as better tillage, the development of new disease-proof heavy-yield seeds, the eradication of plant and animal pests. These efforts, however, cannot get very far, unless the farmers can make necessary improvements for sanitation, housing, fencing, and use more scientific methods. This made the introduction of supervised farm credit in both Brazil and Venezuela, a most important part of the general program.

Take the Brazilian state of Minas Gerais, where living standards have been generally lower than elsewhere in the country, and take the case of Sebastião Onofre da Silveira, who owns a 140-acre farm and works it diligently and intelligently but with barely enough success to support his family of fifteen. In 1948, his home lacked sanitary facilities, the water supply was unsafe, some of the children were ill, and Sebastião had to sell half his cattle to raise enough money to put in a new crop. Credit was out of the question for Sebastião because he would have had to pay around 20% interest.

In 1948 the state government invited AIA to assist in solving the agricultural credit problem. In collaboration with an autonomous agency, the Associaçao de Credito e Assistencia Rural—$450,000 were put up jointly to set up local offices in seven districts to provide financial and technical aid to farmers. A state bank agreed to make loans at 8% where the AIA field workers certified that the borrower was willing and able to cooperate in improving production.

When the program was explained at a village meeting, many farm people, including Sebastião and his wife, were suspicious and reluctant to accept the supervision necessary to obtain a loan but they finally decided to participate. Their application for a 30,000 cruzeiro loan was approved by the local committee, and AIA experts drew up a program for operation of their farm. Fifteen dairy cows and two oxen of improved breed were purchased. Crop rotation was started with beans, vegetables and sugar cane. Fences were erected, manure waste was ended and crops were properly sprayed.

For the first time, Sebastião planted hybrid corn and got an extraordinary yield. His banana trees, with scientific care, produced better and more abundantly. His cattle not only provided the family with milk but brought in an income of 2,000 cruzeiros a month. The first year, he cleared 12% more than his total loan. He's pretty puffed up about being able to sign his name, and he hangs his account book in the front room for everybody to see. He has found a way to help himself.

He also availed himself of the general help the entire community receives from AIA, cattle-spraying, extermination of leaf-sawing ants and other pests, seed-demonstration plots, soil conservation and preparation. His family is healthier from participating in community health and handicraft services, which include sanitation, education, cooking, nutrition, sewing classes. People are told how to build sanitary privies and the necessary concrete slabs are sold to them at cost.

"In 1950," AIA reports, "more than 300 head of better dairy cattle were introduced into the Santa Luzia area, thus increasing urban milk supply; 116 loans were granted for such things as disc plows, irrigation dams, corn-planters and livestock."

The story of Sebastião has been repeated hundreds of times wherever AIA is at work. Farmers gather regularly, perhaps in the village church, Municipal Palace or schoolhouse, to learn new methods from the AIA and government experts. New and more nutritious vegetables grow in family gardens. Cement floors have been installed. Many young children no longer sleep on floors.

The community services program in Santa Rita de Passo Quatro is unique, for here not the government but the farmers themselves have shouldered half the cost of the AIA. Each member of the farmers' association contributes three days' milk receipts to provide the cash to match AIA funds.

The town government provides office space and other facilities. This activity was begun in 1948 as an outgrowth of a livestock parasite-control program. The farmers' faith in the program has been justified for within a year and a half milk production was increased 25%.

This community is typical of many in Brazil that are in the process of shifting from coffee to dairying and general farming. Coffee production, after exhausting the local soil, moved west— much the same story as the early wheat migration in the United States—and new types of farming had to be developed. But when the farmers turned to dairying, they found ticks as bad as the eroded soil and the broca pest.

The AIA cattle-spraying eliminated the ticks and seemed the answer to their problem. Hard work was put into it. One AIA worker explains: "Three men worked full time spraying forty dairy herds. A simple hand-sprayer was developed, but occasionally one of the four power pumps is loaned to a co-operating dairyman. An average of 5,000 cows and calves are sprayed every month."

Then hoof-and-mouth disease struck. An intensified cattle-vaccination program was added. The Biological Institute of the state of São Paulo supplied the vaccine, and AIA undertook the refrigerated transportation and distribution through the farmers already organized for spraying.

The Santa Rita program kept growing till five separate projects were under way: cattle-spraying and vaccination, artificial insemination for better breeds, health services, a community nursery and club work. Two thirds of the money for such services was put up by private individuals, private organizations and local government agencies. A large local milk concern co-operated with the community program. Eleven posts for artificial insemination were established. At regular meetings, AIA technicians demonstrated new sprays, advised about fertilizers and selected seed-planting and other improvements. They answered countless questions on feeding, pasturage and various livestock problems.

In 1951, the AIA nursery in Santa Rita and three AIA technicians had distributed 500,000 seedling plants and 20,000 tree saplings. Eleven women's hygiene and health clubs were operating and sixteen clubs for boys and girls had planted experimental gardens with new kinds of vegetables and hybrid corn. Some 12,500 persons attended rural health clubs in 1951. A full-time dentist has been added to the services in Santa Rita.

In Venezuela, the community service program followed a pattern similar to that in Brazil. In the village of Peribeca, in the Andean section and not far from San Cristóbal, a local church was used as the community center and, after some hesitation, farmers were persuaded to come twice a month to discuss with experts how to select seed, prepare the soil, use hand sprays and other modern equipment. Eleazar Cárdenas was one of the first to qualify for a loan. He owned only eleven acres, but as a result of better methods and better equipment he increased the value of his farm from about 6,000 bolivares to almost 8,000 bolivares, and was able to rent and cultivate eight extra acres. He raised onions scientifically and got a bumper crop. He also started a vegetable garden so his wife and nine children could have a better diet. The three youngest attend the milk-station school at the community center. Eleazar is proud of his new cement floor (formerly dirt), new zinc roof (formerly thatch), his new clean kitchen and the cupboards his wife learned to make at community classes.

Timoteo Durán got a small loan to improve his twelve and one-half acres, half of which were lying idle, mend his house and buy seeds and insecticides. He also laid out a coffee patio and built a water tank. His daughters learned to make furniture and his sons have whitewashed the house and put in cement floors. He now has a handsome rose garden and tame doves and has renamed his place Flor de Paraíso—Flower of Paradise.

In both countries AIA has pushed various training programs to prepare younger people to continue the work begun. For Venezuela this has been done in three ways. Selected farm boys are sent to the Inter-American Institute of Agricultural Sciences in Costa Rica, to learn practical farming. This Institute was first started by the Co-ordinator's office in Washington when Nelson was head of it. It was continued after 1944 by a joint agreement of all the twenty American republics, and helped by The Rockefeller Foundation, which has made it the chief center for the entire continent for the distribution of scientific farm literature and photostats. AIA gave it an additional $158,000 grant to help expand facilities, and in return the Institute provided AIA with 300 one-year Venezuelan scholarships.

Of the first twenty Venezuelan students, four were awarded an additional year for more advanced study. The others found ready employment on their return to Venezuela. One is now assistant in the Ministry of Agriculture in its anti-cacao disease campaign. Another is conducting potato experiments. Forty other youths had been sent to the Institute for training by 1952.

Training was given in conjunction with AIA work itself, so local assistants will be ready to take over when AIA finally pulls out. In each local AIA office, one or more trainees were placed under a United States technician, participating in regular staff work and assisting in office activities. Gradually the assistants were given regular assignments and responsibilities in planning and administration. Progress from traineeship to responsible position has been rapid. Today all but three of the technicians are Venezuelans.

A third phase of training is to give certain farmers specialized knowledge, plus over-all instruction in sound methods. This was particularly successful in Valencia where AIA managed 1,800 acres of government land and employed about 100 families, to which it had authorized 167 loans by 1949. The members of this association have been specially trained in the use of machinery and farm management, in insect and disease control.

Thus in both Venezuela and Brazil those who have access to the AIA programs are learning how to break away from the old peonage pattern and to become independent, self-reliant and, above all, hopeful. "What we are doing," Hudgens emphasizes, "is expanding an idea. The most urgent task is to help people apply available knowledge to their own social and economic development. The range and scope of opportunities for private enterprise to help in solving these problems are unlimited. But the people themselves will have to do the work and carry it on if it is to succeed."

A few statistics will suggest how well the AIA has succeeded since 1946. In both Venezuela and Brazil the governments in 1952 raised the AIA program budgets for the following three years to about twice what they had been during the first or trial period of three years' actual operation. In other words, the AIA's objective of getting the local governments to take over and run and expand the programs is showing good progress. The new over-all budget in Venezuela will be $5,000,000, of which the federal government will contribute two thirds as compared to its 50% contribution to a $2,500,000 budget in the previous period. In Minas Gerais the state will provide four fifths of the new budget of $930,000, which is roughly double the previous budget. In São Paulo, state agencies and some private concerns are expected to multiply by several times a fund of $150,000 already committed to rural extension services. In all, government agencies and the AIA will spend around $6,080,000 on rural welfare projects in the two countries in the three-year period from 1952 to 1955.

These figures suggest the readiness of the local governments to support and adopt the AIA programs. But perhaps more important are the reactions of the people themselves. In Minas Gerais, by the end of 1951, 900 loans to about 600 rural families had been made under the credit assistance program. The record showed that 96% of the one-year crop loans made in 1950 had been repaid. One hundred of the borrower families were checked and the investigation showed that their farms had increased in value by an average of 22%. It also showed a twenty-five to thirty acre increase in cultivated land, a 66% increase in dairy cows, a 30% increase in sows and an increase in the gross farm family income in a year from $1,443 to $1,952.

In connection with the AIA program some 3,000 head of cattle were sprayed regularly against insects, 10,700 persons were immunized against diphtheria, smallpox and typhoid and 2,500 persons were treated for intestinal parasites and other diseases. Fifteen rural health clinics were operating in São Paulo and had given 50,000 individual treatments. More than a million plants, both vegetables and flowers, were distributed and regular country fairs were being held by twenty-five youth clubs to check on progress in their production of hybrid corn and foodstuffs.

In Venezuela, figures for 1951 showed that loans had been made to 700 farm families in the lower-income group and that repayment was at the rate of 91%. Increase in the net worth of these families was between 30 and 50%. There was a 7% increase in habitable rooms in their homes, a 14% increase in the number of beds, and a 10% increase in the number of privies. A total of 130 miles of vehicular roads in isolated farm regions had been opened up by road building.

In the progress of the AIA programs, Hudgens sees a far wider significance than merely assistance to Venezuelan and Brazilian farmers. "Private enterprise, one of the foundation stones of the free United States, is coming to recognize more and more the important role it can play and must play in helping underdeveloped regions toward economic and social stability," he explained. "In recent years, business has begun to regard this international responsibility as a real opportunity. We believe that the experience of the AIA will be an important guidepost in other fields and other areas of the world."

The Rockefellers hope and believe that he's right, because that's what they want to do—set up some guideposts.

✻ XVI ✻

ONE SUNNY DAY IN 1947 A BIG, BLOND TEXAN NAMED
C. O. Gingrass drove a jeep up the Chirgua Valley into
the hill country of Venezuela, followed by four snorting tractors, three big bulldozers and three power-sprayers. This mechanical cavalcade turned into historic Montesacro plantation,
about 160 miles west of Caracas, an estate that had once belonged to Simón Bolívar, the great "liberator" of South American history. Gingrass waved his big hat and the bulldozers
moved like a machine-made tornado across the famous estate.
The families of forty tenants watched in awe or, terror-stricken,
retreated with the younger children and the farm animals to the
nearest woods.

Neither awe nor fear lasted long. Modern methods and mechanized farming had come to the back country of Venezuela.

As much as anything the Rockefeller brothers have attempted,
International Basic Economic Corporation symbolizes a modern
approach. It covers a wide variety of activities. It includes a
little of everything from hard-boiled business and high finance
to philanthropy and international relations, plus a touch of
global uplift. "The United States came out of World War II
the greatest industrial power in history," ran the IBEC theory.
"Yet two destructive world wars and the depression between
those wars had damaged severely the world's machinery of
trade and finance, leaving a tangle of exchange restrictions,

tariffs, quotas, defaulted debts and impaired investment confidence."

Under such circumstances, what new mechanism could be set up to serve as a bridge for the movement of trained men, money and machinery to underdeveloped areas of the world? That was the question that Nelson had been trying to answer since the war ended. "Look at it this way," he liked to say. "The United States is a rich and powerful country in a poor world; like a rich family in a poor town. The poor don't want charity. But they would like to be helped to stand on their own feet. In the past, business went into foreign areas to get markets or materials. Maybe the foreign area benefited, but that was incidental. It wasn't planned that way.

"Today, our welfare and security depend on the welfare and security of other peoples. We've got to help them stand on their own feet. We have to form a kind of partnership in which they are given the incentive and the means to progress. And, as partners, we have to work together for mutual gain."

The New York business community failed to run a temperature over Nelson's ideas. Many hard-headed businessmen saw them only as a reflection of the New Deal "do good" theme. They were, in fact, an amalgamation of theories regarding international trade relations that had been kicking around for some time. There was just one big difference. Once they had adopted the idea, the Rockefellers did something about it.

Latin America needed capital and technological knowledge and equipment. It was also an area that had been considerably upset by the abrupt manner in which the United States government had dropped much of its good-will program immediately after the war. It seemed a logical field in which American private capital with a new approach and a broad vision might accomplish a great deal. As soon as IBEC had been established, economists were sent to Brazil and Venezuela to study the factors retarding economic development and to determine the major bottlenecks and recommend what, if anything, could be done about them that would benefit both the communities involved and the investors. The answers that came back were varied and the recommendations covered a wide range. In Venezuela, for example, with its rich oil fields and its high cost of living, the first problem obviously was that of providing food at a reasonable cost.

With this objective in mind, IBEC joined with the oil companies—which have invested about $12,800,000 in nonvoting preferred stock—to form the $14,000,000 Venezuela Basic Economy Corporation (VBEC) as a subsidiary. VBEC, in turn, set up a number of experimental business and farming enterprises in co-operation with the Venezuelan government and local capital. The government temporarily acquired some $4,500,000 worth of nonvoting preferred stock and IBEC retained control of the voting stock, which is mostly in Nelson's hands. In the end, a series of subsidiaries and sub-subsidiaries was created in what became a complicated corporate structure for a nonindustrialized country such as Venezuela.

One of these subsidiaries was called Productora Agropecuaria, C. A. (PACA), a company established with capital of $3,000,000 to produce food and introduce modern farming methods. And it was PACA that had brought Gingrass and his parade of agricultural machines to Bolívar's historic plantation. Gingrass had worked for years in Latin America and was experienced in tropical farming. He put in 110 acres of potatoes on former coffee land that had been denuded by his bulldozers. He used a mechanical combine planter to open furrows, seed in the potatoes, add fertilizer and cover the furrows in a single operation at the rate of eight and a half acres a day. Overhead sprinklers were installed to prevent loss of the crop during the dry period and automatic power-sprayers kept down the weeds and killed off the usual pests. On harvesting day, an automatic digger rooted out the potatoes, gathered them and deposited them free of dust for sacking. A herd of prize Duroc-Jersey hogs also was imported and within a few years provided almost a thousand animals a year for slaughter. The tenant farmers on the hacienda became field workers at good wages, and improvements were made in their homes.

In a similar fashion, Hacienda Bolívar, an 8,000-acre plantation near Santa Barbara, and Agua Blanca, a 20,000-acre estate south of Barquisimeto, were turned into modern livestock and grain farms. For these estates, PACA imported Jersey, Chabra, Zebu and Texas St. Gertrudis cattle, seeking to combine high meat and milk production with resistance to sun and heat. Experiments in crossbreeding also were made with imported Brahmans which flourish in hot climates. The best offspring were used to increase the PACA herds and the rest were sold to other cattlemen in the area. Careful inspection, spraying, vaccination, dehorning and horn-tipping were introduced, as were Argentine rollers, more efficient than hand labor, to keep pastures free of fast-growing weeds and brush. At Agua Blanca, 250 acres were cleared and plowed and 100 acres were reseeded with Brazilian Para and Yaragua grasses. Experiments also were started with sweet Sudan and Kudzu grasses. By these methods, PACA in a few years doubled the number of cattle that could be raised on a given acreage.

At Hacienda Bolívar, 400 acres were set out to plantains and, with improved fertilization and pruning, the yield rose to 8,000 bunches per month. A drainage system was installed in low areas and, by using fertilizer with a high nitrogen content, a heavier and better colored fruit was produced in a shorter period. Additional roads were built through the plantation so that none of the fruit had to be carried more than fifty yards to be loaded for shipment. PACA also set up a modern poultry farm at Dos Caminos, on the outskirts of Caracas, where 3,500 chicks were flown in each week and raised as broilers.

All of these enterprises were experiments, chiefly in the initial period of operation from 1948 to 1950, as IBEC experts were feeling their way toward a proper course. Technologically, they got off to a good start but that did not, of course, mean that they had found the answer to successful business operation. Countless difficulties arose and there were a good many blunders, some of them little tragedies and some almost comic. Early in the experimentation, some 2,000 acres on three plantations were devoted to growing corn. The natives knew the problems of growing corn in that area but the "silly Gringos" put a great deal of faith in standard American sprayers to kill weeds with chemicals. They doused the rapid noxious growths with enough poison to destroy a forest. The crop, however, was not harvested before the end of the rainy season and, in that period, the leaves folded over, letting the hot sun strike the moist rich earth. The jungle growth shot up like Jack's beanstalk. The first corn crop stood fourteen feet high, but higher still rose a jungle of giant mint which no chemical sprayer could discourage. It enveloped entire fields. The only way the corn could be harvested was to slash down the whole jungle and sort out the ears, which yielded twenty bushels to the acre.

Later, the experts built a special ten-row sprayer but it still failed to keep back entirely the late period growth of weeds. Still later, Robert P. Russell, VBEC's vice-president, was inspecting a fine stand of corn in Brazil where there was similar tropical weather. He was amazed that there was no weed problem. The answer was that, after the early chemical treatment of weeds, the Brazilians had planted a hardy voracious type of pig bean called *fiejao de porco* between the corn rows. It choked out the weeds and at the same time added nitrogen to the soil. The beans also were good feed for hogs. Knowing the complicated restrictions on taking new seeds into Venezuela and wishing to use them as soon as possible, Russell imported some beans, and successfully employed the same methods in the Venezuelan corn fields.

Meanwhile, despite the technological progress that had been made, the PACA experimentation was proving expensive and under the prevailing conditions it became obvious by 1950 that some of the enterprises were not going to pay their own way within a reasonable time. The entire setup was reconsidered as a result of this experience and some drastic changes were made. The Chirgua and Agua Blanca properties were liquidated by PACA, with the former being taken over personally by Nelson as an experimental farming project. The Agua Blanca property went to the government for further experimental use in developing modern techniques. The Dos Caminos poultry operation, a success from the technical standpoint, failed to make a profit and was abandoned. The big Hacienda Bolívar, which is mainly a livestock operation, continued as the principal PACA enterprise.

In connection with these ventures, it is important to note that important gains were made even in instances where a project might not be financially successful. One significant gain has been the introduction of better strains of livestock in Venezuela. It was also interesting that the yield and the profits from Nelson's farm at Chirgua were increased in 1952 through the use of herbicides, insecticides and other chemical controls. In one year's operation the corn yield was increased from thirty-three to fifty-four bushels per acre. In the same period, the net income per acre rose from minus to around $75 per acre. Cost of operation per acre also was reduced and was believed to be about the same as in the United States.

Agricultural improvement was not, of course, the entire

answer to the Venezuelan food problem and VBEC had simultaneously branched out into other fields that were regarded as essential to over-all success. One such field, the experts decided, was the fishing industry. Off the coast of Venezuela were famous fishing grounds that teemed with such fine varieties as red snappers, groupers and Spanish mackerel; yet fish—which should have been plentiful and cheap—were expensive and provided only a small part of the national diet. Only one fair-sized fishing company was in operation, most of the fishing was done by sailboats on a local basis for nearby markets, and there were no adequate refrigerating plants or means of safely distributing fish to interior markets. To the experts, it looked like a perfect opportunity to go into action.

With a capital of $1,500,000 a VBEC fishing subsidiary known as Pesquerías Caribe, C. A. (PCCA) was formed. It built a five-hundred-foot pier and an $800,000 refrigeration and ice-making plant at Puerto La Cruz, and machine shops on Margarita Island. Refrigerated boats were purchased to bring the Margarita catch to the mainland plant, and nine refrigerated trucks were added to carry it to Caracas and eleven other suburban markets. A fleet of small motorboats was purchased to be manned by hired fishermen under direction of North American experts and it was also arranged for individual fishermen to buy, on easy installments, iceboxes and motors for their sailboats. Fish would be bought from all fishermen at a fair price.

The setup looked good. With modernized boats the fishermen could go farther and bring back a bigger catch; they would be guaranteed a steadier income; there would be a constant supply of fish for the market at a reasonable price and, in all, a notable contribution would be made to solution of the food problem. Furthermore, the investors should realize a profit. The whole proposition was foolproof—on paper. In practice, it made a technological contribution to the local fishing industry and otherwise fell flat on its face.

It proved difficult to put a finger on the exact cause for failure. The introduction of high-cost, imported equipment and scientific methods into a low-geared agrarian economy, without adequate parallel industrial expansion, is always likely to create peculiar stresses and contradictions. It is out of line with the price structure, jolts the industry, violates established work habits and ideas, damages existing vested interests and upsets cultural patterns. The ingrained habits of the fishermen were one obstacle. Those on the well-equipped company boats brought in small catches and the sailboat fishermen at first refused to sell to PCCA. Later, the company cut down its own fleet and equipped independent fishermen with special gear and offered them and the sailboat fishermen a steady price. Then the fish came flopping in almost too fast. There were still plenty of problems but eventually, according to PCCA figures, boat owners were averaging $450 a month clear as compared to about $180 previously and crew members were making $150 as compared to a previous $60.

Other troubles, however, plagued the company, especially in regard to marketing and consumption. The most difficult of all was the task of trying to alter the eating habits of the people in order to create an adequate market. When the fish began reaching the market at the rate of about fifty tons a month the Caracas housewives shied away from them. They weren't accustomed to serving fish to their families, their mothers had served very little fish to *their* families and they just didn't buy. The company had been moving as rapidly as possible—perhaps a bit too rapidly—in the hope of making a quick showing, and, as one of the experts put it, "we discovered that you can't change the eating habits of a lifetime in a hurry."

In addition, the price at retail was not as low as had been

hoped. The fishermen were receiving a little more than thirty cents a pound for their catch. Fish at that time reached the Caracas market at a price that was not out of line with other prices but nevertheless it was a high price for the average Venezuelan, and fish remained a luxury item in a country where rice and beans are the basis of the worker's diet. PCCA could not get on a money-making basis and, after four years, its prospects for survival were uncertain.

In addition to efforts to increase and improve food production, VBEC established another subsidiary—Distribuidora de Alimentos, C. A., or CADA—to streamline the problem of food distribution. CADA was designed to purchase foodstuffs and bring them directly from farmer to consumer, to provide farmers with a wider market, to import foods not obtainable locally, to provide storage facilities and to stabilize consumer prices. It started out with a single warehouse at Valencia and a large part of CADA's goods originally came from the three VBEC plantations and the poultry farm, although it also contracted for the output of the only large canning factory, which was expanded with CADA funds. Other warehouses were opened but CADA did not prove a success—perhaps because of excessive overhead costs—although it did help bring down prices and thus made a contribution to the national economy.

The status of these various enterprises after several years of operation might have been highly discouraging for IBEC's sponsors had it not been for other and more successful ventures. A milk company which VBEC organized in partnership with Golden State, Ltd., of San Francisco, for distribution of cheese, ice cream and milk in sanitary paraffin containers, showed signs of success almost from the beginning. The milk company, known as INLACA, began with a run-down pasteurization plant in 1949 when output was between 8,000 and 12,000 quarts daily. This capacity was increased to 37,000 quarts daily and, in two years, the company put on the market 90,000 quarts of ice cream, 70,550 quarts of chocolate milk and 12,500 pounds of cottage cheese. The chocolate milk and cheese had never before been produced locally.

The company also put pasteurized milk on a daily delivery route to fifteen towns and villages and introduced sanitary paper containers. These advances proved popular and the company in 1952 had become one of the most successful and profitable of the IBEC-VBEC enterprises. A second company was organized in Maracaibo but, more important, the number of dairymen selling milk to the pasteurization plant had more than doubled and the prospect of a stable income had enabled them to purchase equipment for more efficient and hygienic operations. Moreover, the advances were being adopted by other Venezuelan milk concerns, some of which began extending distribution of pasteurized milk to small towns, suggesting that the IBEC efforts to set a pattern that would eventually affect the entire country were getting results.

The retail food stores also proved successful and have, significantly, been attracting more and more Venezuelan capital. Operated by subsidiaries of VBEC, they are the TODOS (Everything) store in Maracaibo, which serves about 2,000 customers a day, MINIMAX (Minimum Cost, Maximum Quality) supermarket at Caracas, about one hundred miles from the capital. The stores are modern, neon-lighted establishments that carry a complete line of foodstuffs and small household articles. They have the latest technical devices for handling food, air conditioning and parking space for customers. The majority of employees in the stores are Venezuelans who have been given thorough training. Thirty-five per cent of the food sold by the stores comes from Venezuelan sources, and in 1951 native frozen fish fillets from the PCCA fishing project were introduced in one-pound packages.

The success of these modern stores has been particularly interesting to the Rockefellers because they have been a test of how United States methods of food retailing can be adapted to a typically Venezuelan environment. A number of new markets have been opened by other interests and have been guided by the VBEC experience, while established stores have also been modernized and have taken up the new methods. And that, when all is said and done, was a basic purpose of the whole IBEC operation—setting a pattern that others could follow and one that, through modern methods, would enable the people to live better at lower prices.

Now all of these Rockefeller efforts to break up the food bottleneck in Venezuela were scientifically planned and backed by men who were willing to risk large sums of money to achieve a goal and to earn a modest return over a long period. They have, in 1952, brought significant signs of change, but obviously the going has not been smooth even in the most successful projects nor were these efforts always welcomed by the people they were intended to help. Many Venezuelans for many different reasons, including politics, have opposed various aspects of the Rockefeller program and, after a change of leadership, the Venezuelan government's stock participation in the VBEC operating enterprise was liquidated by a property exchange and reorganization, leaving VBEC entirely a private enterprise by 1952.

There also was some popular opposition to the VBEC operations in the early phases of work. The Chirgua Valley plantation once owned by Simón Bolívar, for example, became a point of controversy. Nobody had ever bothered to improve it or to turn it into a national shrine. Even so national pride was injured, just as Americans would be shocked if a big British corporation bought up George Washington's Mount Vernon plantation on the Potomac, moved in with bulldozers and bowled over ancient trees—some planted by the father of our country—in order to establish a mechanized truck and hog farm. Some politicians and the Communists quickly fanned this resentment and many untrue stories were spread that the ancient Bolívar chapel had been smashed down and that the tenants on the estate had been "cruelly" forced to give up their homes and their way of life.

"Complaints and lamentations mean nothing to these North Americans," one hostile newspaper said, "and the disinherited can only look on as the Yankee machines go by, breaking down their fields of grain, destroying their humble houses." And the nonpartisan Caracas newspaper *El Universal* asked why does Rockefeller "take over producing farm land instead of developing new plantations so greatly needed. . . . There is plenty of land never ruffled by the plow."

In addition to these editorial complaints, some fear and resentment arose among small farmers who could not hope to compete with the IBEC operations because they could not afford expensive farm machinery, fertilizers, selected seed and insecticides. The small farmers had the benefit of many new ideas and many modern methods that VBEC introduced but it was an indirect benefit and many of them feared they would eventually lose their land and have to become wage workers or tenant farmers. Many large plantation owners also were concerned because they did not have sufficient capital to modernize their operations and might be pushed to the wall by a triple squeeze of improved wages for workers, more efficient production and superior products. And the fact that the PACA and VBEC personnel generously assisted both large and small farmers, that information, better seeds, artificial insemination, efficient pasture care and "hospital pastures" for ailing stock were provided (sometimes for a modest fee) could not entirely dissipate these fears. ("Hospital pastures!" snorted one hostile politician. "Too few persons in Venezuela get any medical care at all and fewer still have access to a hospital!")

It soon became evident that no matter how laudable IBEC's intentions or how valuable its long-range contributions, many persons were going to be disturbed and resentful or damaged. It also was evident that the program would be the target of criticism in especially heavy doses because its methods were new and because it was run by foreigners. The fact that the foreigners were mainly Rockefellers could only open the way for widespread suspicion that the whole thing was an oil company plot to get some kind of advantage out of Venezuela.

The antigovernment weekly *U. R. D.* summed this feeling up in a cartoon of two figures labeled "Roke" for Rockefeller and "Romu" for President Rómulo Betancourt, standing in swimming trunks under a shower of oil spurting from a pipeline. But past abuses and fears of Yankee imperialism prompted critical questions from many other newspapers, too, in connection with charges that the real purpose of the program was to provide oil workers with cheaper food so that the companies would not have to shell out dollar exchange for expensive imports and could keep wages down. "Rockefeller extends another of his tentacles," said the magazine *Así Es*. "He will have access to usable land not because he is a producer without lands but a capitalist with gall; he will . . . have access to markets because Rockefeller is not Rockefeller—he is a powerful expansionist state."

The VBEC milk company operations caused trouble with small milk operators who felt they were being squeezed. There were complaints at one time in the newspapers about the mixing of milk powder with "Orinoco River water and fresh milk," despite the fact that this "reconstituted milk" had a high nutritional value and its use was a stopgap until local production could be increased. Charges were made that the VBEC subsidiary was trying to get a monopoly in the Valencia region and that large quantities of milk had been dumped—this was not true—to keep the price up. There also was resentment that the price of milk rose to about thirty-two cents a liter, a high rate for the average Venezuelan, at a time when the milk company was showing a good profit.

In the beginning, VBEC retail stores also came in for serious attack on charges that they tend to control farmer output, to eliminate Venezuelan wholesalers and damage other retailers if the goal of lower prices is to be achieved. Small farmers were afraid they might lose their independent market outlets and large plantation owners were disturbed by the idea that they might be chained to one large retail outlet. These fears were voiced by the leading technical business journal *Venezuela Económica*. Protest meetings were held by the National Merchants-Employers' Syndicate and the National Merchants' Union. The President of the wholesale merchants' organization contended that even if VBEC sold more cheaply it would only bring "misery to thousands of persons directly or indirectly dependent upon the nation's business" and that there was no guarantee that, once competition had been stifled, the low prices would be continued.

VBEC aims "to monopolize food and its distribution in all Venezuela . . . to become dictator of the market," said *El Nacional*, the largest daily. "Why," asked *El Universal*, "does he [Rockefeller] come down here to destroy the small corner grocery?" *U. R. D.* published a cartoon showing a fat "Rockefeller" storekeeper under fancy neon lights, while across the street a scrawny Venezuelan storekeeper tacked up a sign on his shabby store saying: "Forced to close." Local storekeepers charged that since CADA had government money it was relieved of many taxes that they must pay and that the MINIMAX stores were free from the high local taxes which others must bear.

They contended that CADA was charged only 7% duty on imported foodstuffs whereas some merchants pay up to 100%. Newspapers reported that VBEC could get foreign exchange 26% cheaper than most Venezuelan importers and that it bought goods abroad more cheaply because its imports were either from oil company commissaries or from a VBEC buying subsidiary in New Orleans which was able to make large savings by bulk purchases.

All of this would suggest that everybody in Venezuela was ready to throw out all VBEC operations, and the Rockefellers too, but that would be far from the truth. An analysis of the Caracas press on the basis of circulation over a four-year period, for example, showed that about 42% of comment was neutral (that is, sometimes critical and sometimes friendly) ; that 21% was pro-Rockefeller and 37% was consistently hostile and often bitter. This survey did not concern the AIA, and all of the newspapers, including those hostile to VBEC, regularly featured AIA news releases on such subjects as nutrition and home care.

VBEC had strong support from a solid section of the press. *El Gráfico*, a leading Caracas newspaper, summed up this attitude by saying: "The investments made by VBEC in the production of food in Venezuela should be accepted and backed by those interested in improving the system of living in our country." This attitude has been strengthened and criticism has been on the decline as the operations and intentions of the Rockefellers become better known. IBEC wants local capital. The TODOS store, for example, had about half Venezuelan capital by 1952. IBEC emphasizes the hiring and training of local employees in all levels of work, and by 1952 VBEC personnel was Venezuelan with the exception of some technicians. It makes the welfare of the people affected by its enterprises as important as profits. And, in the original arrangement, it agreed to pull out of the enterprises completely as soon as local companies were going concerns and could be disposed of to local capital. A ten-year period was set originally for development or abandonment of the projects, after which all stock would be offered to local investors, but this arrangement was disrupted and left up in the air in 1951 by the withdrawal, as noted above, of government participation in VBEC. The principle, however, remains unchanged in the minds of the Rockefellers, despite the fact that experience has shown some of their high hopes of 1947 were unrealistic.

When and whether local capital can take over, only the future can tell, but there is a good example of the Rockefeller attitude in the history of the Avila Hotel. In 1939, Nelson was riding through the suburbs of Caracas with the President of Venezuela, who remarked on the need of the city for a modern hotel. The Rockefeller brothers promptly took up the idea as one of their first enterprises in South America. In addition to the Rockefellers, the oil companies, various business firms and about 300 individual Venezuelans invested in the project and Wallace Harrison designed the building. The gleaming, modern hotel was opened in 1942 and became one of the best known on the continent. It has 114 rooms, a fourteen-room apartment house, a ten-room residence and a seven-room annex for staff quarters.

The Avila was highly profitable from the beginning and was an excellent investment in 1951, when the Rockefellers carried out their plan of making the stock available to local capital once they had demonstrated that the enterprise could be successful. By the end of 1951, they had sold the controlling stock to Venezuelan and other investors for about $800,000.

The first five years of IBEC operations in Venezuela are not easy to measure in terms of success and failure. It appears certain now that some enterprises were started on too large a scale and some were pushed too rapidly or without sufficient investigation and preparation. Overall, VBEC assets in 1952 were estimated at around $7,000,000—which meant a loss of about half of the $14,000,000 total investment. But it must be remembered that VBEC began as a pioneering effort in international development, introducing new ideas and feeling its way into unexplored fields. It will eventually be judged with that in mind rather than on the basis of profits or losses in 1952. There were certain to be disappointments such as the farming projects that successfully applied new methods of production but couldn't make a profit, or the fishing enterprise that couldn't quite make the grade. Yet even these disappointing efforts have been important in demonstrating what not to do in future ventures and they have also contributed something that will not be entirely lost. An eastern fishing port has been developed, for example, native fish products have been introduced in the Venezuelan market and a contribution has been made toward stabilizing the supply and price of fish.

On the credit side of the books there were gains and good future prospects in connection with the financial success of the supermarkets and milk companies. Seen at longer range, the over-all results were neither sensationally good nor sensationally bad in terms of new business ventures. But in the wider and more important field of technological progress and in the effort to establish a mechanism for co-operation in the advancement of underdeveloped areas, VBEC enterprises have been highly significant as guideposts to new forms of partnership enterprise on an international scale.

❊ XVII ❊

A LMOST EVERYONE THINKS OF BRAZIL AS THE WORLD'S
greatest coffee-producing country as, indeed, it is. But
it is not so well known that Brazil is the fourth corn-producing
country of the world despite the fact that its yield per acre
is low and much of its crop is lost each year because of improper
handling, uncontrolled pests and rodents and inadequate storage and shipping facilities.

"Coffee has long been king in Brazil," Berent Friele once
remarked. "But corn is grown more widely in every part of the
country except the Amazon basin. As food, as feed and in
industry, corn is in great demand. Coffee and corn are the twin
pillars of Brazil's agricultural strength, coffee chiefly for export and corn mainly for domestic consumption. Improvement
of corn is one of the productive ways of helping the Brazilian
farmer help himself through new technology."

The role of corn in the Brazilian economy was very much in
the minds of the Rockefellers when IBEC undertook operations
in that vast land. There was a difference between IBEC activities in Brazil and Venezuela. In the latter country, it was hoped
that an impact could be made on the economy generally. But
Brazil was so large that limited and specialized operations were
necessary, although it was intended that they establish a
formula for improvements that in time would affect the whole
country. In other words, IBEC in Brazil tended to assume a
special service character instead of a direct and sizable venture

in production of food. Furthermore, it operated through direct subsidiaries for which additional capital was secured locally from Brazilian sources as well as from United States concerns that participated in the IBEC program. But no Brazilian government capital was subscribed.

One of the first considerations of IBEC in Brazil was corn production. "Simply by a shift to hybrid corn there would soon be an enormous lift to the entire national economy," in the opinion of John B. Griffing, who had been director of the Agricultural School in Minas Gerais state and who became technical director of IBEC activities in this direction. To start the enterprise, capital of $163,000 was provided for a hybrid seed company known as Sementes Agroceres, S.A., or SASA, which IBEC established in 1947.

Much of the ground work for hybrid corn production already had been done. The government had carried on experiments at the Instituto Agronomico of São Paulo and was then marketing considerable quantities of seed. Other state and federal agencies also were developing new strains, but the most notable private achievement had been made by Dr. Antonio Secundino de São José, a Brazilian trained in the United States. After about ten years' experimentation with more than a thousand varieties of Brazilian, Texan and Oriental corn, he had developed two pure strains. One was from hard Brazilian corn and the other from a cross of Texas and Brazilian soft corn. These two strains when recrossed produced a remarkably strong and prolific hybrid, resistant to disease, wind and drought.

When SASA entered the field, Secundino already had formed his own company, Agroceres, Ltda., and turned out about twelve and a half tons of commercial seed. But he and his co-worker, Dr. Gladstone Almeida Drummond, collaborated with SASA so that additional production could be started at once. SASA bought an 867-acre fazenda in Jacarezinho, Paraná state, which was an extraordinarily fertile region where the soil is known as "terra roxa" or "purple land."

A few tons of hybrid seed corn were harvested the first year. The following year there was a severe drought that destroyed much of the Brazilian corn crop. But the farmers who had planted the SASA seed were able to save their crops and, in fact, got a larger than ordinary yield. "Bad conditions," one technician explained, "seem to bring out the fighting spirit of the hybrid. A scorching dry period gives it great advantage over the usual kinds. A high wind often levels ordinary corn, but the hybrid has vigorous prop roots and it proudly holds firm against a gale."

The drought so dramatically demonstrated the superiority of the hybrid that, for a while, SASA could not keep up with the demand from farmers, although its 1950 crop was up to about 1,250 tons or enough to plant some 250,000 acres—about 10% of all cultivated corn land in Paraná and São Paulo states. Secundino's company also expanded, increasing output to about 1,500 tons and, with the government efforts and the output of smaller firms, the total Brazilian hybrid corn production increased in 1950 to about 20,000 tons or enough to increase the country's corn yield by about a million tons.

By this time, however, production of seed corn had caught up with the demand and exceeded it. Although SASA had shown profits of more than 25% in the first few years, it was in the red in 1951 because of expansion costs and overproduction although showing good financial promise for the future. At this time, the company was merged with Secundino's Agroceres, Ltda., giving SASA two more producing units at Ubá and Patos de Minas in the state of Minas Gerais. The combined company now operates four units and, with additional funds from IBEC, the total capital has been raised to about

$375,000, part of which is held by the Brazilian specialists working in the concern.

Most of the seed corn is raised by farmers near the units working under company supervision and is turned over to SASA for processing. A comprehensive program has been undertaken since the merger to educate farmers to wider use of hybrid seed. Motion pictures showing the planting and harvesting of seed corn on SASA farms were produced for exhibition at farmers' meetings and thousands of farmers received brightly colored pamphlets explaining in simple language and pictures how farm income could be increased by planting hybrid seed. The upward trend in sales of hybrid seed has continued and in 1951 SASA's producing centers disposed of considerably more seed than did the four producing units in the previous year. The success of efforts to improve the country's corn crop also was reflected in the increased hybrid output by government agencies and by other private producers who came into the field in the last few years.

Meantime, IBEC was giving attention to the handling of the corn crop. In the past much of Brazil's corn has been destroyed by rats, weevils, and worms which robbed the grower of a large part of his crop. Or it was destroyed by the weather or by being stored in leaky sheds and barns or by rotting on railroad sidings. It was customary for corn to reach the railroads at the same time the coffee crop was being moved, and custom as well as the power of the coffee growers, who operate on a large scale, had always given that product the right of way and often left the corn to spoil.

To help correct this situation, IBEC went into the bulk grain handling business with Cargill, Inc., a Minneapolis grain company with long experience. Almost a million dollars capital was provided and two elevators to store corn, seed, oil and other products were built in São Paulo and Paraná, the largest corn-producing states. The elevators have a capacity of 150,000 bushels. The new company also provided direct service to farmers by going into the fields to pick up the corn, shell it, treat it against weevils and store it on a bulk basis.

In the past, Brazilian farmers had always shipped their corn in sacks and some of them were suspicious of the new bulk system, which was the common practice in the United States. The farmers had always been able to count their sacks of corn and knew how much each one should bring but when it was purchased in bulk, by the pound or bushel, it was not always easy to convince them that they were not being cheated. One farmer was given a kilo-weight receipt for his crop but refused to accept it.

"Give me a receipt for the number of sacks," he insisted.

The clerk figured out how many sacks of corn he would have had if he had not sold by bulk and made out the receipt for the number of sacks.

"Now," said the farmer as he took the receipt, "let me count the sacks so I'll be sure you're right."

These were small problems, however, and the elevator program went along rapidly. There were some skeptics who expressed fears about foreign monopoly in a vital food field and there were occasions when the manager of the big 3,000-ton elevator in São Paulo state found Communist denunciations painted on the building when he arrived for work in the morning. But generally the program was accepted, and in October of 1951 the company passed an important milestone in the farm-to-market flow of commodities in Brazil. Then, for the first time, shelled corn was moved in bulk from the São Paulo grain elevator in twenty-nine boxcars to the hold of a ship in the port of Santos. That such a practice had never been tried before suggests the wide open possibilities for future improvement in speeding commodities from farm to market, and in

1952 the company was conducting a study of how further warehouse space could be provided to facilitate handling of the corn crop. In general, the Cargill-IBEC operation has been successful and profitable since it was started in 1948.

A natural side industry of corn growing is hog raising. In 1947 a big gap was torn in Brazilian livestock statistics by a cholera epidemic that wiped out half the hogs in the country. IBEC helped to meet this disaster by setting up several 300-acre experimental farms to improve and modernize methods of raising hogs and to introduce hardier animals. A new, inoculated breed was imported, and raised scientifically by a $326,000 company under management of S. A. Debnam, an experienced Texas hog raiser. Part of the money for the company was subscribed by resident American meat-packing subsidiaries and, by 1950, some 3,200 hogs were being handled.

Although the hog company got off to a good start, it had some unfortunate experiences, especially during the year of severe drought when the price of feed skyrocketed. This and other factors made it difficult for the enterprise to show a profit, and in 1951 it was liquidated. The enterprise also had been harassed by unfounded charges that the Rockefellers were seeking to destroy local meat-processing operations and give United States concerns a monopoly.

"Who," snorted one left-wing opposition newspaper, "is silly enough to believe for one minute that the great Rockefeller is interested in raising pigs? This whole farm business of his doesn't amount to a hill of beans: It is just a scheme to get hold of future oil lands. Note that . . . he and the Brazilian wife of his chief assistant in Brazil (Mrs. Friele) have been buying up great tracts in Mato Grosso, Paraná and other states where the prospects for oil are good."

Brazil for years had been engaged in sharp controversy over whether foreign capital should be permitted to engage in the oil business, and the percentage of minority participation to be allowed foreign countries in any given company. When the Rockefeller operations through IBEC began it was only to be expected that the name would be drawn into the debate. "Mr. Rockefeller," said *Diario Popular*, "is merely waiting for the new oil laws when he will revert to the principal field." "Ah, how well he can figure out things!" lamented *Diretrizes*, while *O Globo* spoke of "preparation for the petroleum kill."

To such attacks, *Diario de São Paulo* replied that the work was bound "to provoke . . . indigenous nationalism, that mongrel stupidity that confounds national society with closed frontiers and forbids the entry into the country of valuable contributions such as those brought by the American millionaire and businessman. They [the contributions] will bring about a profound transformation in Brazil." And *A Revista do Fazendéiros*, an organ of large landowners, called Nelson "a man who can show us the advantages of rationalizing agricultural activities. His are the fundamental beliefs of Christian democracy."

More important than the criticisms or praise, in Nelson's mind, was the obvious fact that many Brazilian farmers were getting new and modern ideas about how to improve operations and were enthusiastically putting into practice some of the methods that were demonstrated on the IBEC farms.

Coffee is still the most important export crop and IBEC Research Institute has done some experimental work in that field, seeking to introduce modern methods. Experimental trees were planted on the hybrid seed corn plantation and a helicopter-spraying company, called HELICO, was established to attack the dread broca pest that has infected some 250,000,000 trees in Brazil and driven coffee entirely out of some areas.

The insecticide was shot out of the helicopters and driven downward by the force of the whirling blades. In one year,

5,000,000 trees were sprayed and contracts were made to spray 6,000,000 the following year, but drought stopped the spread of the disease and only about 4,000,000 were sprayed. The effort was well received, although one newspaper criticized the fact that it was hit-and-miss spraying, covering only those plantations whose owners could afford it instead of being an over-all campaign to control the disease. For this it blamed, not IBEC, but the government. The HELICO company did not turn out well financially, however, because the machines could be used only five months of the year, although there were crews to be paid and overhead to be carried for the other seven months. Some slack was taken up by other small spraying contracts but eventually it was decided to abandon the enterprise.

Improvement of corn and coffee growing is only a part of the problem of making Brazilian agriculture more productive. "The country," Friele points out, "also needs machinery, fertilizers and better livestock if the living standards are to be raised." Industry, on which Brazil pins fantastic hopes, has been expanding much faster than farming or transportation and as a result food costs have gone up rapidly in large and growing industrial cities. "If Brazil is to realize her industrial aspirations," Friele adds, "she must find means to increase the productivity of workers, releasing workers from the land and expanding per unit farm output to feed the increasing population in the cities. That can be done in part through mechanization, supplemented by other advances in farm technique."

There were only 4,000 tractors in all Brazil in 1947 as compared to some 4,000,000 in the United States. When this fact was pointed out publicly by the IBEC experts, one newspaper angrily proposed that they be thrown out of the country immediately for being so unpatriotic and ungentlemanly as to mention such a discrepancy. But Nelson felt that IBEC could play an important role in helping to solve this problem. His idea was not to try to catch up with the United States at once in the number of tractors, but to form a service company that would have the latest in mechanized equipment and would be available for contracts to clear land and cultivate and plant and perform other tasks that could be done more efficiently with modern machines. He set up the Empresa de Mecanização Agrícola, S.A., a service company that was fondly called EMA. Capital of $635,000 was provided and, to get started, $375,000 worth of new farm machinery was imported from the United States. The company formed three original units for service in the states of Paraná and São Paulo.

Nelson went to Jacarezinho in southern Brazil in 1948 for the inauguration of EMA. He gathered with a crowd of farmers, some of whom had come one hundred miles, and watched a big tractor jerk a huge stump out of the ground in five minutes. "That," said a wizened old Brazilian standing next to him, "would have taken me five weeks of hard work."

Again, there were times when the "silly Gringos" made some errors. In October, which was the dry season, EMA contracted to destump a large tract of land the following January. The land was surveyed on horseback in October, plans were completed and the fee arranged. But when the big tractors clattered around to do the job in January they couldn't even find the tract of land. The wet season and the hot sun had produced a tremendous jungle growth so dense that every square foot had to be combed merely to find the stumps. EMA made no profit on that job.

But, despite such setbacks, it was obvious almost from the start that EMA was a move in the right direction, and by 1952 it was one of the most successful IBEC projects. Almost a million dollars' worth of farm machinery was imported in the first four years. Two more units had been formed—making five in all—and others were being formed or were contemplated. Work was steadily increasing. In 1951, a total of 18,540 acres were destumped as compared to 8,500 acres in 1950; 15,000 acres were ploughed and 7,590 were harrowed. The company worked 63,000 tractor hours, including thousands of acres of planting and miles of terracing.

Such work not only is profitable to the company but has started a highly important change in Brazilian farm economy. A powerful piece of equipment known as a TD-18, with two tractor drivers, can destump and clear ten acres of rugged terrain in a day—a task that was almost impossible for farmers who once depended upon the *enxada* or oversized hoe for clearing and tilling. Near the town of Jacarezinho, in the state of Paraná, for example, a farmer named Mario Zacarelli hired EMA to clear one hundred acres. For a small farmer it was an expensive operation, but the crop he grew the next year not only paid his running expenses but paid for the cost of clearing the land. That year Zacarelli was offered twice as much for his hundred acres as he had paid for them. In the Rio Pardo valley, EMA experts used a tractor with a bulldozer blade to dam a small tributary, cut a canal that would deliver water to fields along the river bottom and throw up terraces that would aid in irrigation. The owner grew potatoes on the irrigated land and was able to pay EMA's bill with the income from three acres of his vastly improved farm.

The enthusiasm of Brazilian farmers for EMA's heavy equipment has been steadily increasing, even in areas where light tractors have been used for years. At the farm community of Lins, in western São Paulo state, many farmers were accustomed to mechanized equipment but they were not able to do destumping and other rugged clearing jobs. EMA set up a special unit in the community and, in two months, destumped and cleared about 950 acres, ploughed 350 acres, harrowed 500 acres and planted 175 acres. The value of the land was almost doubled as a result of the permanent improvements made.

In three years' operation EMA covered some 125,000 acres in the states of São Paulo and Paraná, clearing fertile farm land, planting, cultivating, building roads and even constructing small airstrips for farmers. This work has done a great deal to overcome the labor shortage in Brazilian farm areas and has made it possible to increase production greatly. But most important of all, EMA is contributing significantly to Brazil's solution of the long-range farm production problem. All of the farm equipment operators are Brazilians, most of them between eighteen and twenty years old, and the top man is João Toledo, a husky young graduate of the São Paulo State Practical Schools of Agriculture at Piraçunnunga and Jabotica- bal. He succeeded the late Carl Schneider who had been in charge of EMA when it was started.

The manner in which the IBEC experts trained young Brazil- ians for the work was a surprise to local officials. One news- paper editor, invited to inspect the EMA operations, watched enthusiastically as a TD-18 operator cleared a small patch of wooded land. "Ah!" he exclaimed, "you American mechanics can achieve wonderful things." His hosts promptly escorted him over to the roaring, panting TD-18 and introduced him to its operator—Eliseo Alves de Lima, a recent graduate of the Jaboticabal Practical School. The editor went back to his office and wrote an editorial about Brazil's new generation of mechanized farmers.

As a part of its over-all program, IBEC has inaugurated or taken part in a considerable number of other enterprises in Brazil and elsewhere in Latin America in an effort to stimulate technological progress in line with President Truman's Point Four program. These endeavors reach into widely divergent fields and are financed in various ways. Some are short-term or stopgap efforts but others are designed as permanent contributions of an expanding economy.

The IBEC Research Institute, for instance, is for the improvement of tropical and semi-tropical agriculture and is a nonprofit organization, operating in Brazil and Venezuela. The Institute seeks to establish methods for improving production of basic food crops, to make these discoveries known to farmers and to encourage their application in a practical manner. An important experimental program in seedbed preparation was undertaken in Venezuela because the soil there was typical of the excessively wet and dry soils of most of the tropics. Methods were worked out for reducing the cost of preparing seedbeds and controlling weeds. In addition several promising methods of chemical weed control were tried out and may lead to general progress in that direction. IRI also is experimenting with mechanical weeding and mechanized compost production and handling in an effort to reduce labor requirements in the Brazilian coffee industry.

The IBEC Technical Services Corporation, which illustrates how private business can supplement the Point Four idea, dispenses technical skill of all kinds on a fee basis, sending specialists and engineers almost anywhere to make surveys and recommendations for development projects. For example, the growth of industry in the thriving city of São Paulo created many problems in the last few years. Transportation was too slow. Office buildings were crowding the center of the city. There was a shortage of parks and playgrounds, and public utilities were lagging behind the population growth. IBEC Tech made a contract with the city to draw up a plan for future improvement and it brought in a group of experts, including Robert Moses who had wide experience in such work in New York. The experts made a study of São Paulo and a comprehensive report that recommended many changes and improvements from the development of a network of arterial highways to the straightening of the Tiete River. Methods of financing the program of public improvements also were included in the report. IBEC Tech has done a number of similar jobs in scattered parts of the Western Hemisphere, including traffic and water improvements in Venezuela; power and land development in Brazil; economic development in Cuba and a survey of ways to increase production and trade in Newfoundland.

In other projects, IBEC has worked as a minority participant in developing new enterprises, particularly in Brazil. A drop-forging project financed largely by Brazilian capital was an example of such efforts as was an effort in 1950 to alleviate a paper shortage for Brazilian newspapers. In the latter instance, IBEC was the intermediary in getting newsprint by arranging for the purchase of the Gould Paper Company of Lyons Falls, New York, by a Brazilian-IBEC group. Then IBEC took over the managerial responsibilities of the company and the newsprint went to Brazil. In 1950, IBEC also got into manufacturing in Brazil by minority participation in the Regencia Company in São Paulo to manufacture medium-priced clothes and both Brazilian and American money was put into the enterprise. Again it participated in a Brazilian-French project for production of low-cost fertilizer.

Probably the most important effort along this line in 1952 was the inauguration by IBEC of a new plan to marshal capital that would help speed Brazilian economic progress on a broad scale. To do this, IBEC and the Chase Bank of New York joined with a group of Brazilian banks to organize a financing company along the lines of modern investment banking. The joint enterprise is known as the Inter-American Finance and Investment Corporation, with the long-range objectives of financing increased production in Brazil, assisting in development of a Brazilian capital market and establishing an investment pattern that can be followed in other countries in similar stages of development. The company has an authorized capital of about $2,700,000, of which the Chase Bank and IBEC hold 51 per cent.

"Expanding Brazilian economy needs vast amounts of capital for roads, electric power, heavy industry, mineral and agricultural development, education and other public facilities," sponsors of the enterprise said. "With a population of 50,000,-000, increasing at the rate of a million a year, and with rich natural resources, Brazil has a development potential comparable in many respects with that of the United States in about 1880." Basically, the sponsors felt that there was a great need for new facilities for distributing securities in the rapidly expanding Brazilian economy and that such a security market was essential to continuation of rapid growth in the manufacturing, steel and similar industries.

All in all, IBEC's enterprises in Brazil proved more successful financially in the first four or five years of operation than they did in Venezuela. (It should be mentioned that IBEC also made an unsuccessful venture into mechanized farm services in Ecuador, particularly in an effort to extend the rice cultivation program. It was a smaller operation in which the long rainy season interfered with the work and it was later liquidated by sale of the equipment to the government.) In the period up to 1952, about $30,000,000 went into the various business enterprises and nonprofit activities in which the Rockefellers were interested in Venezuela and Brazil, including Rockefeller money, local capital, government funds and funds from the oil companies and others. Out of these various projects came some profits and some losses—and a great deal of valuable experience.

Any pioneering enterprise must be flexible and in the case of the Rockefeller activities in Latin America there have been many changes, many variations of method and many revisions of plans on the basis of experience in the field. Projects that showed no hope of future profit have been dropped, while some that were unexpectedly profitable have been expanded and will be pushed in the future. By 1952, the record showed that IBEC had paid-in capital of some $12,455,000 and that the total investment in companies set up by it was around $22,000,000. The actual profit and loss record of the various IBEC enterprises was not particularly significant at this point in their development because some projects were just getting on their feet and had good future prospects. For the record, however, in 1952 three Venezuelan enterprises (the milk companies and the supermarkets) were profitable and three others (CADA, the farming company and the fish company) were either liquidated or losing money. In Brazil, the mechanized farming operation and the grain-handling enterprise were successful, the seed-corn company was momentarily in the red but with good prospects and the hog-raising project as well as the helicopter-dusting experiment was abandoned.

It was too early in 1952 to try to predict the future for IBEC, but because of the wide variety of its activities the outlook could be considered as better than indicated by the specific financial rating of its major projects in Brazil and Venezuela. In general, the Rockefellers considered over-all progress as encouraging, if not extraordinary. They are not unmindful of the fact that they set out to establish new patterns that would aid in raising living standards; that they would like to show how private capital can make a vital contribution to international co-operation in a free world.

In 1950-51, Nelson served as chairman of the International Development Advisory Board which, at President Truman's request, made extensive recommendations for carrying out the Point Four program of extending technological aid to underdeveloped areas throughout the world. The Board expressed the belief that strengthening of the economies of the under-developed regions and an improvement of their living levels must be a vital part of the United States' own defense mobilization.

"Some people would say that in the present world emergency we cannot afford to concern ourselves with these problems," Nelson remarked later. "They would say that the only thing that counts is military strength. But I say that careful consideration of these problems was never more important. In the face of the threat of Russian imperialism the underprivileged of the free world must have tangible and continuing evidence of our spiritual and moral dedication to this cause."

In an era when American industry was becoming increasingly dependent upon imports, the Rockefellers have devoted a tremendous amount of time, energy and money to a search for an effective mechanism whereby the United States can provide effective leadership of a co-operative program for economic and social development in the free world and thereby safeguard our own future security and well-being. Regardless of eventual success or failure, IBEC and AIA constitute one of the most significant experiments in the postwar world, an experiment in which all of the people of the Americas and a billion others around the world have a tremendous stake.

❈ XVIII ❈

AT CERTAIN INTERVALS MEMBERS OF THE BOARD OF THE
Rockefeller Brothers' Fund, of which John is president,
give formal approval to various charitable expenditures in
which all of the brothers are interested such as the Red Cross or
the Young Men's Christian Association. These meetings are
normally routine because the experts have drawn up a list of
contributions after prior discussion, but sometimes a question
arises to lift the session out of the ordinary, as was the case
when a young associate of the Rockefellers happened to be
present.

"I was there for some technical reason or other," he said
later, "and I guess I was a little surprised by the routine manner
in which various large donations were approved. Somebody
would read one item on the list. Maybe it was $10,000 to some
well-established organization in the philanthropic field. None
of the brothers paid much attention. They just said okay—
$10,000 to that one. It was the same with the others. Maybe
$20,000 here or $30,000 there. Okay. No questions. Just okay.

"They finally worked through the list without any questions
or objections and everybody seemed happy to get it over with
so they could go on about their business. But then one of the
office associates said that he wanted to mention something
before the meeting broke up. He said plans had been made to
switch some of the furniture around in the offices and he assumed it was all right with everybody. Suddenly all five of the

Rockefellers woke up! They wanted to know the details and some of them didn't like the idea at all. The furniture was okay. Why move it? Well, let's give it a little thought, anyway. Here they had been handing out thousands without blinking but when it came to moving the furniture around—well, there was hell to pay before it was settled!"

The associate's account of the Rockefellers' attitude toward philanthropic gifts was amusing but misleading, because a great deal of work and effort had gone into the preparation of the list prior to the meeting. Planning is behind all such family affairs.

The development of the South American enterprises represented a remarkable but perfectly normal advance in Rockefeller philanthropic methods over a stretch of three generations. In the beginning, it did not, of course, involve more than a small fraction of almost a billion dollars that the family has put into philanthropic enterprises. But it was aimed at a highly significant goal and it demonstrated a conviction of the third generation that not merely the giving of money but direct and energetic personal participation is essential to success in such enterprises.

"Welfare is everybody's job," Winthrop once remarked. "It is not enough to contribute money. People must make the gift of themselves, of their own time, their creative talent and spiritual strength."

Throughout their lives, the Rockefeller brothers have set an unusual record in giving time, talent and strength as well as money to a wide range of civic affairs. Not a few of these affairs, it is interesting to note, are those in which their father or their grandfather or both were also interested. This is illustrated, for example, by the restoration and reconstruction of Williamsburg as it was in the days when it was the capital of the colony of Virginia, a labor of love started by Mr. Rockefeller, Jr., and later carried on by John D., 3rd, and Winthrop

Into the work went the intimate supervision, the care and thought as well as deep affection of Mr. Rockefeller, who has contributed $44,500,000 to the reconstruction.

When the work began, it was obvious that only part of Williamsburg could be "restored" as it was in colonial days. Too much had been destroyed or allowed to crumble away and had to be reconstructed. The first work then was patient, tedious historical research in an effort to establish with infinite exactitude the architectural specifications of the original buildings. No effort was spared, and no expense. The search of records extended to England and other foreign lands. At times it seemed hopeless, but determination and occasional strokes of luck brought impressive results at last and architects and workmen began the painstaking task of reconstructing the original government buildings, the gracious homes and business houses. The project was officially opened to the public in 1934 when President Roosevelt described its main public way—Duke of Gloucester Street—as "the most historic avenue in all America." But the work was by no means completed. The war forced a suspension of work but in December of 1948 an additional program was started to reconstruct and restore a hundred additional buildings and to expand facilities to handle the thousands of visitors that throng the town throughout the year.

"The job is just getting started," John explained soon afterward. "The building program is well along, but the educational and interpretive program is only beginning."

In John's view, Williamsburg is not just a place of beauty and tourist interest, but a stage for a deeper spiritual presentation of the inspiring story of early democracy in America. "We are," he said, "thinking increasingly of the broader significance of this community as a reflection of the character and faith of the people of colonial America by whom it was built. Williamsburg was a vital force in the life and thought of eighteenth-century

America. We hope and intend that it shall be a living force in the twentieth century."

As chairman of the board of Colonial Williamsburg, John has emphasized the importance of getting the story to all parts of America. Something like a quarter of a million persons visit the reconstructed capital each year but that is only a fraction of the number who hear the story. Other hundreds of thousands of persons—800,000 school children alone in 1949—see a colorful motion picture of Williamsburg each year. Other millions are reached by a campaign of lectures, radio and television programs and photographs in a program that is expanded almost every year.

Much of the appeal of Williamsburg is made to school children, reflecting, perhaps, John's long-standing interest in the education and the affairs of young people. He was at one time head of a national committee that was instrumental in bringing about important reforms in treatment of juvenile offenders against the law and, after the war, he took a special interest in the development of American Youth Hostels, Inc., of which he was president until 1951. The Youth Hostels movement, first organized in Germany to promote international understanding and good will, later spread to twenty-two countries but only after the war did it acquire a substantial membership in the United States. The organization encourages and assists young people to make hiking and cycling tours that will make them better acquainted with their own and other countries.

In 1952, John made a grant of $250,000 to Princeton University in order to establish a program of awards for outstanding public service by civilians in any branch of the federal government. The Woodrow Wilson School of Public and International Affairs of Princeton was authorized to administer the five-year program under which grants will enable the recipients to spend from six to twelve months in residence at any college or university, or in some comparable activity such as educational travel. The awards will not carry a fixed amount of money but will be enough to enable the recipients to detach themselves from active duty for an agreed period at no financial sacrifice. Government officials will nominate candidates for the awards.

John's greatest postwar interest, however, has been in the Far East, particularly Japan, and in 1952 he became president of Japan Society, Inc., which has the purpose of helping to bring the people of the United States and of Japan closer together in their appreciation and understanding of each other and each other's way of life.

"It is our hope that a vigorous Japan Society can be of real benefit by functioning as a private, nonpolitical organization interested in serving as a medium through which both our peoples can learn from the experiences and the accomplishments of the other," he said later. "Membership is open to individuals, organizations and companies interested in furthering the objectives of the Society."

The Society arranges meetings at which prominent Japanese visitors to the United States and others can discuss matters of common interest and it assembles information on significant activities in both countries. It also serves as a channel of contact between individuals and institutions in the two countries and assists in developing programs of cultural interchange such as a Japanese art and national treasures exhibition which is planned for the United States in 1953. The Society assists Japanese students in this country.

John had visited Japan on various occasions before World War II and had been greatly interested in the country. He returned after the war and then accompanied the John Foster Dulles mission to Tokyo when the peace treaty was being negotiated. At that time he met with many Japanese in all stations of life and out of those discussions began to emerge a plan for a cultural center that would work for harmony between the two peoples. A preparatory committee of Americans and Japanese was created in 1951 and in 1952 John again visited Japan to complete final arrangements for establishment of a Tokyo international center to promote a program of international understanding and culture.

Such enterprises as Colonial Williamsburg and the Japan Society are, of course, only examples of the various philanthropic and civic activities in which John takes part. Each of the brothers has a number of such interests, involving perhaps a score of different organizations or institutions, some of which call for short-term efforts and some of which are continuing. Nelson, for instance, served after the war as chairman of the initial drive of the New York City for the Victory Clothing Collection, an effort to help in relief of war-damaged countries. In two years, the organization sent nearly a quarter of a million pounds of clothing to Europe and Asia.

In 1946, Nelson became chairman of the nonsectarian Community Committee of New York in behalf of the United Jewish Appeal to aid a million and a half displaced Jews in Europe. The next year he was a member of the National Christian Committee for the United Jewish Appeal. His efforts in this direction were not restricted to charity appeals. He has deep convictions regarding the equality of citizenship and he worked hard for two years in behalf of the Ives-Quinn bill, in the New York State Legislature, to prohibit racial and religious discrimination.

One of the great interests of the Rockefeller family has long been centered around conservation measures. Mr. Rockefeller, Jr., has devoted much time and money to such projects and the family interest has been carried on by his sons, especially Laurance. This interest probably started on some of their childhood journeys with their father to Wyoming, where in

1926 Mr. Rockefeller authorized the purchase of about 40,000 acres of private land for a total of $2,000,000 in the Jackson Hole area. His purpose was an unusual one. He was enthusiastic about the country around Jackson Hole and particularly the wonderful view of the Grand Teton mountains. But he was distressed that countless hot dog stands and bill boards were being erected along the road across the valley near Jackson Hole, where visitors got the most perfect view of the Grand Tetons. As a result, he decided to buy the land in the valley and give it to the National Park service in order to preserve the natural beauty of the foreground of the famous mountains. Although he began purchasing the land in 1926, controversy arose over the project and it was not feasible for the arrangements to be completed until 1949, when 33,562 acres were turned over to the Department of Interior by Laurance acting for his father.

As far back as 1909, the founder of the Rockefeller fortune had been elected a Founder of the New York Zoological Society. Ten years later Mr. Rockefeller, Jr., also was elected a Founder and, in 1935, when Laurance showed an interest in the work of the organization after his graduation from college, he was made a trustee of the Society. Five years later he was elected a Founder, also becoming the second vice-president and, later, chairman of the executive committee.

At first, Laurance was thinking mainly in terms of conservation but once he had found out exactly what the Society was doing to provide recreation and entertainment for the public— that is, the zoos—he became fascinated by the work, to which he devoted not only money but considerable personal effort. "Laurance has an ability to put money into organizations like the Society without making it seem like a personal gift or donation," one member of the Society said later. "He isn't modest or inhibited about it and he doesn't make gifts anonymously.

It's as if he were doing a perfectly natural thing and that is a very subtle quality. Not many rich men can claim it."

Laurance's talent in that direction may have been enhanced by his enthusiasm for the denizens of the zoo. Once after the war when he was about to make a journey to Africa on business he discovered that the Society then had a collector of animals in the Belgian Congo. Laurance was fully briefed on the work and, while in Africa, he took a special interest in the collecting and otherwise facilitated the project. Then, when the animals finally arrived in New York by air, he was waiting at the airport for the crates and cages to be unloaded.

"I was amazed to find him scrambling all over the place," one officer of the Society recalled later. "He was like a kid at the circus and he took dozens of photographs. His enthusiasm is tremendous and it stirs up enthusiasm in everybody else." He paused and turned to a colleague for confirmation. Then, just to make sure that there was no misunderstanding, he continued in a conservative manner. "Of course, you understand that Laurance is definitely not an expert in this field. He wouldn't, for example, be likely to appreciate fully the excitement of getting—ah, say a woolly tapir—but he's done wonders for the Society."

The Society, as a matter of fact, was largely a local organization before the war, exhibiting animals for the education and enjoyment of the people of New York City. Since 1944, however, its membership has greatly increased and it has undertaken much broader work in research and conservation—fields in which Laurance had a special interest. It was Laurance who arranged for the Society, co-operating with the State of Wyoming, to establish the Jackson Hole Wildlife Park on 1,000 acres of the land his father had purchased there. Laurance had, meantime, become a trustee of the Zoological Society's Conservation Foundation, which carries out research and educational work in co-operation with government agencies, universities and other private institutions.

Again it should be pointed out that the Zoological Society is but one of a number of organizations of this nature in which Laurance is interested and to which he gives considerable time. He is active in the American Geographical Society, the American Museum of Natural History, the New York Botanical Gardens and the New York State Forestry and Park Association. He devotes time to preservation of the natural beauties and resources of Westchester County, where he has a home, and was instrumental in working out plans for an airport that would not damage the watershed area there. As a member and secretary of the Palisades Interstate Park Commission, he sponsored the idea of developing a public park and a scenic drive along the towering cliffs that rise from the Hudson River near New York. In this connection, he purchased Dunderberg Mountain, a landmark along the Hudson, for $25,000 and presented it to the Park Commission in order to make sure that no commercial enterprises would be started there and mar the scenic beauty of the area. Mr. Rockefeller, Jr., at one time had owned large tracts along the Hudson River and had disposed of them in a way that safeguarded the southwestern side of the Palisades Interstate Park from commercial or industrial encroachment.

In another field, Laurance has carried on the interest of his father in the Memorial Center for the Treatment of Cancer and Allied Diseases, in New York, one of the greatest cancer enterprises ever established and one to which he has devoted himself unstintingly. In the later 1920's, Mr. Rockefeller, Jr., gave the hospital its present site of two blocks on the upper East Side of Manhattan and in 1950, Laurance was elected president of the Board of Managers.

Another field in which the Rockefellers, especially Winthrop, have been active concerns race relations. Winthrop, who once remarked that "democracy is a very personal thing when you don't have it," has been a leading figure since before the war in the National Urban League, which deals with social and economic problems of Negroes in urban areas, and has affiliates in fifty-nine cities and thirty states. He helped to organize the first Urban League group in the Bronx and took an energetic part in its activities, raising funds, interviewing employers, traveling about the country and investigating cases of discrimination.

When the League was started in 1910, the Negro was largely rural, untrained and the object of almost universal discrimination. Forty years later, about 15,000,000 Negroes had become city dwellers and much of their progress toward social maturity and enjoyment of equal civil rights can be attributed to the Urban League. One of the biggest steps forward came after the war when two advisory councils—one of management and the other of labor—were set up to work for racial equality of economic opportunity. An intensive campaign was carried on among employers. Representatives of many large corporations were persuaded to go to the campus of Howard University and other Negro schools and offer employment to qualified Negro graduates on nearly all levels. The League also began interviewing more than 50,000 Negro job applicants a year and finding places for a large percentage of them.

"No doubt many of these men and women would have found jobs on their own," Winthrop pointed out, "but the League has played a vital part in getting them equality of opportunity." One check-up by the League on 261 Negroes that it had placed in higher than ordinary jobs showed that after a few years their combined income was almost $4,000,000 a year.

Winthrop's excellent work as vice-chairman of the Greater New York Fund in its initial year, 1938, has already been noted.

After the war he also became a trustee of the Public Education Association and took an active part in strengthening the New York educational system and in preparing the way for establishment of New York State University.

Perhaps his greatest interest and hardest work, however, has gone into his job as chairman of the Board of Trustees of the New York University-Bellevue Medical Center, a $33,000,000 project started in 1948 and designed to bring to New York's East Side one of the world's finest institutions for teaching, for research and for care of the sick. The Medical Center does not confine its operations to New York, but through a Regional Hospital Plan also serves eleven hospitals in four states under a reciprocal arrangement for training and facilities. Four New York hospitals are under its direct supervision and seven others lend their facilities for student training. Four research institutes are maintained, for industrial medicine, heart diseases, cancer and physical rehabilitation—the latter a much publicized new phase of medicine under the direction of Dr. Howard Rusk, who gained fame for techniques developed in the armed services during the war. Other fields of research cover almost every phase of medicine from alcoholism to skin diseases, enabling the Center to give the student who intends to be a general practitioner experience with almost every known human ailment.

"The Center has been called the outstanding example of the partnership of public agencies, private agencies and individuals," Winthrop said in summing up the enterprise. "It grew up on a century-old marriage between the medical faculty of New York University and the city's Bellevue Hospital. On this foundation, doctors, educators and laymen built a bold new concept of a modern medical center to serve the community and also the nation through an integrated program of medical research, training and care. More than 14,000 individuals, business firms and philanthropic foundations so far have made contributions.

"The dollars and the labor that go into the operations are important only as they help human beings to become productive, adjusted citizens. Thus the Center will be a means of enabling practicing physicians to keep abreast of the newest approved developments because many other hospitals will be affiliated."

David Rockefeller's activities have reflected an intense interest in planning for the future, not only in community affairs but in keeping the peace of the world. Education and understanding are a key to peace and David has been busy in educational matters connected with the universities of Columbia, Harvard and Chicago and in religious and educational affairs of the Greater New York Interfaith Committee as well as in various Protestant organizations. Since 1947, he has been chairman of the executive committee of the New York International House, oldest of four such establishments set up by his father to foster international understanding and friendship among students attending universities in countries other than their own. To strengthen the ties of friendship among such students, he helped form an organization among former foreign students in America with the objective of working in almost every country for peace among nations.

David also has been active in the Carnegie Endowment for International Peace and was instrumental in planning the Endowment's new $3,800,000 international center being erected opposite the United Nations Building in New York. It will be a home for organizations working for harmony among nations. David has devoted great effort to mobilizing the Endowment's efforts toward support of the United Nations.

An illustration of David's emphasis on future planning is a nonprofit community organization called Morningside Heights,

Inc., of which he is president. Morningside Heights is a part of New York City, an area that stretches over a hill between 108th and 125th streets not far from the Hudson River. Half a century or so ago this was the site of wealthy estates. It was convenient to the business section of Manhattan but it also commanded a beautiful view of the River and the Palisades.

About the turn of the century the character of the neighborhood began to change. There were several large institutions there and more came in—Columbia University, the Jewish Theological Seminary, Juilliard School of Music, and International House, to name a few. It is, incidentally, also the site of the Cathedral of St. John. The new institutions spread out, the old ones expanded; the wealthy residents began to move out of Morningside Heights and it lost its fashionable atmosphere. By the time of World War II it was an important cultural and educational center but it was also crowded and getting more so every year. The population pressure—about 60,000 persons live there—and the lack of city planning caused living conditions to deteriorate and, in David's words, "poverty, poor sanitation and all the other ills of underprivileged people took their toll." The contrast between the great centers of learning and the woeful living conditions which surrounded them was striking and grievous.

It was to correct this situation that Morningside Heights, Inc., was organized to carry out community research and planning for the area. The work was financed privately by member institutions and a small staff was set up to get an exact picture of living conditions and the attitude of the residents toward future improvements. Citizens Committees were organized to assist in preparing and executing local improvements and to work for outside help in behalf of schools and housing. A businessman's group was formed to organize a systematic campaign for cleaning up and improving the appearance of buildings and stores.

Another committee explored the problems created by crime and juvenile delinquency and worked out plans for better recreation facilities for young people in the neighborhood. Slowly, these efforts began to be felt. Slum clearance progressed and, through the efforts of the organization, two housing projects were proposed.

One of these projects was for low-income families, to be built by the New York City Housing Authority and to cover an irregularly shaped six-block area. The other was a co-operative housing project for middle-income families on a two-block area. There was no question that the section of the city involved was overcrowded and deteriorating, but the middle-income project encountered stiff opposition from neighborhood groups that contended the rentals would be too high for most of the families then living on the site. David took a vigorous role in the successful fight to carry out the proposed improvements, arguing that the city needed housing in the middle-income group as well as in the low-income group.

"City planning," he said later, "has come of age. It is no longer the exclusive province of the dreamer. It is the province of the economist, the businessman, the government official and, most important of all, the citizen. I am in this work because planning is essential to any institution that is dynamic in growth. Any intelligent person should look ahead and plan for an objective. And I believe in the enterprise system—not in planning for socialism."

✳ XIX ✳

THE THEME OF WORLD PEACE AND INTERNATIONAL understanding has been a major factor in three generations of Rockefeller family affairs. This is particularly true of the third generation and they have pinned a great deal of faith on the future of the United Nations as an instrument for world harmony, or at least as a hopeful means of preventing world conflict. They have, too, put a great deal of effort into justifying that faith, although only on rare occasions has this been a matter of public record.

There is, however, a kind of monument to their industry and determination in this regard—the massive bulk of the United Nations buildings that rise along the East River in midtown Manhattan. Stone and glass and mortar can contribute little to the fulfillment of the idea of international understanding; yet the story of the establishment of the headquarters of the United Nations may well fill a page in history and the Rockefeller family will merit at least a footnote. Better than any other venture perhaps, it illustrated how the Rockefellers could work together under pressure toward a common goal.

The story began in 1946 when Nelson was working as a member of the Mayor's Committee which was attempting without much success to persuade the United Nations to construct permanent headquarters in New York City. The Committee was authorized to offer the organization the old World's Fair site at Flushing meadows as a gift, but the UN was unanimous in rejecting this. Engineers estimated that to sink foundations in the filled-in swamp land would cost $35,000,000 before a single building could be erected.

Other sites were considered. The preferred places could not be obtained because property owners put up too rugged a resistance. Less favored sites were prohibitive in cost.

At one time Nelson became enthusiastic about the possibility of using Rockefeller Center Theater as the meeting place for the General Assembly and was severely disappointed when that proved impossible because of contract obligations. Meantime other cities were bidding strongly for the headquarters, and it appeared likely that Philadelphia would be the chosen center, though one prominent UN delegate expressed the fear that absenteeism would be great.

Nelson was in Mexico when he learned that a final vote would be taken on December 11. He flew home on December 9 to make a last-ditch effort to find a suitable New York site. At Lake Success he was given a discouraging report that the decision was virtually in the bag for Philadelphia.

Late that night a New York political reporter phoned Frank Jamieson, former newspaperman, Pulitzer Prize winner and in recent years the brothers' public relations chief, and said New York still had a chance.

"The delegates," he reported, "really want New York if they can get a good site."

At noon the next day, twenty-two hours before the deadline for bids, Nelson met in his own office with Jamieson, Wallace Harrison and John E. Lockwood, the brothers' legal adviser. His first remark was typical: "There's something we can do. What is it?"

"All I am sure of is that we have today to do it in," Jamieson replied.

"They'll come here if we find the right place," somebody remarked. And then, referring to the Rockefeller estate near Tarrytown up the Hudson River: "How about Pocantico Hills?"

Only a member of the family could fully appreciate the implications of this suggestion. The estate had been established by the boys' grandfather. It is the spot their father loved more than any other in the world. The brothers and their sister had considered it "home" from the time of their childhood, and their own children are growing up there now. Yet . . . it might be the answer.

At once Nelson called John, who was in Williamsburg. He explained the idea and asked: "How do you feel about giving up your house at Pocantico Hills? Yours would be the first to go."

"I just finished building it and I certainly don't want to give it up," he answered painfully, but added almost in the same breath, "If that's the best way to solve the problem I'll do it."

Nelson called in Laurance whose office is across the hall. Laurance also said at once he would go along. He not only offered his 250 acres, his home, but also cash for additional land if it should be needed.

They phoned David to come up at once from his Wall Street office, and they put in a long-distance call for Winthrop who was somewhere in South America.

David arrived and heard the story, too. "Isn't there any other way?" he asked. "Couldn't I give money to buy other land?" It seemed unlikely and he said, "All right. Count me in."

By then it was one-thirty. Maps were spread out on Nelson's desk, and they studied possibilities. An air of excitement built up in the office.

The telephone operator reported that it was impossible to reach Winthrop. The others talked it over. They all agreed that

Winthrop would co-operate and that they could go ahead on that supposition. One big question remained. Their father.

It would hurt him worst of all. Would he have to give up his home there entirely? Perhaps it would be possible to save part of the estate for him if other additional land could be purchased. They leaned over the maps. Nelson called several influential friends near Pocantico Hills and started them secretly getting the necessary options on the desired additional land.

They got hold of Mr. Rockefeller, Jr. and told him of their plans. Nelson said they hoped to save part of his estate, but he replied simply that it would be all right with him to give up his entire 3,000-acre estate if necessary.

That afternoon the work went on at high speed. It was decided that the family would give 1,000 acres from their various estates and buy an adjoining 2,000 acres. By evening the necessary options had been obtained.

Meanwhile Harrison went to consult with United Nations officials. A little later, Mr. Rockefeller called up to suggest that Nelson make certain whether the UN would prefer to be in the suburbs or in the city.

They phoned Warren Austin, the United States delegate. He said apparently the delegates wanted to be as near the center of the city as possible. Harrison came back with a similar impression; probably the Pocantico Hills offer would be rejected. It would then be too late to hit upon anything else.

There were phone calls, many conferences. Discouragement was settling heavily over Nelson's office.

Just before dinner time, Nelson, Harrison, Lockwood and Jamieson wearily pushed the maps and notes aside, and sat down to check over all results. It was a pessimistic round-up.

Nelson reached his hand out for the phone and called his father.

"I guess they'd rather have some place in Manhattan, Pa," he said.

There was a pause. Then Mr. Rockefeller mentioned an area of several blocks on the East Side of Manhattan, where William Zeckendorf, a New York realtor, was planning to tear down a slum section and build a $150,000,000 skyscraper project. The plans were well along, but maybe that property could be purchased. No actual work had been started.

Harrison, whose firm was designing the Zeckendorf skyscraper center, said cautiously that though the property was publicized as being worth $25,000,000, it might be had for $8,500,000, which he was sure was more than Zeckendorf and his partner, Henry Sears, had paid. Nelson relayed this information to his father.

"Well," Mr. Rockefeller replied. "I think that's all right, Nelson. You're authorized to negotiate the purchase at that price. If you can get it, I'll give it to them."

A great smile broke across Nelson's face. "Pa!" he exclaimed. "Why, Pa, that's wonderful."

The conference room came to life again with a new hum of excitement and planning. By then it was seven-fifteen. The deadline was only fifteen hours away. It was already the dinner hour, offices were closed, people hard to contact. Nobody knew whether Zeckendorf would sell or whether he could be found.

But they went ahead. They got in touch with Commissioner Robert Moses. He was enthusiastic and believed the city would cede the necessary streets, the water front and agree to condemn several small pieces of land. Negotiations were also started with federal officials in Washington by long-distance phone. Among other things, John D., Jr., felt that he should not have to pay a gift tax which would be heavy.

The coast was clear, apparently. All that was left to do was to buy the property, draw up the proper papers and get them to

Warren Austin at his hotel in time for him to take them to Lake Success by ten-thirty the next morning.

Harrison undertook the purchasing job. He went on a hunt for Zeckendorf and finally located him and Sears late that night at the Monte Carlo night club where they were celebrating an anniversary.

Harrison got them off by themselves at another table, spread out the roll of blueprints and explained the situation. Would they abandon their project and give Mr. Rockefeller an option to buy the land for $8,500,000? Harrison asked above the blare of the dance orchestra.

There was some argument, but in the end, Zeckendorf picked up Harrison's red pencil and scribbled along the margin of the blueprint on which the area had been marked: "8.5 million— United Nations only. December 10 for 30 days."

The partners signed it, and Harrison put a circled A and B on the two sections of the map involved and added his initials to show they were both part of the same document. A description of the area was also written on the map.

Harrison left the night club shortly before midnight and stopped at a pay phone to call Nelson. "It's all set," he reported.

"Great, Wally! Let's celebrate. Stop on your way for a bottle of champagne."

Ten minutes later Harrison arrived in Nelson's office with the blueprints.

"Where's the champagne?" Nelson demanded.

Harrison grinned sheepishly. "When I started to buy it, I discovered I had only a dollar and eighty cents in my pocket."

"That's great! You just put over an eight-million-dollar deal and you haven't enough money to buy us a drink of champagne."

It also occurred to Harrison that he had successfully talked

himself out of an enormous architectural fee for the Zeckendorf project.

Lockwood looked at the blueprints. "It's the most unusual
legal document I have ever seen," he said. "But it's legal and
binding."

It took him several hours to draw up the other necessary
legal papers and then after a few hours' sleep, he joined
Nelson and Jamieson at Mr. Rockefeller Jr.'s apartment for a
seven-thirty breakfast.

Everything was reviewed and approved. Time was really
getting short now, and Nelson scooped up all the papers and
prepared to dash to Austin's hotel.

Mr. Rockefeller touched him on the arm and, obviously
thinking of earlier frustrations, asked, "Does this make up for
giving up the Center Theater idea, Nelson?"

Nelson nodded happily and ran out the door.

As Nelson arrived at Senator Austin's hotel suite, a call from
Secretary of State Byrnes at Washington gave assurance that the
government would agree to the terms of the gift and that it
would be tax-free.

Presently a letter arrived from Mayor William O'Dwyer
agreeing that New York would cede the necessary street inter-
sections.

A lot of people had been busy that night.

Austin sent word to the chairman of the United Nations
Headquarters Committee, Dr. Eduardo Zuleta Angel of
Colombia, who was ill at the Presbyterian Hospital, and then
hurried on to Lake Success with all the papers that in all
likelihood would bring an epochal decision.

Exactly at ten-thirty, Dr. Zuleta, who in his excitement had
left his hospital bed to come to the session, arose to present to
the delegates of all nations the news of the Rockefeller gift.

It was a moment of some significance in the history of the

United Nations and the history of the world. It was significant, too, in the story of the third generation of Rockefellers, none of whom was present at Lake Success. Its significance depended, however, not on the fact that their father happened to have enough money to make a gift of land, but on the energies and talents of a father and his five sons and their willingness to use them in behalf of what they believe to be the common good.

It will be some time before history can judge of the success of the United Nations in its gleaming skyscraper home in Manhattan, which eventually Harrison was to help design. And it will be some time before anyone can judge finally the success of the brothers' efforts to set up a new economic pattern in underdeveloped areas or its effect, if any, on the position of the United States in world affairs. But win, lose or draw, the Rockefellers at least will have demonstrated that in a time notable for indecision and uncertainty they had the courage to try.

Index